INTERRELIGIOUS STUDIES

Dispatches from an Emerging Field

Hans Gustafson

Editor

BAYLOR UNIVERSITY PRESS

Book and cover design by Kasey McBeath
Cover art by Alex Wong/Unsplash

Library of Congress Cataloging-in-Publication Data

Names: Gustafson, Hans, editor.
Title: Interreligious studies : dispatches from an emerging field / Hans
   Gustafson, editor.
Description: Waco : Baylor University Press, 2020. | Includes index. |
   Summary: "An interdisciplinary exploration of definitions, method,
   issues, and opportunities for interreligious studies as an academic
   field"-- Provided by publisher.
Identifiers: LCCN 2020020811 (print) | LCCN 2020020812 (ebook) | ISBN
   9781481312547 (hardcover) | ISBN 9781481312585 (pdf) | ISBN
   9781481312578 (mobi) | ISBN 9781481312561 (epub)
Subjects: LCSH: Religious thought. | Religion. | Religions. | Religious
   pluralism.
Classification: LCC BL85 .I688 2020 (print) | LCC BL85 (ebook) | DDC
   201/.507--dc23
LC record available at https://lccn.loc.gov/2020020811
LC ebook record available at https://lccn.loc.gov/2020020812

NATIONAL
ENDOWMENT
FOR THE
HUMANITIES

Interreligious Studies has been made possible in part by a major grant from the National Endowment for the Humanities: Exploring the human endeavor. Any views, findings, conclusions, or recommendations expressed in this book do not necessarily represent those of the National Endowment for the Humanities.

Printed in the United States of America on acid-free paper with a minimum of thirty percent recycled content.

CONTENTS

FOREWORD

Anna Halafoff

This impressive volume—a timely dispatch from what was certainly an emerging field at the time that this edited collection was first conceived—reports on the most salient contemporary issues in interreligious studies (IRS). These include debates concerning terminology and the status of the field; a shift from a focus on world religion to the complexities of embodied and lived religion; considerations of secular contexts and of the rise of the nonreligious; emic and/or etic differentiation, including scholar-activist perspectives; the importance of sacred places and natural and built environments; interactive approaches that consider the more than human lifeworld; the need to decolonize religious studies and IRS; and arguments for more engagement with critical and intersectional theories examining religions' ambivalent roles in violence and peacebuilding. In so doing, this volume marks a significant moment for IRS, of an emerging field approaching maturity.

Paul Numrich[1] identified three criteria necessary to distinguish a distinct field of study: specialization, organization, and publication. This volume demonstrates that all three of these factors are now present in IRS. Contributors to this collection include leaders in the field who have established or work in specific IRS departments or centers that provide specialized scholarly training in this area in Norway, the Netherlands, Germany, the United States, and Singapore. Professional associations such as the European Society for Intercultural Theology and Interreligious Studies (ESITIS) and the American Academy of Religion's Interreligious and Interfaith Studies Unit hold regular meetings and conferences. An increasing amount of Ph.D. dissertations, scholarly peer-reviewed articles, edited books, and books have been published on the subject in recent years, notably *Interreligious Studies: A Relational Approach to Religious Activism and the Study of Religion*[2] and *Interreligious/Interfaith Studies: Defining a New Field*.[3] There are also several journals dedicated to IRS, such as *Interreligious Studies and Intercultural Theology, Studies in Interreligious Dialogue*, and the *Journal of Interreligious Studies*.

Numrich added that a field's maturity can be measured by its capacity for internal critique and debate, and its level of cross-disciplinary engagement. Another sign of development of a field may also be how genuinely international it is. A robust self-reflexivity regarding IRS's coherence in deliberations of the field's main issues is certainly evident in this volume. However, while IRS scholarship is certainly cross- and multi-disciplinary, it is still primarily situated within the humanities. In addition, and as the volume's editor Hans Gustafson and contributors Kevin Minister and Paul Hedges have flagged, it is still largely dominated by Western European and North American scholarship.

Consequently, as a sociologist of religion, based in Australia, with expertise in interfaith/ interreligious studies, worldviews education, and Buddhism and gender, I am a somewhat unusual choice of author for this volume's foreword. Yet, including me in this way actually provides further proof of IRS's maturation as a field of study.

In terms of ways forward from here toward further sophistication, I call, alongside many of the volume's contributors, for further expanding the IRS conversation to include more voices from the Global South and East, as well as North and West, mindful that our identities with regard to location are increasingly complex and hybrid. I also agree that while the securitization of religion at the turn of the twenty-first century certainly propelled religion and interreligious relations into the public mind, we must respond to political imperatives for social cohesion critically, so as not to further entrench existing power imbalances and injustices.

In this volume, Minister, citing Lori Patton, stresses that the capacity for IRS's success depends on how liberatory it can be. To what extent can IRS be a field of resistance against Western hegemony, capitalist neoliberalism, authoritarianism, and intersectional violence of all kinds, direct and structural? Whose voices, asks Gustafson, "are unheard or left out?" These are, in my opinion, the most pressing issues facing IRS raised by chapter authors including Minister, Hedges, Marianne Moyaert, Anne Hege Grung, Kate McCarthy, Brian K. Pennington, Russell C. D. Arnold, Rachel S. Mikva, and Jeanine Hill Fletcher. They are also the questions that I am tackling in my own research and teaching on critical religious pluralism,[4] which has been increasingly focused on the nexus between human and animal rights and religious freedom. I concur that race, gender, sexuality, and multispecies diversity are not yet receiving sufficient attention in IRS.

However, I do not think there is a need for all IRS scholars to subscribe to a critical theory, scholar-activist stance. It seems the best way forward would be for the field of IRS to embrace its own complexity, when studying the complexities of interreligious relations and theology. We need to embrace that there are myriad ways of approaching IRS, theoretically and methodologically, and how they can both complement and/or contradict one another.

At the same time, I am wary of arguments that favor agonistic respect, and of agreeing to disagree, especially regarding that which is intolerable. Our current global post-truth world in which we are witnessing a rise of religious vilification against Muslims and Jews, of xenophobia, and of widespread climate change denial results in serious harms that need, I believe, to be countered by a more robust focus on certain freedoms not impinging upon the rights of others. Empathy, as Catherine Cornille highlights in her chapter, can be cultivated through IRS. Our research in Australia has also demonstrated that education about diverse religions can play a significant role in interreligious understanding and peacebuilding more broadly by contributing to more positive views of religious minorities.[5]

Finally, while IRS has established itself now as a distinct field—with subfields that remain important within it centered on, for example, Christian–Muslim relations or interreligious theology—the question remains regarding whether the focus on religion in its terminology impedes it from being genuinely inclusive. Given the complexity of religious, spiritual, and nonreligious identities, beliefs, and practices, as well as overlaps between them in contemporary society,[6] the IRS boundaries may need to expand and engage more with the emerging field of worldview studies and to focus on multiple ways of knowing or lifeways, rather than stress religious ones, to be truly liberatory. This can perhaps be the subject of future inquiry that may enrich the debate and thereby ensure IRS's ongoing maturity and relevance.

Notes

1   Paul Numrich, "North American Buddhists: A Field of Study?" in *North American Buddhists in Social Context*, ed. Paul Numrich (London: Brill, 2008).

2   Oddbjørn Leirvik, *Interreligious Studies: A Relational Approach to Religious Activism and the Study of Religion* (New York: Bloomsbury, 2014).

3   Eboo Patel, Jennifer Howe Peace, and Noah Silverman, eds., *Interreligious/Interfaith Studies: Defining a New Field* (Boston: Beacon, 2018).

4   Anna Halafoff, "Multifaith Movements and Critical Religious Pluralism," How We Come Together (Cohesion) Plenary, International Conference on Cohesive Societies, June 19–21, 2019, Singapore.

5   Andrew Singleton, Mary Lou Rasmussen, Anna Halafoff, and Gary D. Bouma, *The AGZ Study: Project Report*, ANU, Deakin University, and Monash University, 2019.

6   Singleton et al., *AGZ Study*.

References

Halafoff, Anna. "Multifaith Movements and Critical Religious Pluralism." How We Come Together (Cohesion) Plenary, International Conference on Cohesive Societies, June 19–21, 2019, Singapore.

Leirvik, Oddbjørn. *Interreligious Studies: A Relational Approach to Religious Activism and the Study of Religion*. New York: Bloomsbury, 2014.

Numrich, Paul. "North American Buddhists: A Field of Study?" In *North American Buddhists in Social Context*, edited by Paul Numrich, 1–17. London: Brill, 2008.

Patel, Eboo, Jennifer Howe Peace, and Noah Silverman, eds. *Interreligious/Interfaith Studies: Defining a New Field*. Boston: Beacon, 2018.

Singleton, Andrew, Mary Lou Rasmussen, Anna Halafoff, and Gary D. Bouma. *The AGZ Study: Project Report*. ANU, Deakin University, and Monash University, 2019.

PREFACE

I did not set out to edit a volume of this size. In fact, I was not particularly interested in wrangling and prodding thirty-four accomplished scholars from across the globe to produce original and unpublished chapters to be revised several times over. It sounds exhausting. It was not. In hindsight, I can now fortunately admit that if I ever must wrangle thirty-four scholars again, I want it to be these thirty-four insightful professionals, all of whom are simply downright good human beings. My initial intention was to wrangle a mere four or five scholars to write short, sweet, straight-to-the-point, three-to-five-page essays on defining the nascent field of interreligious studies (or interfaith studies if you prefer) with a special focus on scholarship and research (more on that below). I was interested in this question and could not find much written about it. So, in a fit of measured self-interest, I invited scholars whom I admire to write something.

There is significant work on defining interreligious studies as an academic field in the context of pedagogy and leadership development. Most recently, the outstanding volume *Interreligious/Interfaith Studies: Defining a New Field* edited by Eboo Patel, Jennifer Peace, and Noah Silverman comes to mind.[1] I have learned much from these three leaders and scholars over the years and count them among my most esteemed colleagues and friends. Their volume contains full-length chapters on defining the field, many of which focus on curricular and program development. It contains some excellent chapters that certainly touch on interreligious studies as a field of research. To be sure, the present book is in no way meant as a response to, a replacement for, or a rebuttal to the Patel, Peace, and Silverman volume. If anything, this book is a complement to it—a cohort or companion to it. Moreover, this book, as the introduction explains below, focuses primarily on research and scholarship and not on pedagogy and curricular development (although, at some point, research and pedagogy interrelate as some of the contributors point out).

Many academic journals periodically publish short related articles in a "roundtable" format. These articles range from one to five pages and often address the same prompt or question. Recently, I read a roundtable titled "Exploring the Field of Intercultural Theology."[2] After reading it, I thought to myself, "That was nice. Each essay took only fifteen minutes to read. And now I have some sense, from nine distinct leading voices, of the current contours and dynamics in the field of intercultural theology," a field with which I am not terribly familiar. I also thought to myself, "Why not try to curate a roundtable like this for the field of interreligious studies?" Thus, my initial intention (stated above) was to invite four or five scholars to write short essays responding to the basic question of defining interreligious studies in the context of research and scholarship.

Why research and scholarship? As noted above, we have some great resources on teaching, pedagogy, curricular development, and leadership competencies in the field (of course, we always need more). However, there is still not much about defining the field for research and scholarship. Certainly, there is, and has been, research carried out that investigates questions that fall within the purview of interreligious studies; however there are few texts that focus on defining the field for research and that ask questions about its object(s) of study, histories, methodologies, challenges, opportunities, ethics, and politics among others.

When I began to invite scholars to contribute to my envisioned roundtable, and when I casually discussed it with colleagues in the area of interreligious studies, I received an overwhelming, immediate, and enthusiastic response, which I did not anticipate. The response pushed me to reconsider my tack. Are five scholars enough? Is one basic question enough? Might there be more hunger here than I originally thought? The roundtable grew to include thirty-four scholars, and I want to thank all of them for their diligent work, prompt revisions, and inspirational encouragement. In particular, I thank Barbara McGraw who suggested we consider Baylor University Press to publish this volume. Her council proved wise, as Baylor University Press editors Carey Newman and Cade Jarrell saw immediate value in the project and chaperoned it with first-class professionalism and collegiality. I also thank Martha "Marty" Stortz for her sage insight and counsel in reviewing an early version of the manuscript.

Needless to say, this volume grew to include, in my view, many of the leading thinkers in this field today. Undoubtedly, there are countless others who ought to be included in this volume. We need their wisdom as well. My hope is that this volume furthers the conversation and draws those missing voices into future publications. Perhaps the next stage entails the spawning of several subthemed roundtables on the guiding questions of this volume to be published in various journals committed to promoting and growing the field of interreligious studies (or interfaith studies if you prefer).

Hans Gustafson
Summer 2019 | Minnesota

1   Eboo Patel, Jennifer Howe Peace, and Noah Silverman, eds., *Interreligious/ Interfaith Studies: Defining a New Field* (Boston: Beacon, 2018).

2   "Roundtable: Exploring the Field of Intercultural Theology," *Interreligious Studies and Intercultural Theology* 1, no. 1 (2017): 91–151.

1

Introduction

Hans Gustafson

If it is true, as many argue, that interreligious studies (IRS) is energetically growing as a field of instruction, what then might it mean for scholars to conduct research in this field? What primary disciplines and methodological approaches are employed, and what are its historical precedents? Who is researching in this field, what are they investigating, and how does their work relate to other fields? What limitations and challenges, contemporary and historic, surface? What voices are unheard or left out? Are scholars in this field making assumptions, what are they, and how do they influence their research? Are there any unique ethical mandates or normative obligations that researchers in this field ought to strive for? Ought we to distinguish between the academic field of IRS and the so-called interfaith movement, and, if so, how? Why is the field important, and how might it contribute to the world and to knowledge generation? What epistemological methods prove useful in such knowledge generation, and how ought researchers recognize any inherent flaws or biases contained therein?

These are among the many questions addressed by the thirty-four "dispatches" in this volume. By no means the first or final word on IRS, this volume gathers voices to address the contemporary parameters (definition) of the academic field of IRS in the context of research and scholarship. To be sure, several texts have been published in the last decade dedicated to this field in one way or another.[1] Many research projects examining interreligious encounter or applying interreligious practice to a particular context, and thus falling within the basic field of IRS, have recently been published as well.[2] Furthermore, scholars have now begun to peer back into the archives for shining models of IRS.[3] In the United States in particular, there is significant energy around cultivating pedagogy and fostering instructional design for interreligious and interfaith studies programs at the undergraduate and graduate/ seminary level, due in large part to the relentless efforts of the Interfaith Youth Core.[4] There are substantial academic journals[5] and guilds[6] now dedicated to the field. Although the primary audience of this volume includes scholars, researchers, and students engaged in academic work, practitioners, pedagogues, and policy makers will certainly benefit from the deeper understanding presented in this volume concerning the major currents and nuances streaming through this nascent field.

Notes on Terms

A couple of notes are in order here about the term "dispatch" and the field of "interreligious studies." The term "dispatch," utilized as both verb and noun, dates to the 1500s from the Spanish *despachar*, which can mean "to expedite," "to deal with," "to hasten," "to send off," and the like. As a noun, it is often used to refer to a brief message sent off in an efficient and timely manner. A dispatch combines efficiency with purpose. It is sent with promptness and the air of authenticity—that is, sent from the lived reality on the ground written with an intent to represent, to the extent one is able, the concrete reality as it is experienced, and with an earnest attempt to forecast future events resulting from any impending actions. The dispatches in this volume are not necessarily written in a hasty manner; however they are certainly crafted with brevity and promptness in mind (especially in an era of proliferating verbose academic prose), and from positions from within the field reporting on the pressing issues and questions relevant to the contemporary world.

In a word, this edited volume is a collection of dispatches from the field of "interreligious studies." The dispatches come from contemporary scholars from around the world, mostly the Western world. As such, the volume lacks a balance of non-Western voices, a limitation that continues to plague much of Western scholarship. The dispatches come from scholars operating with different methods, disciplinary tools, and modes of scholarship. They certainly do not all agree on the boundaries of the field, how to research the field, the role of the scholar within the field, or what the major questions are. Some prefer "interfaith studies" to "interreligious studies" or vice versa (sometimes, along the lines distinguished in table 1.1.),[7] while others use these interchangeably or in tandem,[8] or to refer to different foci. For the purposes of this volume, no attempt was made to impose a standard on the contributors in this regard. Rather, they were granted free rein to deploy either or both terms in ways that best suit their chapters. Here we might imagine two basic (and thus still yet oversimplified and problematic) ways to distinguish between interfaith studies and interreligious studies, among others. The first way distinguishes them along the well-worn lines of confessional/caretaker (interfaith) versus critical (interreligious)—a distinction known all too well among confessional theologians and non-confessional scholars of religion. The rehashing of these categories as interfaith versus interreligious yields the following sometimes problematic, and all too general and binary,[9] distinctions:

Interfaith Studies	Interreligious Studies
emic / insider	etic / outsider
confessional, normative, and prescriptive	critical and descriptive
promotes civic leadership, pluralism, cohesion[10]	promotes detached knowledge generation
closely allied with the so-called interfaith movement	intentionally distinct from the so-called interfaith movement

Table 1.1: "Interfaith Studies" vs. "Interreligious Studies"

This volume does not endorse or reject the above binary chart. In my view, the two modes can blend in various contexts and under certain conditions to function in a complementary and constructive mutually upbuilding manner.[11] Leaving aside this binary chart above, a second way to distinguish between interfaith studies and interreligious studies is to posit the former having for its object of study the so-called interfaith movement,[12] while the latter is understood to be the broader and include the study of all encounters and relations that take place between, among, and within religious identities and communities, including personal, local, and geopolitical conflict and violence. In this case, interreligious studies encompasses interfaith studies, and interfaith studies refer more particularly to the study of the interfaith movement.[13] Furthermore, research initiatives that fall within the field of comparative religion, and that perhaps do not always explicitly address relations among or within traditions, might also fall under the broad canopy of IRS since not only do they often implicitly include, compare, and examine multiple traditions, but they also often recognize that religious people "intermingle and interact with the 'other,' folks whose beliefs, cultures and languages differed from theirs."[14] Such intermingling, in turn, influences the self-understanding and construction of religious traditions, and thus projects of comparative religion can become simultaneously projects of IRS under certain conditions.

For the purposes of this volume, and in the spirit of a broad understanding of interreligious studies, "interreligious" is used more often than "interfaith." Moreover, the majority of scholars in this volume use "interreligious" over "interfaith," but not necessarily by a significant margin. The reader will notice that some contributors prefer "interfaith" to "interreligious" or vice versa and will therefore often explain their rationale.

Given then the welcome diversity of thought exhibited in this volume around the parameters and boundaries of the field and definition of interreligious studies, it may be helpful here to offer, at the very least, a basic understanding of interreligious (or interfaith) studies around which many contributors would agree. If such a definition exists, it would be that IRS as an academic field of inquiry examines, by one or several disciplinary methods, encounters that take place and relations that exist or existed, in the contemporary world or historically, between, within, and among groups with significant difference in worldview or lifeway, including religious, nonreligious, and secular traditions. The question of how a scholar ought to go about researching and attending to these encounters, and the implications and normative assumptions they take on, creates an interesting context for the scholarly conversation that emerges in this volume. Several approaches are identified by various scholars. These include a descriptive, critical, and nonnormative approach; an agenda-driven, normative, activist approach; a theological and/or philosophical truth-seeking approach; and a civic approach imbued with leadership capacity training, among others. The diversity of methods, approaches, and norms of this field demonstrate, in my view, not a weak disjointed pursuit of dissimilar aims; rather they proclaim a resilient commitment to the generation of historical and practical knowledge through various avenues. Such diversity, I believe, vigorously surfaces in the chapters that follow.

Overview

Part 1, "Sketching the Field," opens the volume with the attempt to provide some context and contours to the academic field of IRS. Oddbjørn Leirvik discusses the relation between area, field, and discipline in the case of IRS, followed by Geir Skeie, who asks whether it is justified to speak of IRS as a field of research in its own right. In particular, Skeie, in the process of raising questions about the relationship between the object of study and research context, draws on experiences and results from an international research project, "Religion and Dialogue in Modern Societies" (ReDi),[15] that combined theological and empirical studies. Eboo Patel's chapter highlights an inspiring example of interfaith civic leadership and explains how a well-structured interfaith studies research agenda and academic program would prepare students with the vision, knowledge, and skills to do similar civic work. Marianne Moyaert identifies, examines, and deconstructs overcharged claims to the disciplinary boundaries between three scholarly profiles, each with their own primary discipline, that have contributed to the emergence of IRS in the academy: the interreligious scholar in religious studies, the (comparative) theologian in theological studies, and the activist bridge builder engaged in the so-called interfaith movement. Mark E. Hanshaw presents the reader with an engaging case study of his experience with the cult of Maximón of San Simón, the colorful Mayan deity and Catholic folk saint popular in Guatemala, to identify the parameters of study for the field. Jeanine Diller, drawing insight from Spinoza's "infinite attributes," argues why the field of IRS should be interdisciplinary. Anne Hege Grung explores how the term "transreligious" challenges and enriches IRS and fosters constructive interreligious dialogue by destabilizing the image of fixed boundaries between religious traditions in addition to including a feminist perspective.

Part 2, "History and Method," probes questions relating to forerunners in the field and historical examples of interfaith dialogue, and it offers various approaches and methods employed to examine interreligious encounter. Thomas Albert Howard opens the section with a look to history in search of some early precedents for interfaith dialogue. Frans Wijsen then explores the shift from religious studies to IRS in terms of its history, epistemology, and methodology. Chapters from Nelly van Doorn-Harder, Hans Gustafson, and Ånund Brottveit follow by looking at ethnographic (van Doorn-Harder), lived religion (Gustafson), and empirical (Brottveit) approaches to interreligious encounter. Aaron Hollander's chapter offers insight into the relationship between IRS and the older intellectual framework of ecumenical studies by identifying them as mutually inclusive insofar as the border between "inter" and "intra" religious difference is porous and unstable, and insofar as the social realities shaped by these differences are often entangled or even identical. Timothy Parker's chapter concludes part 2 with an examination of how perspectives of architectural history and theory contribute to the field of interreligious studies by considering its relation to the study of the built environment in which religion is enacted.

Part 3, "Theological and Philosophical Considerations," raises questions pertaining to the place of theological and philosophical truth-seeking in the context of interreligious encounter, and offers some visions of what responses to such questions might look like. J. R. Hustwit's chapter makes the case for how IRS has helped support, give rise to, and provide valuable data for four important theological subfields: theology of religions, missiology, comparative theology, and transreligious theology. Wolfram Weisse then reflects on the approach of dialogical theology, which "primarily focuses on the extent to which core elements in the basic theological foundation of all religions substantiate both dialogue and the acceptance and appreciation of people of other religious and cultural affiliation,"[16] as a promising means not only for the study of interreligious encounter but also (a) for the development of an academic theology appropriate for humankind in plural modern societies and (b) serving as backdrop to legitimize interreligious dialogue in school and society. Perry Schmidt-Leukel then takes up the age-old question of religious truth, but he pursues it in the perhaps new context of a collaborative effort unbound to a single source or tradition (whether this be called multireligious, interreligious, transreligious, or "whatever it may be called"; Schmidt-Leukel is not into labels). He speculates that the future of theology and its analogues in every religious tradition will increasingly become interreligious. Jeffery D. Long concludes the section with a sketch of Swami Vivekananda's pluralist-inclusive philosophy of religion and its implications for interreligious dialogue.

Part 4, "Contemporary Challenges," turns to some of the most pressing questions and concerns for IRS in our present world. To begin, Kevin Minister and Paul Hedges argue for the decolonization of the study of religion (Minister) and of IRS (Hedges). Minister argues that IRS makes an essential contribution to theories of religion that redresses major, contemporary critiques of theories of religion, including decolonizing the study of religion; Hedges argues that decolonizing methodologies remain important in order to establish IRS on a sound basis and, at the same time, also shows that it has an implicit trajectory that aligns it with such concerns. Kate McCarthy's chapter contends that the emerging field of IRS has the twofold "secular imperative" to (a) distinguish itself from its faith-based lineage with a clearly defined secular purpose unallied with predetermined pluralist ideals and (b) take on the work that such a subdiscipline entails, which is to say that IRS must be secular, and the secular world must make sense of its own interreligiosity. Brian K. Pennington's chapter logically follows, and, in identifying the relationship between IRS and the modern university's diversity and inclusion agenda, he argues that classically liberal notions of personhood and society and the logic of global capitalism, both of which significantly shape university curricula, pose the most serious challenges to the legitimacy and longevity of this budding field. Russell C. D. Arnold's chapter addresses the limitations of using religious identity as the starting point for interreligious engagement, and it proposes a constructive, story-based, and intersectional approach that allows participants to break free from the religious identity paradigm and create spaces truly inviting to all. In so doing, Arnold's chapter offers a resource to be utilized by scholars to appreciate the complexity of identities in research that examines interreligious encounter. Rachel S. Mikva's chapter addresses the need for IRS to respond to our current reality in which the politicization of religious difference presses for contemporary theorization about constructions of the "other." She pays particular attention to Islamophobia, antisemitism, and the racialization of religious identities. Caryn D. Riswold and Guenevere Black Ford's coauthored chapter explains how and why xenoglossophobia, the fear of "foreign" languages, serves as a barrier to constructive interreligious engagement, and it argues that naming and confronting it can lead to positive responses to further develop the field. Peter A. Pettit concludes part 4 with a case study on the intra-religious influences in the responses to the *Kairos Palestine* document, insofar as they collectively offer an informative perspective on the intersection between interreligious study and engagement with the internal diversity of religious traditions.

Part 5, "Praxis and Possibility," concludes the volume with a turn toward a recognition of the practical knowledge and wisdom that the field of IRS might generate in various contexts. Barbara A. McGraw opens by arguing that IRS, as a multidisciplinary field of inquiry, can help to operationalize and optimize cultural studies, leadership studies, and especially the practice of cross-cultural leadership by providing the proper knowledge of every region's deeply rooted cultural values, but also by generating insight about how various religious communities and regions interact with traditions outside it. Therefore, she points out, a growing area of prominence and discovery for IRS is one of fostering meaningful and practical knowledge for effective cross-cultural leadership with interfaith competence at its core. Catherine Cornille follows with a chapter that examines the role of empathy, which she locates "somewhere on the border between knowledge and skill," in the context of interreligious encounter and makes the case not only for why IRS plays an important role in cultivating interreligious empathy but also for why IRS should critically reflect on variables that enhance or impede empathy. Or N. Rose's chapter, a constructive effort to learn from our forebears, offers a particular case study of the relationship between two pioneering figures in the North American interreligious movement, Howard Thurman and Zalman Schachter-Shalomi. Navras J. Aafreedi's chapter offers ways IRS might play a role in the prevention of intolerance and promote peacebuilding, primarily through providing educational opportunities. In a similar fashion Asfa Widiyanto's chapter explores modalities of interfaith activism for peacemaking, assesses its potential contributions to nation building (especially within the framework of post-secular nation-state), and suggests an appropriate model of religious education for such a nation. Widiyanto further argues that scholars of IRS ought to take on the responsibility of scholar-activist, especially since their contributions to the field can help to build peace, deepen social and national cohesion, and substantially contribute to a religious education curriculum that values and accommodates minority faiths. In a similar vein, Jeannine Hill Fletcher's chapter looks to Max Horkheimer's foundational definition of "critical theory" to encourage scholars of IRS to adopt methods of scholar-activists in responding to contemporary currents in political landscapes, especially in the United States. Douglas Pratt and Deanna Ferree Womack conclude the volume with chapters on perhaps the most-pressing interreligious encounter for our time (in the Western world): that between the world's two most-dominant traditions, Christianity and Islam. Pratt argues that IRS can offer a worthwhile contribution to Muslim–Christian relations by focusing on the dynamics of dialogue and the deep scrutiny of the narrative structures that yield insight into the religions themselves and between them. Womack pays attention to the often-overlooked subject of gender in Christian–Muslim studies, and observes, on a broader level, that gender is not yet a significant subject for IRS in general.

Looking Ahead

The limitations that plague this book are not unique to most scholarly collections coming out of the West today. In particular, there is a need for more non-Western voices. As Hedges and Minister point out, this will continue to be a priority. Certainly, there are scores of pressing topics not addressed in this short volume of brief dispatches. Some topics deserving of attention include a greater analysis of the geopolitical dimensions of interreligious encounters and conflicts (at the global and local levels, and their resulting glocal implications), a need for a deeper look at the place of IRS within the academy vis-à-vis various institutional contexts (certainly "one size need not fit all"), a rigorous analysis of the relationship between the academic field of IRS and the interfaith movement, and a continued effort to recognize and evaluate how power and privilege remain formative for this field and for the voices and topics it highlights, ignores, and marginalizes. Perhaps a second volume of "dispatches" will be called for in several years. For the present, my hope is that this volume energizes the conversation around, and beckons more clarity of, the academic field of interreligious studies for research and scholarship in the contemporary world.

Notes

1   See the following resources for authoritative attempts to define this field of study: American Academy of Religion, "Interreligious and Interfaith Studies Unit," https://papers.aarweb.org/content/interreligious-and-interfaith -studies-unit; Jeannine Diller, Eboo Patel, Jennifer Peace, and Colleen Windham-Hughes, "Toward a Field of Interfaith Studies: Emerging Questions and Considerations," *Journal of Interreligious Studies* 16 (2015): 5–13; Hans Gustafson, "Interreligious and Interfaith Studies in Relation to Religious Studies and Theological Studies," *State of Formation*, January 6, 2015; Paul Hedges, "Editorial Introduction: Interreligious Studies," *Journal for the Academic Study of Religion* 27, no. 2 (2014): 127–31; Hedges, "Interreligious Studies," in *Encyclopedia of Sciences and Religion*, ed. A. Runehov and L. Ovideo (New York: Springer, 2013), 1176–80; Hedges, "Interreligious Studies: A New Direction in the Study of Religion?" *Bulletin of the British Association for the Study of Religions*, November 2014; Interfaith Youth Core, "The Field of Interfaith Studies," in *Interfaith Studies: Curricular Programs and Core Competencies* (2016); Oddbjørn Leirvik, "Interreligious Studies: A New Academic Discipline?" in *Contested Spaces, Common Ground: Spaces and Power Structures in Multireligious Societies*, ed. Ulrich Winkler, Lidia Rodriguez, and Oddbjørn Leirvik (Leiden, Netherlands: Brill Rodopi, 2016), 33–42; Leirvik, *Interreligious Studies: A Relational Approach to Religious Activism and the Study of Religion* (New York: Bloomsbury, 2014); Leirvik, "Interreligious Studies: A Relational Approach to the Study of Religion," *Journal of Inter-Religious Studies* 13 (2014); Eboo Patel, "Toward a Field of Interfaith Studies," *Liberal Education* 99, no. 4 (2014); Eboo Patel, Jennifer Howe Peace, and Noah Silverman, eds., *Interreligious/Interfaith Studies: Defining a New Field* (Boston: Beacon, 2018); Joshua Stanton, "Inter-religious Studies: A Field of Its Own," *Huffington Post*, April 24, 2014; Ulrich Winkler and Henry Jansen, eds., *Shifting Locations and Reshaping Methods: Methodological Challenges Arising from New Fields of Research in Intercultural Theology and Interreligious Studies*, Interreligious Studies 12 (Berlin: Lit Verlag, 2018).

2   See, e.g., Julia Ipgrave, Thorsten Knauth, Anna Körs, Dörthe Vieregge, and Marie von der Lippe, eds., *Religion and Dialogue in the City*, Religious Diversity and Education in Europe 36 (Münster: Waxmann, 2018); Julia Ipgrave, ed., *Interreligious Engagement in Urban Spaces: Social, Material, and Ideological Dimensions* (Cham, Switzerland: Springer Nature, 2019); Elisabeth Arweck, *Young People's Attitudes to Religious Diversity* (London: Routledge, 2017); and Barbara A. McGraw, "From Prison Religion to Interfaith

Leadership for Institutional Change," in Patel, Peace, and Silverman, *Interreligious/Interfaith Studies*, 183–95.

3   In this volume, see chapters from Howard and Rose.

4   Pedagogical approaches to the field often articulate normative and prescriptive dimensions by applying them to professional and vocation contexts that emphasize practical skills and leadership competencies. For Eboo Patel, the applied dimension is perhaps paramount to what he believes serves as a major part of what the field should be about: "nurturing a cadre of professionals," a group he refers to as "interfaith leaders" (Patel, "Toward a Field of Interfaith Studies"). Patel's organization, the Interfaith Youth Core, of which Patel is founder and president, reflects this in its mission (on its website) "to make interfaith cooperation the norm in America" (Interfaith Youth Core, "Mission," accessed March 27, 2019, https://www.ifyc.org/mission). He argues that a key goal is to "recognize the importance of training people who have the knowledge base and skill set needed to engage religious diversity in a way that promotes peace, stability, and cooperation—and to begin offering academic programs that certify such leaders" (Patel, "Toward a Field of Interfaith Studies"). Wakoh Hickey and Margarita M. W. Suárez, professors who teach in the field, agree. They argue, "Interfaith studies has the explicit goal of promoting pluralism as a social norm" ("Meeting Others, Seeing Myself," in Patel, Peace, and Silverman, *Interreligious/Interfaith Studies*, 109).

5   E.g., *Interreligious Studies and Intercultural Theology* (Equinox), *Studies in Interreligious Dialogue* (Peeters), *Journal of Interreligious Studies*, *Journal of Ecumenical Studies* (University of Pennsylvania Press), *Ecumenical Trends* (Graymoor Ecumenical and Interreligious Institute), and *Studies in Jewish-Christian Relations, Islam and Christian–Muslim Relations* (Taylor and Francis).

6   E.g., European Society for Intercultural Theology and Interreligious Studies (ESITIS), established in 2005 in Amsterdam; and Association for Interreligious/Interfaith Studies (AIIS) established in 2017 in the United States.

7   Faith and religion do not always refer to the same concept, so on a literal and technical level it is reasonable to distinguish between inter*faith* and inter*religious* (see Hans Gustafson, "'Interfaith' Is so 1970s!" *State of Formation*, April 12, 2018). Oddbjørn Leirvik argues that interreligious studies needs "the critical outside perspective of religious studies in order not to be controlled by the dialogue of the insiders who are well aware of their role as agents but perhaps not always able to see themselves from a critical distance." Leirvik, "Interreligious Studies" (drawing on David Cheetham, "The University and Interfaith Education," *Studies in Interreligious Dialogue* 15, no. 1 [2005]: 16–35). Kate McCarthy agrees, arguing that it is precisely this "scholarly and religiously neutral quality" of interreligious studies that establishes it as an academic field, and that "[Russel T.] McCutcheon is right that it should not be the task of interreligious relations scholars to be caretakers of the traditions." McCarthy, "(Inter)Religious Studies," in Patel, Peace, and Silverman, *Interreligious/Interfaith Studies*, 12. Leirvik's concern brings out a crucial distinc-

tion between IRS and the generally less- or non-academic activist grassroots community-level "interfaith movement" that aims to foster civic pluralism, mutual understanding, peacebuilding, and social cohesion (admirable aims often shared by many curricular and cocurricular programs at colleges and universities, especially at the undergraduate level). To pronounce the separation between the academic field and the community movement is one reason, among others, that scholars such as McCarthy and others advocate for "interreligious" over the "interfaith" when referring to the field of study. If interreligious studies, McCarthy writes, "is to be an academic discipline suitable to secular higher education, it must not be construed as an auxiliary of the interfaith movement." McCarthy, "(Inter)Religious Studies," in Patel, Peace, and Silverman, *Interreligious/Interfaith Studies*, 10. On the other hand, scholars in this volume who tend to use interfaith over interreligious (whether intentional or not) include Eboo Patel, Catherine Cornille, Mark Hanshaw, and Barbara McGraw to name a few.

8   E.g., the group dedicated to this field at the American Academy of Religion is named the "Interreligious and Interfaith Studies Unit"; the most recent authoritative publication on this field is titled, *Interreligious/Interfaith Studies: Defining a New Field*, edited by Eboo Patel, Jennifer Howe Peace, and Noah Silverman.

9   Several scholars have made the point, like Perry Schmidt-Leukel, that "there is no such thing as completely disengaged, disinterested or impartial studies of religion. . . . No scholar comes to his or her field as a *tabula rasa*." "Why We Need an Engaged Interreligious Theology," *Interreligious Studies and Intercultural Theology* 2, no. 2 (2018): 131. Schmidt-Leukel here recalls Rita M. Gross' statement that "there is no neutral place from which one can objectively study religion. Everyone has an agenda and those who claim they are outsiders to religion are insiders to and advocates of some other belief about religion." Gross, "Methodology: Tool or Trap?" in *How to Do Comparative Religion? Three Ways, Many Goals*, ed. René Gothóni (Berlin: De Gruyter, 2005), 150; quoted in Schmidt-Leukel, "Why We Need an Engaged Interreligious Theology," 132. Oddbjørn Leirvik (drawing on Gavin Flood) critiques "the idea of 'the detached, epistemic subject penetrating the alien world of the other through the phenomenological process.' Instead, Flood writes, 'the subject must be defined in relation to other subjects.' Flood goes as far as to say that religious studies thus become 'a dialogical enterprise in which the inquirer is situated within a particular context or narrative tradition, and whose research into narrative traditions, that become the objects of investigation, must be apprehended in a much richer and multi-faceted way." Leirvik, "Interreligious Studies," 15; citing Flood, "Dialogue and the Situated Observer," in *Beyond Phenomenology: Rethinking the Study of Religion* (London: Cassell, 1999), 143. Both Leirvik and Flood are cited in Gustafson, "Interreligious and Interfaith Studies."

10   See footnote 4 for more about how this is pedagogically manifested.

11   In a forthcoming publication, I argue for interreligious and interfaith studies to be closely allied with, and yet clearly distinct from, the so-called interfaith

movement in ways analogous to how a coach or trainer is related to an athlete or competitor.

12 I.e., the generally less- or non-academic activist grassroots initiative at the community level (beyond, but also within, the walls of the university) that aims to foster, among religious persons and communities, civic pluralism, mutual understanding, peacebuilding, and social cohesion. These admirable aims are also often shared by many curricular and cocurricular programs at colleges and universities.

13 Many scholars recognize that "the idea of pluralism that underlies much of the discussion of interfaith and interreligious work in the United States is due for particular scholarly scrutiny, and *theoretical framing* is a critical part of the endeavor." McCarthy, "(Inter)Religious Studies," in Patel, Peace, and Silverman, *Interreligious/Interfaith Studies*, 13 (emphasis in original). Kate McCarthy insists that for interreligious studies to "achieve the status of an academic discipline, central theoretical constructs . . . must be subject to critique and reformulation." These constructs include Western civic pluralism and idealism, the universalizing of elite cultures, the almost never-ending incorporation of identities "into configurations of difference that make real difference invisible" (McCarthy, "[Inter]Religious Studies," in Patel, Peace, and Silverman, *Interreligious/Interfaith Studies*, 13), and "neoliberal projects of the postcolonial nation-state" (Amy L. Allocco, Geoffrey D. Claussen, and Brian K. Pennington, "Constructing Interreligious Studies," in Patel, Peace, and Silverman, *Interreligious/Interfaith Studies*, 48).

14 Jeanne Halgren Kilde and Marilyn J. Chiat, "Twin Cities Houses of Worship: 1849–1924," University of Minnesota, accessed April 12, 2019, https://housesofworship.umn.edu/home. Kilde and Chiat report, due to the complexity and dynamism of religion and religious people, that although their "study initially focused on houses of worship (churches and synagogues) as a means to explore the complexity of religious life and ethnic interaction during [1849–1924] in the Twin Cities as new immigrants acclimate themselves to the region, [the authors] soon realized that other sites needed to be included as well: specifically, places where these diverse people found solace among like-minded individuals, such as social clubs and ethnic/religious institutions, and places where they had to intermingle and interact with the 'other,' folks whose beliefs, cultures and languages differed from theirs."

15 See, in this volume, Skeie, "Identifying the Field of Research," note 1.

16 In this volume, chapter from Weisse, "Dialogical Theology and Praxis."

References

Allocco, Amy L., Geoffrey D. Claussen, and Brian K. Pennington. "Constructing Interreligious Studies." In Patel, Peace, and Silverman, *Interreligious/Interfaith Studies*, 36–48.

American Academy of Religion. "Interreligious and Interfaith Studies Unit." Accessed April 12, 2019. https://papers.aarweb.org/content/interreligious-and -interfaith-studies-unit.

Arweck, Elisabeth. *Young People's Attitudes to Religious Diversity*. London: Rout- ledge, 2017.

Cheetham, David. "The University and Interfaith Education." *Studies in Interreli- gious Dialogue* 15, no. 1 (2005): 16–35.

Diller, Jeannine, Eboo Patel, Jennifer Peace, and Colleen Windham-Hughes. "To- ward a Field of Interfaith Studies: Emerging Questions and Considerations." *Journal of Interreligious Studies* 16 (2015): 5–13.

Flood, Gavin. "Dialogue and the Situated Observer." In *Beyond Phenomenology: Rethinking the Study of Religion*. London: Cassell, 1999.

Gross, Rita M. "Methodology: Tool or Trap? Comments from a Feminist Perspective." In *How to Do Comparative Religion? Three Ways, Many Goals*, edited René Gothóni, 149–66. Berlin: De Gruyter, 2005.

Gustafson, Hans. "'Interfaith' Is So1970s!" *State of Formation*, April 12, 2018.

———. "Interreligious and Interfaith Studies in Relation to Religious Studies and Theological Studies." *State of Formation*, January 6, 2015.

Hedges, Paul. "Editorial Introduction: Interreligious Studies." *Journal for the Academic Study of Religion* 27, no. 2 (2014): 127–31.

———. "Interreligious Studies." In *Encyclopedia of Sciences and Religion*, edited by A. Runehov and L. Ovideo, 1176–80. New York: Springer, 2013.

———. "Interreligious Studies: A New Direction in the Study of Religion?" *Bulle- tin of the British Association for the Study of Religions*, November 2014, 13–14.

Hickey, Wakoh, and Margarita M. W. Suárez. "Meeting Others, Seeing Myself." In Patel, Peace, and Silverman, *Interreligious/Interfaith Studies*, 108–21.

Interfaith Youth Core. "The Field of Interfaith Studies." In *Interfaith Studies: Cur- ricular Programs and Core Competencies*, 2016, 3–5. Accessed December 5, 2019. https://www.ifyc.org/resources/interfaith-studies-curricular-programs -and-core-competencies2.

———. "Mission." Accessed March 27, 2019. https://www.ifyc.org/mission.

Ipgrave, Julia, ed. *Interreligious Engagement in Urban Spaces: Social, Material, and Ideological Dimensions*. Cham, Switzerland: Springer Nature, 2019.

Ipgrave, Julia, Thorsten Knauth, Anna Körs, Dörthe Vieregge, and Marie von der Lippe, eds. *Religion and Dialogue in the City*. Religious Diversity and Educa- tion in Europe 36. Münster: Waxmann, 2018.

Kilde, Jeanne Halgren, and Marilyn J. Chiat. "Twin Cities Houses of Worship: 1849–1924." University of Minnesota. Accessed April 12, 2019. https:// housesofworship.umn.edu/home.

Leirvik, Oddbjørn. "Interreligious Studies: A New Academic Discipline?" In *Con- tested Spaces, Common Ground: Spaces and Power Structures in Multireligious Societies*, edited by Ulrich Winkler, Lidia Rodriguez, and Oddbjørn Leirvik, 33–42. Leiden, Netherlands: Brill Rodopi, 2016.

———. *Interreligious Studies: A Relational Approach to Religious Activism and the Study of Religion*. New York: Bloomsbury, 2014.

———. "Interreligious Studies: A Relational Approach to the Study of Religion." *Journal of Inter-Religious Studies* 13 (2014): 15–19.

McCarthy, Kate. "(Inter)Religious Studies." In Patel, Peace, and Silverman, *Interreligious/Interfaith Studies*, 2–15.

McGraw, Barbara A. "From Prison Religion to Interfaith Leadership for Institutional Change." In Patel, Peace, and Silverman, *Interreligious/Interfaith Studies*, 183–95.

Patel, Eboo. "Toward a Field of Interfaith Studies." *Liberal Education* 99, no. 4 (2014) Accessed April 12, 2019. https://www.aacu.org/publications-research/periodicals/toward-field-interfaith-studies.

Patel, Eboo, Jennifer Howe Peace, and Noah Silverman, eds. *Interreligious/Interfaith Studies: Defining a New Field*. Boston: Beacon, 2018.

Schmidt-Leukel, Perry. "Why We Need an Engaged Interreligious Theology." *Interreligious Studies and Intercultural Theology* 2, no. 2 (2018): 131–40.

Stanton, Joshua. "Inter-religious Studies: A Field of Its Own." *Huffington Post*, April 24, 2014.

Winkler, Ulrich, and Henry Jansen, eds. *Shifting Locations and Reshaping Methods: Methodological Challenges Arising from New Fields of Research in Intercultural Theology and Interreligious Studies*. Interreligious Studies 12. Berlin: Lit Verlag, 2018.

I
SKETCHING THE FIELD

2

Area, Field, Discipline

Oddbjørn Leirvik

Since 2013, following an increasing growth in the scholarly study of interreligious relations, several attempts have been made to define "interreligious" or "interfaith" studies as a new academic field or discipline. In an article from 2013 titled "Toward a Field of Interfaith Studies," Eboo Patel of the Interfaith Youth Core wrote:

> As an academic field, interfaith studies would examine the multiple dimensions of how individuals and groups who orient around religion differently interact with one another, along with the implications of [these] interactions for communities, civil society, and global politics.[1]

From Area to Field

Terminologically, Patel distinguishes between "areas" and "fields." He notes that academic fields are "useful because they are formal spaces for a group of colleagues to engage in long-term data gathering, sustained reflection, and extended discussion." "Clearly," he adds, "[interfaith studies] would be an interdisciplinary field."

From the perspective of Bourdieu's field theory, when an area becomes a field it also becomes a battleground for struggles over academic capital.[2] In the case of interreligious studies, it is becoming valuable and thus contested. From a power-critical perspective, interreligious studies already competes—

17

for prestige and money—with established fields and disciplines such as religious studies and theology (and the rest of the humanities).

Interfaith / Interreligious

In attempted definitions of the field, one notes a certain fluctuation between the expressions "interfaith" and "interreligious," as reflected in the title of an edited book from 2018 titled *Interreligious/Interfaith Studies: Defining a New Field*.[3] The terminological ambivalence might reflect William Cantwell Smith's distinction between dynamic faith and institutionalized religion. It seems, however, that the term "interfaith" is the preferred expression when referring to academic initiatives with a strong practitioner dimension oriented toward personal formation (cf. Patel's emphasis on educating "interfaith leaders"). "Interreligious," by contrast, concentrates more on analytical approaches, studying the complex interaction between religions from theological, religious studies, or social science perspectives.

In academic practices, however, one witnesses a cross-fertilization between the two approaches. Moreover, interfaith and interreligious studies are similar in their emphasis on agency perspectives—be it (in the legacy of practical theology) personal formation or (in the perspective of critical theory) analytical awareness of the student's role as an agent of change or conservation in the spaces between religions and secularities.

From Field to Discipline?

As regards the relation between religious and interreligious studies, Kate McCarthy defines "(inter)religious studies" as a "subdiscipline of religious studies." Its aim, according to McCarthy, is to study "the interactions of religiously different people and groups, including the intersections of religion and secularity."[4] Emphasizing the "scholarly and religiously neutral quality" of interreligious studies (which establishes its place in the academy), McCarthy also raises the question of whether interreligious studies—beyond its emerging status as a field of its own—might also achieve the status of "an academic discipline." Becoming a discipline would require, McCarthy suggests, a "theoretical framing" in which "central theoretical constructs . . . must be subject to critique and reformulation."[5]

Obviously, the two foremost disciplinary neighbors to interreligious studies are religious studies and theology, both of which can offer a broad array of methodological approaches and critical theoretical perspectives that inform interreligious studies. In an article from 2013, Paul Hedges suggests that interreligious studies may actually be seen as "an interface between a more traditionally secular Religious Studies discipline, and a more traditionally confessional theological discipline."[6] The difference to both, he suggests, would be that interreligious studies is "more expressly focused on the dynamic encounter and engagement between religious traditions and persons."[7]

A Relational, Self-Implicating Approach

I sympathize with Hedges' reasoning, which goes well together with my own attempt to define interreligious studies as "a relational approach" to the study of religion.[8] But is the relational approach something exclusive to interreligious studies, in contrast with religious studies and theology? That clearly depends on how one sees the two more established disciplines.

Religious studies have traditionally been seen as more neutral and less self-implicating than theology and (by implication) interreligious studies. There are several examples, however, of how religious studies may actually incorporate a relational approach to the relevant areas of study. An interesting example is Gavin Flood's remarks on "dialogue and the situated observer" in his book *Beyond Phenomenology* (1999). Referring to the shift to language and the sign as the focus of religious and cultural studies, Flood criticizes the old idea of "the detached, epistemic subject penetrating the alien world of the other through the phenomenological process." Instead, Flood writes, "the subject must be defined in relation to other subjects." Religious studies thus becomes

> a dialogical enterprise in which the inquirer is situated within a particular context or narrative tradition. . . . The relationship between the situated observer and situation of observation becomes dialogical in the sense that the observer is thrown into conversation with people and texts of the object tradition.[9]

"Rather than the disengaged reason of the social scientists observing, recording and theorizing data," Flood suggests, "we have a situation in which research is imaged as 'conversation,' or more accurately 'critical conversation,' in which the interactive nature of research is recognized."[10]

In light of Bourdieu's power-critical view of a social field, and Flood's dialogical perspective on religion-related research, one must ask: Who is not part of the spaces between religious cultures and secularities? Who is not already a positioned agent in those spaces, when undertaking a particular study? Thus with a view to the many tensions between the religions, and not least between religion and non-religion, interreligious studies therefore examines conflicts that you are already part of.[11]

If doing interreligious studies means to be implicated as an agent in the field of study, it should be no surprise that this emerging field or discipline has evolved from theology rather than from religious studies. Emphasizing the agency perspective, Scott Daniel Dunbar (1998) argues that what he calls "interfaith studies" in the academia (in the legacy of theology) should be experiential and prescriptive, not just descriptive.[12] However, as David Cheetham (2005) has emphasized, the new field needs the critical outsider perspective of religious studies in order not to be controlled by dialogue insiders who are well aware of their role as agents but perhaps not always able to see themselves from a critical distance.[13]

Interreligious studies needs both: self-implication and self-critique.

Interreligious Theology

While defining interreligious studies as a field (in Bourdieu's sense) of its own, I would leave the question open of whether interreligious studies can also be seen as a discipline. Maybe it is more fruitful to see interreligious studies as a multi- or cross-disciplinary field.

Theology is obviously one of the relevant disciplines, just as interreligious theology is one out of many manifestations of interreligious studies. Interreligious studies, in the academy, is not only influenced *by* theology, rather due to its pluralistic and relational approach; it may also reflect back *on* theology. It pushes the question of whether and how university theology, in a situation of accelerated theological pluralization, can be done in an interactive, relational mode inspired by interreligious studies.

The issue of theology and pluralization calls for a reflection on the relation between "interreligious" and "comparative" theology. In the understanding of the Catholic theologian Francis Clooney, *comparative theology* is "faith seeking understanding" across religious barriers, in theological efforts based in a particular faith tradition but venturing into "learning from one or more other faith traditions."[14] In comparison with dialogical or interreligious theology, Clooney states, "[c]omparative theology is primarily and usually a form of reading," whereas interreligious dialogue (in his understanding) is "usually a form of conversation."[15]

Clooney, then, seems to look upon religious plurality and interfaith dialogue merely as raw material for theological reflection. In my understanding, which differs from that of Clooney, the defining features of *interreligious* theology are the *relational* and *cooperative* nature of doing theology in this way.

Theology done in this mode often springs from personal experiences with crossing borders, and is dialogical in and of itself.[16]

Interreligious theology, then, distinguishes itself from comparative theology by inviting researchers, teachers, and students from different religious backgrounds to take part in a critical and constructive interpretive work, which might also be called *collaborative*. Linda Hogan and John D'Arcy May, in an article from 2011, note that "there is already much activity in the field that has come to be called 'comparative theology.'" What they envisage, however, is "something more like a 'collaborative theology' which would not stop short at identifying ways of tackling similar or perhaps identical problems but would actually set about doing so."[17]

This has methodological implications, although not fixed in advance. For instance, "representatives of different faiths would thus deploy their inherited resources together, working out the methodology for doing so as they went."[18]

A Joint Academic Framework

Interfaith/interreligious studies has already evolved from being merely an *area* of study to become a (contested) academic *field*. This requires a further reflection on whether interreligious studies can also be associated with certain methods and theories—thus becoming an academic *discipline*.

Thus in the perspective of Hogan and D'Arcy May, the question of method and theory in the field of interreligious studies is something that must be worked out in collaboration—between different disciplines in the academy and between scholars with different life stances but a shared institutional framework in academia.

For interreligious studies to live up to its defining feature of being *relational* studies, the academy (and other relevant institutions) must make *space* for interreligious collaboration—as when European universities and theological faculties during the last decade have established chairs, courses, and study programs in Islamic theology alongside Protestant and Catholic theology. This (and similar developments in other contexts) opens new ground for doing university theology in an interreligious mode.

Notes

1   Eboo Patel, "Toward a Field of Interfaith Studies," *Liberal Education* 99, no. 44 (2013).

2   David L. Swartz, "Bourdieu's Concept of Field," *Oxford Bibliographies*, 2016, DOI:10.1093/OBO/9780199756384–0164.

3   Eboo Patel, Jennifer Howe Peace, and Noah J. Silverman, eds., *Interreligious/Interfaith Studies: Defining a New Field* (Boston: Beacon, 2018).

4   Kate McCarthy, "(Inter)Religious Studies: Making a Home in the Secular Academy," in Patel, Peace, and Silverman, *Interreligious/Interfaith Studies*, 2.

5   McCarthy, "(Inter)Religious Studies," in Patel, Peace, and Silverman, *Interreligious/Interfaith Studies*, 13.

6   Paul Hedges, "Interreligious Studies," in *Encyclopedia of Sciences and Religion*, ed. A. Runehov and L. Ovideo (New York: Springer, 2012), 1077. Cf. Hans Gustafson, "Interreligious and Interfaith Studies in Relation to Religious Studies and Theological Studies," *StateofFormation.org*, January 6, 2015.

7   Hedges, "Interreligious Studies," in Runehov and Ovideo, *Encyclopedia of Sciences and Religion*, 1077.

8   Oddbjørn Leirvik, *Interreligious Studies: A Relational Approach to Religious Activism and the Study of Religion* (New York: Bloomsbury, 2014).

9   Gavin Flood, *Beyond Phenomenology: Rethinking the Study of Religion* (London: Cassell, 1999), 143.

10   Flood, *Beyond Phenomenology*, 143.

11   Leirvik, *Interreligious Studies*, 10–11.

12   Scott Daniel Dunbar, "The Place of Interreligious Dialogue in the Academic Study of Religion," *Journal of Ecumenical Studies* 35, no. 3–4 (1998): 455–70.

13   David Cheetham, "The University and Interfaith Education," *Studies in Interreligious Dialogue* 15, no. 1 (2005): 16–35.

14   Francis X. Clooney, *Comparative Theology: Deep Learning across Religious Borders* (Chichester: Wiley-Blackwell, 2010), 10.

15   Francis X. Clooney, "Comparative Theology and Inter-religious Dialogue," in *The Wiley-Blackwell Companion to Inter-religious Dialogue*, ed. Catherine Cornille (Chichester: Wiley-Blackwell, 2013), 54.

16   Oddbjørn Leirvik, "Interreligious University Theologies, Christian/Islamic," *Islam and Christian–Muslim Relations* 4 (2018): 509–23. See also Leirvik, "Comparative or Interreligious Theology?" in "Special Issue 1: Comparative Theology," guest ed. Ulrich Winkler, *Frankfurter Zeitschrift für islamisch-theologische Studien* (2017): 11–24.

17   Linda Hogan and John D'Arcy May, "Visioning Ecumenics as Intercultural, Interreligious, and Public Theology," *Concilium* 1 (2011): 76.

18   Hogan and D'Arcy May, "Visioning Ecumenics," 76.

References

Cheetham, David. "The University and Interfaith Education." *Studies in Interreligious Dialogue* 15, no. 1 (2005): 16–35.

Clooney, Francis X. "Comparative Theology and Inter-religious Dialogue." In *The Wiley-Blackwell Companion to Inter-religious Dialogue*, edited by Catherine Cornille, 51–63. Chichester: Wiley-Blackwell, 2013.

———. *Comparative Theology: Deep Learning across Religious Borders*. Chichester: Wiley-Blackwell, 2010.

Dunbar, Scott Daniel. "The Place of Interreligious Dialogue in the Academic Study of Religion." *Journal of Ecumenical Studies* 35, no. 3–4 (1998): 455–70.

Flood, Gavin. *Beyond Phenomenology: Rethinking the Study of Religion*. London: Cassell, 1999.

Gustafson, Hans. "Interreligious and Interfaith Studies in Relation to Religious Studies and Theological Studies." *StateofFormation.com*, January 6, 2015.

Hedges, Paul. "Interreligious Studies." In *Encyclopaedia of Sciences and Religion*, edited by A. Runehov and L. Ovideo, 1076–80. New York: Springer, 2012.

Hogan, Linda, and John D'Arcy May. "Visioning Ecumenics as Intercultural, Interreligious, and Public Theology." *Concilium* 1 (2011): 70–84.

Leirvik, Oddbjørn. "Comparative or Interreligious Theology?" In "Special Issue 1: Comparative Theology," guest edited by Ulrich Winkler, *Frankfurter Zeitschrift für islamisch-theologische Studien* (2017): 11–24.

———. *Interreligious Studies: A Relational Approach to Religious Activism and the Study of Religion*. New York: Bloomsbury, 2014.

———. "Interreligious University Theologies, Christian/Islamic." *Islam and Christian–Muslim Relations* 4 (2018): 509–23.

McCarthy, Kate. "(Inter)Religious Studies: Making a Home in the Secular Academy." In Patel, Peace, and Silverman, *Interreligious/Interfaith Studies*, 2–15.

Patel, Eboo. "Toward a Field of Interfaith Studies." *Liberal Education* 99, no. 44 (2013).

Patel, Eboo, Jennifer Howe Peace, and Noah J. Silverman, eds. *Interreligious/Interfaith Studies: Defining a New Field*. Boston: Beacon, 2018.

Swartz, David L. "Bourdieu's Concept of Field." *Oxford Bibliographies*. 2016. DOI: 10.1093/OBO/9780199756384–0164.

3

Identifying the Field of Research

Geir Skeie

It is certainly both appropriate and necessary to give an overview of inter-religious studies and to discuss the achievements in this field of research.[1] However, the present article does not give this overview. Rather, it reflects on some issues relevant to interreligious studies as a field of research, based on experiences and results from an international research project (ReDi),[2] which combined theological and empirical studies, though mainly separate from— but also in discussion with—each other.[3] The constant deliberations that arose between researchers of theology, religious studies, religious education, and social sciences, all with common interest in the practice and theory of dialogue and interreligious relations, proved to be challenging. At the same time, they served as stimuli to investigate the issues at stake on a meta level. Terms like "dialogue," "religion," "worldview," "normative," and "descriptive" were often on the agenda in addition to issues related to the object of study and the research questions.

This chapter does not focus on the entire scope of the ReDi project; rather it focuses on the empirical study of dialogue between religions and worldviews, both in urban settings more generally and in education (particularly religious education). There is no doubt about the existence of interreligious studies as a new area of academic study, with the establishment of recent study programs, research projects, conferences, and journals.[4] The issue on the table here is whether it can be justified as a field of research in its own right.

For ReDi, "interreligious studies" was not the key phrase from the start; rather, "dialogue" was. At an early stage, our research staff meetings revealed that several of the empirical researchers had more trouble with the term "dialogue" than did the theological researchers. The empirical researchers tended to use "interreligious" rather than "dialogue" because "interreligious" was perceived to be more descriptive, while "dialogue" was seen as more normative. On the other hand, in the empirical field, this dynamic could be turned upside-down. For instance, the actors studied were often talking about "dialogue." Perhaps more importantly, "dialogue" also covered the participation of nonreligious worldviews in the interactions being empirically investigated, while "interreligious" functioned more exclusively.[5] Still, the actors shared a somewhat normative understanding of "dialogue." They did not consider all kinds of activities that included people with different religious or world views to be "dialogue" proper. Some activities were deemed only "cooperation." Such terminological issues mirror the emic/etic differentiation in qualitative empirical research, moving from more experience-near to more experience-distant concepts as part of the analysis. One example of a movement from experience-near to more analytical concepts is the continuum the project found between the more practical "side-by-side dialogue" activities and the more verbal "face-to-face dialogue" activities.[6]

Irrespective of the results coming from individual empirical studies of "interreligious relations" or "dialogue activities between religious and world views," projects like ReDi do not necessarily justify the existence of a distinct field of research. It merely shows there are activities that can be studied as part of the study of religion. In order to speak about interreligious studies as a field of research in its own right, something more is needed. In humanities and social studies, where theory often plays a significant role in defining and constructing both the object of study and the approach to this object, ideas about the field of research as something distinct is not always cherished. Something can be learned from the philosophy of knowledge in natural sciences without adopting their understanding of all the terms used. For instance, the following definition of a "field of research" can be adopted:

> an area of science consisting of the following elements: a central problem, a domain consisting of items taken to be facts related to that problem, general explanatory factors and goals providing expectations as to how the problem is to be solved, techniques and methods, and, sometimes,

but not always, concepts, laws and theories which are related to the problem and which attempt to realize the explanatory goals.[7]

In ReDi, one common problem we identified was, "What are the possibilities and limitations of dialogue between religions and worldviews?" We also
distinguished between (a) a domain consisting of actors in dialogue, (b) content of dialogue, (c) methods of dialogue, and (d) spatial and material aspects
of dialogue. In terms of explanatory factors, the project employed the term
"social capital," which investigated whether "dialogue" contributed to participants acquiring such capital or if "dialogue" was dependent on the existence of
"social capital" among the participants. This proved to be a fruitful approach,[8]
possibly suggesting that the existence of "social capital" is more of a resource
that enables interreligious dialogue rather than an effect of it. The discussion of
social capital raises a broader question about "context." How does the research
distinguish between the object of study (here: dialogue) and its "surround-
ings" (context), and how is the relationship between the two conceptualized?
In ReDi, we presented "dialogue" as something distinct that could be studied
in different contexts in order to understand it better, hence the empirical studies carried out in London, Hamburg, Duisburg-Essen, Oslo, and Stockholm.
However, this research strategy depends on whether "dialogue" in all these
places is the same. In fact, there is no clear difference between object of study
and context. Dialogue, as the object of study, is not already distinct from its
context. Rather dialogue is "separated out" by the researcher from the context
and thereby established as an object of study. As such, a relationship between
the object of study and its context is established.

In order to "separate dialogue out" from its context, the defining characteristics of "dialogue" become central. The definition of dialogue for ReDi was
loose and practice-oriented. It more or less overlapped with interreligious
(and inter-worldview) relations because we wanted to cover a range of practices. In most of them, "dialogue" was a commonly used word. In this way, a
discursive, pragmatic, or functional definition was used, emphasizing the fact
that people with differing religious and/or worldview backgrounds met and
deliberately acted together across lines of division. However, the definition was
not substantial. Certain characteristics had to be in place in order to qualify
an activity or encounter as "dialogue" or "interreligious" in terms of content.
Paul Hedges, for example, proposes one such definition: "Interreligious studies
concerns studies of at least two religions (but it also includes non-religions or
secular worldviews) and the dynamic encounter or relationship this entails."
He adds that it should also be "a dynamic lived reality," "interdisciplinary,"

and "often engaged in activism"; recognize "the researcher as actor"; and push "hegemonic boundaries in disciplines and religious traditions."[9] The two approaches to the relationship between object of study and its context, referred to above, are two different ways of contextualizing the research object. While one is practice-oriented, the other is content-oriented.

In the qualitative empirical studies of the ReDi project, although we mainly drew on the practice-oriented approach to the relationship between research object and context, we observed that the structure of the context in which dialogue activities took place could be differently framed. We differentiated between the urban and the educational setting. In the urban, frames were relatively loose, even if structural, spatial, and social restrictions could be observed. These were particularly visible through the political support and public funding of dialogue activities. This was happening in all settings, but it was generally limited by conditions put on this funding by the local authorities regarding form and content of dialogue. On the other hand, actors needed to be aware of the way the calls for funding were formulated. In educational settings, dialogue was staged and directed by the teacher and was sometimes even supported and assessed by public servants through curricula. In other words, dialogue in educational settings tended to be much more strict, structured, and formally framed. Interestingly enough, the walls between the educational and urban settings were discovered to be, to some extent, porous and in several cases nonexistent. Dialogue practitioners who belonged to the civil sector were often eager to gain access to schools in order to stimulate and support dialogue between religions and worldviews.

Recognizing the differences in the framing of contexts in which interreligious activities are carried out, and the distance between a practice-oriented and a content-oriented approach to the object of research (dialogue / the interreligious), underlines the complexities related to establishing interreligious studies as a field of research in its own right. It also suggests that the relationship between the research object and its social and cultural context plays a key role, and is perhaps one of the main problems this research seeks to understand and explain.

Notes

1   Eboo Patel, "Toward a Field of Interfaith Studies," *Liberal Education* 99, no. 44 (2013).

2   David L. Swartz, "Bourdieu's Concept of Field," *Oxford Bibliographies*, 2016, DOI:10.1093/OBO/9780199756384–0164.

3   Eboo Patel, Jennifer Howe Peace, and Noah J. Silverman, eds., *Interreligious/ Interfaith Studies: Defining a New Field* (Boston: Beacon, 2018).

4   Kate McCarthy, "(Inter)Religious Studies: Making a Home in the Secular Academy," in Patel, Peace, and Silverman, *Interreligious/Interfaith Studies*, 2.

5   McCarthy, "(Inter)Religious Studies," in Patel, Peace, and Silverman, *Interreligious/Interfaith Studies*, 13.

6   Paul Hedges, "Interreligious Studies," in *Encyclopedia of Sciences and Religion*, ed. A. Runehov and L. Ovideo (New York: Springer, 2012), 1077. Cf. Hans Gustafson, "Interreligious and Interfaith Studies in Relation to Religious Studies and Theological Studies," *StateofFormation.org*, January 6, 2015.

7   Hedges, "Interreligious Studies," in Runehov and Ovideo, *Encyclopedia of Sciences and Religion*, 1077.

8   Oddbjørn Leirvik, *Interreligious Studies: A Relational Approach to Religious Activism and the Study of Religion* (New York: Bloomsbury, 2014).

9   Gavin Flood, *Beyond Phenomenology: Rethinking the Study of Religion* (London: Cassell, 1999), 143.

References

Amirpur, Katajun, Thorsten Knauth, Carola Roloff, and Wolfram Weisse, eds. *Perspektiven dialogischer Theologie: Offenheit in den Religionen und eine Hermeneutik des interreligiösen Dialogs*. Vol. 10. Münster: Waxmann, 2016.

Darden, Lindley, and Nancy Maull. "Interfield Theories." *Philosophy of Science* 44, no. 1 (1977): 43–64.

Gustafson, Hans. "Interreligious and Interfaith Studies in Relation to Religious Studies and Theological Studies." *StateofFormation.com*, January 6, 2015.

Hedges, Paul. "Editorial Introduction: Interreligious Studies." *Journal for the Academic Study of Religion* 27, no. 2 (2014): 127–31.

Husebø, Dag, and Øystein Lund Johannessen. "Interreligious Dialogue in Oslo in the Years following the Terror Attacks of 22 July 2011." In Ipgrave et al., *Religion and Dialogue in the City*, 115–40.

Ipgrave, Julia, and Marie von der Lippe. "Interreligious Dialogue and Engagement in the City." In Ipgrave et al., *Religion and Dialogue in the City*, 277–90.

Ipgrave, Julia, Thorsten Knauth, Anna Körs, Dörthe Vieregge, and Marie von der Lippe, eds. *Religion and Dialogue in the City: Case Studies on Interreligious Encounter in Urban Community and Education*. Religious Diversity and Education in Europe 36. Münster: Waxmann, 2018.

Skeie, Geir. "Dialogue between and among Religions and Worldviews as a Field of Research." In Ipgrave et al., *Religion and Dialogue in the City*, 301–16.

Weisse, Wolfram, Katajun Amirpur, Anna Körs, and Dörthe Vieregge, eds. *Religions and Dialogue: International Approaches*. Vol. 7. Münster: Waxmann, 2014.

4

A Civic Approach to Interfaith Studies

Eboo Patel

At the 2018 Parliament of the World's Religions in Canada, I met a young man named Abubakar Khan who told a remarkable story of interfaith leadership. It started with a meeting at city hall in Vancouver in December 2016. Khan and a group of other leaders representing diverse religious communities had been summoned there on short notice. A senior official opened the meeting with these words: "The morgue is full." Vancouver was suffering through the coldest winter in recent memory, and so many homeless people were freezing to death that the city did not know what to do. In a crisis, they had reached out to diverse religious leaders. Khan was twenty-two years old at the time and was the youngest person among the assembled religious leaders by several decades. He was there as a representative of the Al Jamia Masjid. As he listened to the other religious leaders debate back and forth about what might be done, Khan made a decision: he would open Al Jamia as a homeless shelter.

Khan got to work. Convincing the board to open the mosque as a homeless shelter was no easy task. Khan had to highlight both how helping people in this way was a requirement of their Islamic faith and that he would personally assume responsibility for the challenging logistics of the initiative. That included getting volunteers to spend the night at the mosque to "staff" the shelter. This also took some convincing. Whole sets of non-Muslims—both the needy and those who were volunteering to help the needy—would be spending substantial time in the mosque? Abubakar had to remind his own community of the Muslim theology of interfaith cooperation, largely through the prophet

Muhammad's example of welcoming people from different religions into his mosque. Khan then started reaching out to his group of religiously diverse friends and classmates, and he convinced them to participate by reminding them of the command in *their* diverse faiths and worldviews to help those in dire need.

Other logistical challenges arose: the mosque was not equipped to feed large groups of people on a regular basis, and many of the people who volunteered for overnight shifts had to go to work in the morning, meaning that the homeless people using the mosque as a shelter would need to leave and find some other warm place to spend the days. For the evening meals at the mosque, Khan reached out to his friends in the Sikh community. He knew about the Sikh practice of *langar*, religious hospitality through feeding others. He and his Sikh friends arranged for langar to be served to the homeless people and volunteers who gathered at the mosque. For daytime shelter, Khan reached out to his Christian friends involved in churches. He knew that churches, unlike other religious communities, were often staffed during the day and had the facilities for people to gather. But what about food during the day? For that, Khan reached out to friends in the Jewish community. He knew that many synagogues had kitchen facilities, and, while these buildings typically did not have the same full complement of professional staffing during the day that churches did, volunteers could use the synagogue kitchens to prepare food to bring to the churches where people were sheltering.

Abubakar Khan is what I call a civic interfaith leader, by which I mean he had the vision, knowledge, and skills to organize the religiously diverse social capital in a particular civic space to meet a clear social need. I believe interfaith studies as a field of research, teaching, and practice should arrange itself to engage the kind of social problems that emerged in Vancouver in December 2016 and to produce civic interfaith leaders like Abubakar Khan.

It is important to note that I am not making the case that this ought to be the *exclusive* purpose of the field of interfaith studies, simply an important one. There are inclinations within both the academy and interfaith movements that highlight personal spirituality, critical theory, or any number of other interesting and important directions for interfaith studies. In this short chapter, I am not arguing against any of those. Rather, I am only making a case for the significance of research, teaching, and practice for what I call civic interfaith leadership.

A research agenda for a civic approach to interfaith studies focuses on how interactions among diverse orientations around religion—both in the lives of individuals and in the practices of institutions—impact civic space. How do hospitals deal with families from religious traditions that do not allow blood to be removed from the body, or who believe death occurs when breath completely stops rather than when a brain scan flatlines, or who view seizures principally as preparation for shamanhood rather than evidence of epilepsy? What happens to Muslim kids in schools as both Islamic extremism and Islamophobia became more prominent? Should zoning laws be changed as the growing Hindu population seeks to build temples?

Such questions require an interdisciplinary approach. Consider how we might go about answering the question: What would the "good" religiously diverse city look like? We might draw on philosophical perspectives from Plato, theological views from the Bible and the prophet Muhammad's practices in Mecca and Medina, political philosophy from John Rawls and Danielle Allen, and sociological research from Robert Putnam, David Campbell, and Ashutosh Varshney.

Consider the knowledge and skills that Abubakar Khan brought to the table. He utilized a knowledge of the theology of care and interfaith cooperation inspired by his own religious tradition that enabled him to convince a skeptical board to do something unprecedented. He was able to leverage his knowledge of similar threads within other traditions and use his skills to bake that knowledge into an inviting story, to welcome others to participate. His understanding of both the social practices and the social capital within religious communities that were relevant to the situation—the practice of langar in the Sikh tradition, the fact that many Christian churches are professionally staffed during normal business hours, and that synagogues have kitchens—provided the necessary wherewithal to competently design and implement his vision.

An interfaith studies curriculum would center on precisely this type of knowledge and skills demonstrated by Abubakar Khan. A reasonable question remains: If Abubakar Khan managed to pull off his remarkable interfaith civic project without formal training, why cannot everybody else? In other words, why do we need a field of interfaith studies to educate civic interfaith leaders if such vision, knowledge, and skills are instinctive (or God-given) gifts? The answer to this question is multifold and reveals important dynamics related to both civic interfaith leadership and interfaith studies.

First, there are "naturals" in a range of fields. There are people who are instinctively effective teachers, counselors, and basketball players, to offer just a few examples. The existence of such figures is not an argument against schools of education, academic programs in counseling, or team basketball practice. A key reason, of course, is that not everyone is a natural. If we limit the teaching profession to naturals, we would not have enough teachers to staff our schools.

What Abubakar Khan intuited, or learned from experience, when it came to practical theology and mobilization across religious communities, other people will have to learn. Just as a society committed to education needs more teachers than just the individuals who are intuitively gifted at the craft of educating, so religiously diverse democracies need more interfaith leaders than just the Abubakar Khans of the world.

Second, "naturals," naturally, are drawn to the parts of the task that they are natural at. When the task is looked at through a wide lens, that natural will likely need a broader program of education and training as well. It is one thing to be a good three-on-three blacktop basketball player where your ability to make quick drives and long jump shots can dominate most situations. It is a different thing entirely to do the same over the course of an eighty-two-game NBA season when opposing teams have designed their defenses to thwart your athleticism.

Abubakar Khan excelled at the quick mobilization of diverse faith communities to meet the acute social need of housing and feeding homeless people who were freezing to death. But the civic space of interfaith engagement is both wider and more complicated than that scenario. Even in this remarkable situation, there was untapped potential. Since he relied, naturally, on his own experience, personal knowledge, and friendship circles, groups that fell outside of these realms went unengaged. What if Khan had gone through a master's in interfaith studies program where he learned about the practical theology of hospitality in five other communities? What if he understood how diverse faith-based social capital networks operated not just within a tight geographic space but across an entire metropolitan area? The various Catholic institutions in a metropolitan area—churches, schools, health care facilities, social service organizations—are organized into dioceses that make up a network overseen by the archbishop. Different Ismaili jamat khanas work under a single regional Ismaili council; various Church of Jesus Christ of Latter-day Saints wards are organized into a stake. All of these, of course, operate in larger national and global networks as well. Given that people were freezing across the greater Vancouver area, not just in the few miles around where the masjid was located, would a course in the sociology of religion have helped Khan create an even wider interfaith network of care? And when the cold snap breaks, and the immediate need is no longer felt, what happens to the interfaith network? It is one thing to mobilize in times of emergency and is another thing to work together over the long term in order to prepare for the next cold snap or to discern a way forward on issues that reveal various divides (theological, political, and otherwise), such as how to approach teen pregnancy, support services for undocumented immigrants, enact environmental regulations, and affirm diverse sexual expressions.

In my conversation with Abubakar Khan at the Parliament of the World's Religions in Canada, I asked some of these questions and pointed out some of these possibilities. His response to me: "I would love to get a degree in that kind of work."

Abubakar Khan is precisely whom we want in our interfaith studies programs and benefiting from the relevant research agenda described in this chapter.

5

The Scholar, the Theologian, and the Activist

Marianne Moyaert

This chapter identifies three primary fields (and scholarly profiles) that have contributed to the emergence of interreligious/interfaith studies (IIS) in the academy: religious studies (the interreligious scholar), theology (the [comparative] theologian of religions in particular), and the so-called interfaith movement (the scholar-activist). A closer examination of these different profiles helps to deconstruct overcharged claims to the boundaries between theology, religious studies, and activism.

Zooming In on Our Students

IIS programs attract students from a variety of backgrounds and with diverging ambitions. Some students identify as "scholars" who study interreligiosity from an outsider's perspective and with an approach akin to a religious studies classical perspective of the dispassionate and disengaged observer.[1] They do not believe their own "religious" background has any bearing on their studies, nor do they regard themselves as part of the field they examine. Rejecting any self-implication, their primary interest is to analyze critically the dynamic interaction between people who orient around religions differently. Questions that interest them concern the relation between religion and violence, the tension between religion and the secular, and the transformation of religious identities in post-secular societies. Not unlike religious studies scholars, they draw upon several disciplines such as sociology, political philosophy, and psychology.[2]

Since many IIS programs have been established at seminaries or theology and/or religion departments, "theology" students, eager to understand religious diversity from their own confessional background, have taken an interest in this field as well. Theologians were among the first to notice the challenge of religious diversity and to ask what pluralization means for religious traditions and their normative claims about truth, soteriology, and revelation.[3] Different from (inter)religious studies scholars who claim or strive for critical-neutral approaches, theologians self-consciously commence from normative-confessional perspectives to explore the implications of religious plurality for their own tradition and vice versa. An important question is how to move beyond theologies of religions to comparative theologies that draw upon sources from multiple religious traditions.[4]

Some interreligious scholars understand their vocation as scholar-activists. They want to improve interreligious relations, arguing that in religiously plural societies the question of how different religious communities interact is not only of scholarly relevance but also of sociopolitical relevance. They say that interreligious scholarship that limits itself to critical analysis and refrains from activism falls short. In their work they promote "(1) respect for the other (religious, cultural, etc.); (2) appreciating diversity; (3) an awareness that truth is plural and diversely expressed; (4) an interest in social change, particularly involving social cohesion and religious tolerance in society."[5] The vocational aim for these students is to become bridge-builders as either interfaith educators, interreligious leaders, or peacebuilders who mediate conflicts between religious communities.

Blurring Boundaries and Surfaces Entanglements

Together these three student profiles—the *interreligious scholar*, the (comparative) *theologian* of religions, and the *interfaith activist*—reflect the complex genealogy of IIS, which has actually emerged from a complex interaction between religious studies, theology, and the so-called interfaith movement. While some might argue for a clear "division of the estate" that preserves disciplinary boundaries between theology and religious studies, and between scholarship and activism, in my pedagogical approach I take a different stance by encouraging students to adopt distinct "interreligious" profiles to be utilized in critical conversation with each other and experts in the field. In doing so, I at once show how IIS can overcome long-overdue binaries between theology and religious studies, scholarship and activism, and religion and secularity. Given that these binaries are rooted in problematic ideological assumptions that hinder the critical and transformative potential of IIS, blurring their boundaries and complicating their intersections ought to be part and parcel of critical interfaith pedagogy. Recognizing the distinctiveness of these student profiles, I emphasize how each is a product of entanglements between theological discussions, scholarly debates about religion, and interreligious initiatives aimed at building bridges across communities. Rather than denying these entanglements or erecting strong partitions between them, the interreligious educator ought to foreground existing intersections, surface blind spots, and interrogate ideological assumptions and ramifications.

The Theologian

The point of departure for the "theologian," speaking from an insider's perspective and rooted in a particular tradition, is her faith commitment. Her task is to make sense of religious diversity and think through the "im-possibility of interreligious dialogue.[6] Increasingly, theologians realize that they will work in religiously diverse settings, whether they specialize in spiritual care or religious education, become religious leaders in their respective communities, or enter into academia. Their classrooms (like my own) will become more diverse, the families they counsel will be increasingly mixed-faith, and their church will likely share a neighborhood with a mosque and a synagogue in a time of heightened Islamophobia and antisemitism. They will be faced with the choice of closing their doors to outsiders or becoming bridge-builders. Will they reach out to work with leaders and caregivers from other traditions in efforts to develop marital and birth rituals for mixed families? Will they preach and pray in a manner sensitive to the predicaments of those who believe and practice differently? Regardless of whether religious leaders identify with the interfaith movement, being a religious leader today requires knowledge about both religions and interreligious competencies. From this perspective, the line between the interreligious activist and the formally theologically trained is blurry, and that is a good thing because insights from interreligious activism (via testimonies, project work, or even internships) should flow back to, challenge, and interrupt theological reasoning so that the latter does not develop in abstraction.

Inspired by a modern scientific ideal of distanciation, some (inter)*religious scholars* question whether it is possible to understand the religious other when operating out of a confessional perspective. They wonder whether theologians can critically consider their own tradition, especially when it comes to

recognizing the ways it may have contributed to historical oppression and interreligious violence. *Interreligious activists*, on the other hand, might object
to the way theologians overemphasize the importance of theological dialogue
between (usually male) official or ordained representatives and underempha-
size grassroots initiatives by ordinary believers. These concerns have merit and
ought to be discussed. Indeed, critical distanciation ought to be part of good
scholarship, and theological dialogue about conflicting beliefs may very well
be too far removed from lived interreligion. However, given that a goal of interfaith learning is to avoid "othering," I push back against stereotypical and
caricatural depictions of "the" theologian as *per definition* falling outside of the
scholarly realm. First, most theologians today when making sense of complex
contemporary phenomena (e.g., the Anthropocene, beginning or end-of-life
care, responding to migration or diversity) draw on insights from nontheological disciplines such as the natural, medical, and political sciences and the
(comparative) study of religion. Theology done based on half-hearted, shaky,
or biased knowledge is bad theology. Second, it is misguided to assume that
critique is possible *only* from an outsider's perspective. Most religious traditions also contain important resources for critiquing internal theologies that
are too far removed from the daily lives and predicaments of ordinary people.
Third, the theological contribution to the interfaith movement should not be
overlooked.[7] For instance, the decision of the World Council of Churches and
the Vatican to support the so-called dialogical turn gave a tremendous boost
to dialogical initiatives both among so-called religious elites (e.g., clergy, recognized leaders, and authorities) and at a grassroots level.[8] While it is true
that theologians have perhaps focused too much attention on theological dialogues between different traditions,[9] it is not true that theologians involved
in dialogue are necessarily disconnected from lived (inter)religion. Rather, the
biographies of many dialogical pioneers reveal that it was often their close
and sustained interaction with real "others" that incited them to theologically
reconsider traditional claims about those who believe and practice differently.[10] This reinforces the value of experiential learning in the proximity of the
other, not only for theologians but also between academics with different understandings of scholarship.

The Interreligious Scholar

The interreligious scholar claims to speak from an outsider's perspective, and
she values objectivity and neutrality. Indeed, it is precisely "the scholarly and
religiously neutral quality of interreligious studies . . . [that] establishes its
place in the academy."[11] For religious scholars, this "language of neutrality"

is "one of the main things that helps [them] distinguish between an academic and a devotional approach to the study of religion."[12] Scholars of religion are not theologians; they refrain from normative assumptions and strive to steer away from questions of religious truth. Kate McCarthy argues, "Interreligious studies must underline its commitment to critical inquiry by including, among other things, systematic analysis of conflict, domination, and contestation in historical and current interreligious encounters. That is, medieval Cordoba must be set against ISIS and the antigay Westboro Baptist Church. . . . It should not be the task of interreligious scholars to be the caretakers of the traditions."[13] Thus, interreligious scholars should draw on psychology and political science when examining the rise of religious fundamentalism, and they should draw on history, political philosophy, and critical theory when analyzing ongoing European debates about circumcision and the way Muslims and Jews continue to be othered in a (Judeo)Christian Europe. The history and ideological assumptions of the interfaith movement too should be scrutinized in interreligious education.[14]

However, there remains a need to deconstruct some of the clear-cut boundaries between theology and religious studies, which also has repercussions for the self-understanding of the interfaith movement. First, concerning the theology / religious studies binary, we should recognize that the histories of religious studies and theology *are* in fact entangled and that this entanglement resulted in a Christianized, modern-belief-centered, text-focused, and interiorized understanding of religion and the so-called world religions paradigm, which in turn has deeply influenced the interfaith movement.[15] From a scholarly perspective, it makes more sense to expose the entanglement of the study of religion with theology (and its impact on interfaith activism) rather than to artificially erect boundaries that only disenable the interreligious scholar from uncovering the blind spots of his or her discipline. Therefore, the so-called critique of religion should be part and parcel of interreligious studies. Second, building on the above, there is no such thing as a view from nowhere. Everyone, including (inter)religious scholars, speaks from somewhere. Certain pre-theoretical assumptions always play a role in the way one makes sense of interreligious relations. Rather than denying this hermeneutical reality, it is better to be aware of these prejudices so as not let them get the upper hand. In the spirit of self-critique, interreligious scholars see it as part of their scholarly work to explore, test, and revise the "conceptual categories" through which they interpret their data.[16] Finally, as interreligious activists point out, claims to neutrality are not only impossible but often (though not always) voiced by those in privileged positions with the luxury to stay on the sidelines. In the face of the many interreligious tensions in the world today, in which some religious groups are targeted while others enjoy privileges, one cannot but become an advocate dedicated to the cause of transforming structures that lead to unequal and conflictual interreligious relations.

The Interfaith Activist
The interfaith activist wants to learn more about the dynamic interaction between those who orient differently around religion, but especially seeks the skills necessary to become a bridge-builder. Her starting position is one of commitment and involvement. To the activist, the neutral gaze of the scholar misses the urgency of the challenges of our pluralized world. The activist also may not recognize herself in the theologian's commitment to one privileged tradition and community. Activists are dedicated to the interfaith movement as a civic project. Eboo Patel preaches:

> "Civic interfaith work" . . . mean[s] the kinds of activities and conversations that, through addressing diverse faith identities in interaction, strengthen eligiously diverse democracies. An interfaith leader is someone expert in organizing these. . . . Sometimes an interfaith leader has to respond to interfaith dynamics that emerge somewhat surprisingly in a civic space. . . . Other times, an interfaith leader will seek to enrich a civic space by proactively mobilizing interfaith networks.[17]

Some interreligious scholars may worry over whether the commitment to activism obliterates the critical potential of interreligious studies to identify, examine, and deconstruct the ideological assumptions of the interfaith movement. This is a valid concern; however one should not make a caricature of activists, they too desire knowledge about interreligiosity (including the interfaith movement) in order to become better equipped as scholar activists with one foot in the academy and one foot in the interfaith movement. Moreover, it is not the case that critical knowledge is generated within the walls of the academy alone; interreligious encounters at the grassroots most certainly generate critical knowledge and data. For example, encounters at the grassroots often involve people with complex and intersectional identities, which challenges the theological focus on belief-centered dialogical exchanges between representatives of the so-called world religions. Likewise, interreligious scholars and theologians have not always paid sufficient attention to the dimension of power in interreligious encounters and to how religion may contribute to unequal power relations. Rather than upholding the modern scholarly ideal of distanciation, interreligious activists argue that their engagement yields a better understanding of interreligious relations, and history proves them right. Indeed, there is no shortage of examples of theological pioneers who were transformed by close and vivid contact with those from traditions other than their own.

All of this is not to say that there is no distinction between the *interreligious scholar* with a primary commitment to the academy, the *interfaith activist* with a primary commitment to the civically minded interfaith movement, and the *theologian* with a primary commitment to his community in a context of plurality. Rather, this is to say that interreligious studies programs, in my view, function optimally when they speak to and engage all three profiles, which pedagogically thereby transforms the classroom into an interdisciplinary space in one fell swoop.

Notes

1   Russell McCutcheon, ed., *The Insider/Outsider Problem in the Study of Religion: A Reader* (London: Bath, 1999).

2   Eboo Patel, "Toward a Field of Interfaith Studies." *Liberal Education* 99, no. 44 (2013).

3   Gavin D'Costa, *Theology and Religious Pluralism: The Challenge of Other Religions* (Oxford: Blackwell, 1986); Jacques Dupuis, *Toward a Christian Theology of Religious Pluralism* (New York: Orbis, 1997); Paul F. Knitter, *Introducing Theologies of Religions* (New York: Orbis, 2002).

4   Francis X. Clooney, *Comparative Theology: Deep Learning across Religious Borders* (Oxford: Wiley-Blackwell, 2010); Catherine Cornille, *Meaning and Method in Comparative Theology* (Oxford: Blacwell, 2019)

5   Paul Hedges, "Interreligious Studies," in *Encyclopedia of Sciences and Religion*, ed. A. Runehov and L. Ovideo (New York: Springer, 2012), 1076.

6   Catherine Cornille, *The Im-possibility of Interreligious Dialogue* (New York: Crossroads, 2008).

7   Anna Halafoff, *The Multifaith Movement: Global Risks and Cosmopolitan Solutions* (New York: Springer, 2013).

8   Jean-Claude Basset, *Le dialogue interreligieux: Chance ou déchéance de la foi* (Paris: Editions du Cerf, 1996).

9   Marianne Moyaert, "Broadening the Scope of Interreligious Studies: Inter-rituality," in *Interreligious Relations and the Negotiation of Ritual Boundaries: Explorations in Interrituality*, ed. Marianne Moyaert (New York: Palgrave MacMillan, 2019), 2.

10   Paul F. Knitter, *Without Buddha I Could Not Be a Christian* (Oxford: Oneworld, 2009); Jennifer Howe Peace, Or N. Rose, and Gregory Mobley, eds., *My*

Neighbor's Faith: Stories of Interreligious Encounter, Growth, and Transformation (Maryknoll, N.Y.: Orbis, 2012).

11 Kate McCarthy, "(Inter)Religious Studies: Making a Home in the Secular Academy," in *Interreligious/Interfaith Studies: Defining a New Field*, ed. Eboo Patel, Jennifer Howe Peace, and Noah J. Silverman (Boston: Beacon, 2018), 13.

12 Bruce Grelle, "The First Amendment Consensus to Teaching about Religion in U.S. Public Schools: Applications and Assessments," in *Civility, Religious Pluralism and Education*, ed. Vincent Biondo and Andrew Fiala (New York: Routledge, 2013), 138.

13 Kate McCarthy, "(Inter)Religious Studies," in Patel, Peace, and Silverman, *Interreligious/Interfaith Studies*, 12.

14 Kathleen Foody, "Pedagogical Projects: Teaching Liberal Religion after 9/11," *Muslim World* 106 (2016): 719–39.

15 Tomoko Masuzawa, *The Invention of World Religions; or, How European Universalism Was Preserved in the Language of Pluralism* (Chicago: University of Chicago Press, 2005); Marianne Moyaert, "Towards a Ritual Turn in Comparative Theology: Opportunities, Challenges, and Problems," *Harvard Theological Review* 111 (2018): 1–23.

16 Hugh Nicholson, *Comparative Theology and the Problem of Religious Rivalry* (Oxford: Oxford University Press, 2011), 14.

17 Eboo Patel, *Interfaith Leadership: A Primer* (Boston: Beacon, 2016), 6–7.

References

Basset, Jean-Claude. *Le dialogue interreligieux: Chance ou déchéance de la foi.* Paris: Editions du Cerf, 1996.

Clooney, Francis X. *Comparative Theology: Deep Learning across Religious Borders.* Oxford: Wiley-Blackwell, 2010.

Cornille, Catherine. *The Im-possibility of Interreligious Dialogue.* New York: Crossroads, 2008.

D'Costa, Gavin. *Theology and Religious Pluralism: The Challenge of Other Religions.* Oxford: Blackwell, 1986.

Dupuis, Jacques. *Toward a Christian Theology of Religious Pluralism.* New York: Orbis, 1997.

Foody, Kathleen. "Pedagogical Projects: Teaching Liberal Religion after 9/11." *Muslim World* 106 (2016): 719–39.

Grelle, Bruce. "The First Amendment Consensus to Teaching about Religion in U.S. Public Schools: Applications and Assessments." In *Civility, Religious Pluralism and Education*, edited by Vincent Biondo and Andrew Fiala, 128–148. New York: Routledge, 2013.

Halafoff, Anna. *The Multifaith Movement: Global Risks and Cosmopolitan Solutions.* New York: Springer, 2013.

Hedges, Paul. "Interreligious Studies." In *Encyclopaedia of Sciences and Religion*, edited by A. Runehov and L. Ovideo, 1076–80. New York: Springer, 2012.

Knitter, Paul F. *Introducing Theologies of Religions*. New York: Orbis, 2002.

———. *Without Buddha I Could Not Be a Christian*. Oxford: Oneworld, 2009.

Masuzawa, Tomoko. *The Invention of World Religions; or, How European Universalism Was Preserved in the Language of Pluralism*. Chicago: University of Chicago Press, 2005.

McCarthy, Kate. "(Inter)Religious Studies: Making a Home in the Secular Academy." In *Interreligious/Interfaith Studies: Defining a New Field*, edited by Eboo Patel, Jennifer Howe Peace, and Noah J. Silverman, 2–15. Boston: Beacon, 2018.

McCutcheon, Russell, ed. *The Insider/Outsider Problem in the Study of Religion: A Reader*. London: Bath, 1999.

Moyaert, Marianne. "Broadening the Scope of Interreligious Studies: Interrituality." In *Interreligious Relations and the Negotiation of Ritual Boundaries: Explorations in Interrituality*, edited by Marianne Moyaert, 1–34. New York: Palgrave MacMillan, 2019.

———. "Towards a Ritual Turn in Comparative Theology: Opportunities, Challenges, and Problems." *Harvard Theological Review* 111 (2018): 1–23.

Nicholson, Hugh. *Comparative Theology and the Problem of Religious Rivalry*. Oxford: Oxford University Press, 2011.

Patel, Eboo. *Interfaith Leadership: A Primer*. Boston: Beacon, 2016.

———. "Toward a Field of Interfaith Studies." *Liberal Education* 99, no. 44 (2013). Available online at http://www.aacu.org/liberaleducation/2013/fall/patel.

Peace, Jennifer Howe, Or N. Rose, and Gregory Mobley, eds. *My Neighbor's Faith: Stories of Interreligious Encounter, Growth, and Transformation*. Maryknoll, N.Y.: Orbis, 2012.

6

Lessons from a Liminal Saint

Mark E. Hanshaw

As one engages varied communities across the globe, often some of the most unnerving and perplexing cultural expressions experienced stem from encounters with unfamiliar religious and faith systems. From the monolithic gopurams adorning South Indian temples, meant to inspire or instill a sense of awe, to the tranquil scene of a hundred saffron-clad monks chanting praise to the world-healing spirit of Avalokitesvara with the familiar mantra, "Om Mani Padme Hum," such vivid expressions can inspire reverence, wonder, and even confusion. At the same time, such encounters offer an opening.

Encounters with unfamiliar ritual traditions may prompt many questions in the mind of the curious observer and, at least to some degree, the academy, which, through the broad field of religious studies, has sought to systematize the most typical of these inquires and provide a framework for their study and analysis. The questions posed in this field offer critical insight regarding the beliefs, practices, histories, and structures associated with religious communities and systems. Yet, even beyond the objective analysis of religious systems, we have become more attuned to the latent effects that religion may have upon interactions across society, even those that appear nonreligious on their face.

In workplaces, schools, community centers, governmental offices, and every other venue imaginable, individuals informed by differing religious teaching, cultures, and convictions are engaged in daily interactions. This complex social landscape prompts many challenges and questions. How does religion influence routine individual decision-making, even on issues that appear secular in nature? How might individual religious convictions affect interactions between individuals in workplaces, schools, and communities? What are the best approaches for resolving disputes within communities rooted in religious difference?

These complex questions are multidimensional and therefore lean into many different realms of academic and social interest ranging from law and politics to psychology and economics. Yet, there is one common ingredient in such inquiries, and that is the question of the unique influence of religious practice. Such questions have prompted the emergence of contemporary conversations related to the potential need for new methodologies within the academy for the consideration of religion and its effect upon a broad array of social interactions. Among the most recent proposals aimed at addressing emerging areas of inquiry is a focus upon interfaith studies.

In this brief chapter, while first considering the potential parameters of interfaith studies as a possible academic discipline, I reference my own engagement with the cult of Maximón, in Guatemala, as a compelling case study from which to consider vital inquiries implicated through this emergent field. The purpose of the chapter is to consider the appropriate breadth and focus of an academic field of interfaith studies.

Seeking Definition

What is interfaith studies, and what might such a focus add to the already dense field of religious studies? Moreover, should interfaith studies be viewed as a separate field entirely or a defined extension of religious studies?

These questions are complex, and what should not be lost in any consideration of them is the very fact that they are motivated by the strong desire of researchers, scholars, and other thinkers to better understand how religious systems affect, influence, and shape the broader human cultural landscape.

One of the leading voices promoting the potentialities of interfaith studies as a defined discipline of study is the Chicago-based Interfaith Youth Core (IFYC) and its president, Eboo Patel. IFYC defines this emergent methodological system in this way:

> Interfaith Studies is an interdisciplinary field that examines the multiple dimensions of how people who orient around religion differently interact with one another, and the implications of these interactions for communities, civil society, and global politics.[1]

From this definition, it may be gleaned that there are a number of distinct attributes of work that may be classified as "interfaith study." First among these is the express appreciation that religion as a phenomenon cannot be fully understood in isolation. Interfaith study, as it is envisioned, embraces an interdisciplinary approach, precisely because it recognizes the ways in which religious practice both is informed by and colors the many dimensions of an individual's social experience. Thus, the interfaith student would be prepared to consider the ways that particular faith commitments or experiences may shape a variety of interactions taking place between individuals and groups, even beyond the sorts of engagements that we may routinely consider to be religious in nature.

As well, while recognizing that individuals throughout society can and do hold defined religious commitments, the interfaith student is prepared to acknowledge these positions without a confessional motivation and in a manner that privileges the practitioner's own experience. In this regard, the interfaith student desires to understand the multiplicity of views that influence any cross-religious engagement. At the same time, the interfaith student is interested in power dynamics that may affect encounters between religious practitioners and latent biases that may color perceptions, with the aim of ensuring that varied specific individual views are not ignored.

Meanwhile, the interfaith student engages her work with the knowledge that religion is not wholly defined by privatized beliefs, but with the additional awareness that closely held convictions are often externalized, either knowingly or subconsciously, such that they inevitably influence social interactions of every type. The transparent consideration of interreligious engagements as they occur within contemporaneous society will help students to better understand the ways that such encounters have influenced society broadly. As a result, interfaith studies would tend to rely heavily upon applied methodologies, including the use of case studies, which offer specific examples of cross-religious encounters. The goal of interfaith studies would be to prepare students to offer leadership to communities in the facilitation of engagements involving religious difference.

Learning through Encounter

My own consideration of the utility of a formalized framework for interfaith study was fueled, at least in part, by some of my own encounters in the field. One particular episode that provided ample ground for thought occurred while I was in Guatemala some years ago. While I was delving into questions of ancient Mayan history, members of the local community presented me with a challenging contemporary puzzle.

As I was traveling in the southwestern region of Guatemala, I received an invitation to be an honored guest at a festival in the village of Santiago on the banks of the volcanic Lake Atitlán. Though the focus of this celebration was not entirely clear, I agreed to participate, knowing that it would offer a unique opportunity to engage the local community. Once I arrived in the village, after being treated to a wonderful meal, I was taken to a shrine located on the bottom floor of a building in the center of village. This shrine was the beginning point for a religious parade in honor of a deity I had seen before but knew little about. Gathered around me were individuals in a variety of costumes preparing for this important event.

The shrine featured the iconic figure of a mustached cowboy with a cigarette in his mouth (fig. 6.1). He is one of the more curious deities that I have encountered in my travels, and he is variously called Maximón or San Simon. Maximón is believed to be a deity of Mayan origin that some speculate may have originated in the region around Santiago,[2] but who likely has much deeper mythical roots. He is said to be "mitad santo mitad dios," a complex figure who speaks to the routine fears, desires, and experiences of members of the indigenous communities that inhabit this economically challenged region.[3] Curiously, this entity, which holds a nebulous position between saint and deity, reflects aspects of both an ancient Mayan culture that once emerged in this region as early as four millennia ago and the more recently dominant culture of Latin American Catholicism.

Maximón likely takes his name from a combination of the ancient Mayan deity Mam and various figures from the Christian tradition, including the disciple Simon Peter and Judas, the biblical betrayer of Jesus.[4] The mythology associated with Maximón describes the figure as highly promiscuous, a heavy drinker, and a heavy smoker. Through these material foibles, he offers powers that include the ability to spur love interests, insulate women from physical temptations, secure a strong harvest, protect travelers and traders, and cure diseases.[5] San Simon is a trickster and one who appears innately representative of the routine and ordinary challenges that afflict all individuals. Thus, perhaps in certain ways, he may seem far more familiar and compelling to members of the indigenous population than images associated with Catholic saints.

Within the Mayan pantheon, Mam played the special role of supporting the movement of the community through the uncertain transition from one year to the next.[6] Maximón, then, has come to be associated with the movement of the community through the liminal period of Holy Week in the Christian tradition and with the possibilities that lie on the other side of this transition.

Going back to my own experience, I was struck as the figure of Maximón was paraded from his temple and through the streets of the village. The icon was transported to a square located just below the Catholic cathedral, and,

Figure 6.1
Maximón in the Shrine
Santiago Atitlán, Guatemala,
2012
(© 2019 Mark E. Hanshaw)

there, the figure was celebrated with music and dance. I was invited to take a position on a platform set up for the three guests, and we were treated to strong drink and sweet bread, as the festivities ensued.

My raucous encounter with this god saint was perplexing, possessing the aura of a high and holy event, taking place in the shadow of the cathedral, while also possessing an air of debauchery. The experience was curious, but even more puzzling were the questions that I began to entertain in my own mind about how to make sense of these events in light of my own engagement with the field of religious studies.

Deploying Interfaith Study

How might one go about considering the events I encountered in Guatemala? How might one wrestle with the cult surrounding this mysterious figure— Maximón? Indeed, what could be made of the heterodox nature of the Maximón cult and its place within the cultural landscape of this region?

At some level, the presence of the Maximón cult provides a fascinating case study in interaction between faith systems. The syncretic melding of both Christian and Mayan traditions into a composite figure embraced by a significant portion of the community of Santiago represents an important adaptation that holds implications across the local society. For this reason, it seems peculiarly well-suited for interfaith research.

In the field of religious studies, the consideration of a religious system often begins at the center, through the investigation of a perceived orthodoxy, before considering the ways in which heterodox expressions relate to the identified essential norm. The interfaith student is interested in present situations where individual faith practitioners or communities come into contact or conflict with one another. In regard to the cult of Maximón, as it is lived out in Santiago, there are important issues raised concerning the effect of the tradition upon popular perceptions of the Catholic Church and upon attitudes of clergy. As well, there are important questions related to the part that the Maximón cult plays in the shaping of local values, community engagement, and common perceptions of identity. All of these are questions ripe for interfaith study, and they begin not with the consideration of a defined orthodoxy but with present experience.

What would be within the parameters of an interfaith consideration of the Maximón cult? A recent article, "Constructing Interreligious Studies,"[7] helped me to begin formulating a response to my own question. In that article, the authors identify core learning outcomes that were crafted by an interdisciplinary faculty team to support an interfaith studies minor on the Elon University campus. Through that work, six outcomes were developed that students within the program would be required to meet. These thoughtful experiential and curricular objectives seek to encourage student reflection and research in these areas:

1   the production of "nuanced reflections" on interactions between religious systems and traditions;

2   the recognition of the ways in which "religious traditions and interreligious encounters are embedded" within a variety of social settings and situations;

3   the recognition of the "contours of religious difference" between communities;

4   the direct encounter with varied religious communities;

5   the analysis of the field of interreligious studies from both historical and theoretical perspectives; and

6   the critique of models for the facilitation of interreligious encounter.[8]

Under the framework created at Elon, how might an encounter with the Maximón cult in Santiago serve as an appropriate case study for students, and what outcomes might be derived from such an engagement? Indeed, my read of the work of Allocco, Claussen, and Pennington helped me to frame my own experience of years before that took place in Guatemala. In particular, as a focus of study, the Maximón cult offers a number of interesting avenues for the consideration of important interfaith questions.

In terms of reflection upon intersections between religious communities, the Maximón cult offers some vivid opportunities for analysis, with both historical and contemporary dimensions. Central to any study of the community of followers of Maximón must be an inquiry into how this community has engaged the more dominant Catholic community in the region over time. There are many different dimensions of this relationship, including historical interactions between leaders of these communities, the merging of religious symbols, the ways in which these communities have expressed and related to local community political and economic power structures, and much more. The ground is fertile for examination.

At the same time, it is impossible to meaningfully consider this cultic community without seeking to understand how it may be related to various aspects of the societal infrastructure. Undoubtedly, this community—standing in contrast to, and perhaps in competition with, the larger Catholic community—affects political, social, economic, and various other arenas of daily life. The exploration of these effects would demand an interdisciplinary perspective and offers rich opportunities for analysis.

At the heart of any study of this cultic community must also be the further question of how the presence and persistence of followers of Maximón has affected the shape of Catholicism in the region and vice versa. Such inquiries would encompass research questions related to the evolution of these communities over time, as well as the ways in which they interact within a contemporary frame.

Given the relative unfamiliarity that many students would likely have with the Maximón cult, any analysis of the community surrounding this figure would necessarily entail the consideration of ritual patterns and theoretical understandings associated with the tradition. Such consideration would naturally include firsthand experiential accounts and the engagement of individuals affiliated with the cultic community.

Of course, such study would naturally rely upon the utilization of accumulated resources from the religious studies and interfaith studies fields as resources for analysis. At the same time, such a case study would provide ample

opportunity for the purposeful consideration and critique of models for interfaith engagement, as they would relate to both contemporary interactions
with this community and historic engagements between the community of
Maximón and the Catholic Church within the region.

Finally, this consideration of specific types of research questions and directions that might emerge from an engagement by students with the community
surrounding the figure of Maximón in Guatemala is not exhaustive. Still, it
provides a useful vantage point from which to consider the potential parameters of a formal field of interfaith studies.

Interfaith studies programs do not stand as mere theoretical possibilities.
As is true at Elon, many institutions see interfaith studies as an emerging field
that can both help students be better prepared to successfully engage individuals of differing religious perspectives and serve to support healthy broader
community interactions across religious divides. As such, they have already
begun to develop programs, even as the dimensions of the field continue to be
clarified. The precise dimensions of such a field are not fully developed, and,
due to the complexity of the questions that may be included within such an
academic sphere, such dimensions may always be in something of a state of
evolution. Still, those seeking to consider the place of such a field within the
academic landscape are addressing issues of contemporary significance.

As with other aspects of cultural diversity, engagement between individuals and groups representing varied religious beliefs is increasing and must
occupy the attention of institutions desiring to prepare individuals for future
professional roles. Current academic work in the area of interfaith engagement
is setting an important foundation to prepare society to respond to the complex questions that will emerge in the future, as religious communities become
more deeply engaged with one another.

Notes

1   "The Emerging Field of Interfaith Studies," Interfaith Youth Core, accessed
    March 28, 2019, https://www.ifyc.org/faculty/interfaithstudies.

2   Sylvie Pedron-Colombani, "El Culto de Maximón en Guatemala," *TRACE* 54
    (2008): 31–44.

3   Pedron-Colombani, "El Culto de Maximón en Guatemala," 32.

4   Jim Pieper, *Guatemala's Folk Saints* (Los Angeles: Pieper, 2002), 11.

5   Pieper, *Guatemala's Folk Saints*, 34–36.

6   Pedron-Colombani, "El Culto de Maximón en Guatemala," 34.

7   Amy L. Allocco, Geoffrey D. Claussen, and Brian K. Pennington, "Construct-
     ing Interreligious Studies," in *Interreligious/Interfaith Studies: Defining a New
     Field*, ed. Eboo Patel, Jennifer Howe Peace, and Noah J. Silverman (Boston:
     Beacon, 2018), 36–48.

8   Allocco, Claussen, and Pennington, "Constructing Interreligious Studies," in
     Patel, Peace, and Silverman, *Interreligious/Interfaith Studies*, 40.

References

Allocco, Amy L., Geoffrey D. Claussen, and Brian K. Pennington. "Constructing
     Interreligious Studies." In Patel, Peace, and Silverman, *Interreligious/Interfaith
     Studies*, 36–48.
Janson, Thor. "Mayan Patron Saint is an Enigma." *Revue Magazine* 20, no. 4
     (2011): 16–17, 100–107.
Lahnemann, Johannes. "Interreligious Education." In *Interfaith Education for All*,
     edited by Duncan Wielzen and Ina Ter Avest, 31–44. Rotterdam: Sense, 2017.
Mikva, Rachel S. "Six Issues That Complicate Interreligious Studies and Engage-
     ment." In Patel, Peace, and Silverman, *Interreligious/Interfaith Studies*, 124–36.
Patel, Eboo. "Toward a Field of Interfaith Studies." *Liberal Education* 99 (2013).
Patel, Eboo, Jennifer Howe Peace, and Noah Silverman, eds. *Interreligious/Inter-
     faith Studies: Defining a New Field*. Boston: Beacon, 2018.
Peace, Jennifer Howe, Or N. Rose, and Gregory Mobley, eds. *My Neighbor's Faith:
     Stories of Interreligious Encounter, Growth and Transformation*. Maryknoll,
     N.Y.: Orbis, 2012.
Pedron-Colombani, Sylvie. "El Culto de Maximón en Guatemala." *TRACE* 54
     (2008): 31–44.
Pieper, Jim. *Guatemala's Folk Saints*. Los Angeles: Pieper, 2002.
Puett, Tiffany. "On Transforming Our World: Critical Pedagogy for Interfaith
     Education." *Cross Currents* 55 (2005): 264–73.

7

Interreligion and Interdisciplinarity

Jeanine Diller

There is a wonderful passage by Roger Scruton (1999) that for years has been framing the way I think about academic disciplines and how they relate to each other and to reality. Here I will put this passage to use to argue why the field of interreligious studies should be interdisciplinary and then will provide some examples to back up this claim.

A brief backstory: in this passage, Scruton is explaining the thought of Baruch Spinoza, a brilliant seventeenth-century philosopher, focusing particularly on Spinoza's view that reality has "infinite attributes." Though I will not attempt to relay Spinoza's thought technically here, I will be inspired by his idea that the attributes of reality are different ways we can *perceive* it,[1] and that these ways are "*complete*" in themselves and "*incommensurate*" with each other. Specifically, I will suggest that the disciplines each perceive a different attribute of reality, so if we want to understand interreligion—the phenomena that happen when religions meet—it will take many disciplines to do it.

Scruton explains this hard thought with a very helpful metaphor:

> Imagine two people looking at a picture painted on a board, one an optician, the other a critic. And suppose you ask them to describe what they see. The optician arranges the picture on two axes, and describes it thus: "At x = 4, y = 5.2, there is a patch of chrome yellow; this continues along the horizontal axis until x = 5.1, when it changes to Prussian blue." The critic says: "It is a man in a yellow coat, with a lowering expression, and steely blue eyes." You could imagine these descriptions being *complete*—so complete that they would enable a third party to reconstruct the pic-

ture by using them as a set of instructions. But they would have nothing whatever in common. One is about colors arranged on a matrix, the other about the scene that we see in them. You cannot switch from one narrative to the other and still make sense: the man is not standing next to a patch of Prussian blue, but next to the shadow of an oak tree. The Prussian blue is not situated next to a coat sleeve, but next to a patch of chrome yellow. In other words, the two descriptions are *incommensurate*: no fragment of the one can appear in the midst of the other without making nonsense. Yet neither description misses out any feature that is mentioned in the other. This is what Spinoza had in mind with his concept of an attribute: a complete account of a substance, which does not rule out other, and incommensurate, complete accounts of the very same thing.[2]

The painting in Scruton's passage is a metaphor for *reality*. The two descriptions of the painting—namely, the color matrix and imagery—symbolize two distinct *attributes* of reality: they are two ways the painting can be *perceived*, ways so *complete* that we can create an exact duplicate of the painting from either of them, and ways so *incommensurate* that they do not compete but rather state entirely distinct sets of facts about the painting. Scruton's optician and critic are metaphors for *experts* who know about these two attributes of reality. The ideal optician can state a complete account of the "color attribute" of the painting; the ideal critic, a complete account of its "imagery attribute." We fully understand the painting only when we understand *both* its attributes. If we knew the painting just by its color matrix but not by its imagery, or vice versa,[3] we would miss out on an entire set of truths about it.

Spinoza escalates Scruton's metaphor: he takes reality to have not just two but "infinite attributes." He thinks reality is so "multi-attributed," so multifaceted, that if we were perfect perceivers, we could keep producing complete and entirely fresh accounts of it, over and over again, infinitely. Because to know something fully is to know all its attributes, we would need to understand not just two but an infinite number of different, complete accounts of it, on pain of missing out on some of what it is.

Though I am not sure if reality has *infinite* attributes, I am increasingly convinced—from watching the academic disciplines at work, actually—that it has at least *many* attributes. The academic disciplines are producing ever more complete and incommensurate accounts of reality, like the optician and critic give for the painting. For example, if we put academic scientists to work explaining a rock, a chemist would explain what elements compose and bond it together; a physicist, the gravitational pulls it experiences; a geologist, how it came to be produced by the earth's stuff; and so forth. These accounts are in principle complete: ideally, the chemist could recreate the rock chemically, the geologist by moving tectonic plates, and so forth. The accounts are also incommensurate: the physicist leaves the periodic table to the chemist, and both of them leave the magma to the geologist, and all three of them might say to each other: "If you want to see the rock in an entirely different way, look here!"

Interestingly, if we set the academy loose on interreligion, our focus here, we would find even more disciplines germane to studying it, suggesting that interreligion has extra, emergent attributes that the rock lacks. Religion per se can be understood not only by the hard sciences but also by the social sciences and humanities. For example, a single religious ritual such as putting a body on a funeral pyre has physical, chemical, and geologic attributes, but also theological, psychological, economic, and aesthetic attributes, to name a few. If religion has more attributes than a rock, interreligion will have even more: the combinatorial properties alone are immense, not to mention new attributes that may emerge when religion meets religion. So we need a great number of disciplines indeed to understand interreligion, on pain of just skimming its surface.

This Spinoza-inspired theory shows we have a pressing need for interreligious studies to be interdisciplinary. Now for three quick examples to demonstrate the point in practice. To simplify, I will focus these examples on just one aspect of interreligion: multiple religious participation (MRP), the attempt to practice multiple religions in a single life.

First, as an analytic *philosopher*, I find myself interested in the *logic* of MRP. Some religions are harder to participate in together because there are logical contradictions between their beliefs. For instance, Christians commonly believe Jesus is God, Muslims commonly believe that Jesus is not God but a prophet, and Jews commonly believe that Jesus is neither God nor a prophet. This set of beliefs is inconsistent,[4] a fact that forces would-be Jew-Christian-Muslims to hold these affiliations "loosely," as Michelle Voss Roberts says well.[5] For instance, a Jew-Christian-Muslim may choose to stand back from affirming or denying beliefs about Jesus' divine status and from participating in practices (perhaps Communion, or Easter) that may rely on these beliefs. Still, they could lead vibrant spiritual lives by participating in the many beliefs and practices in the intersection set of these faiths.[6]

Second, compare my focus as a philosopher on the logic of MRP to Rory McEntee and Adam Bucko's focus as *practical theologians* on its use in *spiritual formation*. Their recent book offers a practical guide for living a life dedicated to developing spiritually in a way that "cuts across humanity's wisdom and religious traditions"[7] as MRP does. For instance, they recommend a routine of body centering, prayer, and silent practice two times per day for an hour. Body

centering can involve "yogic *asanas*, tai chi, breath work, conscious weightlift-
ing and prostrations," and prayer can be anything from this varied list: "talking
to God," "the prayer of St. Francis," "the prayer of abandonment by Charles de
Foucauld," "the practice of *lectio divina*, . . . a chant . . . [generating] compassion for all sentient beings," or "simply holding one's heart."[8] It is remarkable
that McEntee and Bucko pull Hindu, Daoist, Buddhist, Muslim, and Christian
traditions seamlessly here into a single devoted life.

Finally, consider Francis X. Clooney S.J.'s focus as a *comparative theologian*
on a *theological presupposition* of MRP.[9] As a Jesuit priest working at the border of Hindu and Christian texts, Clooney discovers a particular theology of
"divine accessibility" in some Hindu texts and then re-sees it in a text from his
home tradition. He found this theology first in an account of a ninth-century
Hindu saint named Antal who was invited to marry Lord Narayana. Skeptics
wondered aloud how any woman could marry the lord. Antal replied:

> Whichever form pleases his people, that is his form;
> Whichever name pleases his people, that is his name;
> Whichever way pleases his people who meditate without ceasing, that is his way;
> That one who holds the discus.[10]

As Clooney says well, Antal's point is "if someone loves like a bride, God comes
as a groom."[11] He then discovers this verse's original source,[12] two commentar-
ies on it, and finally a similar verse in the Gita,[13] all of which "confirm the basic
theological point: the Lord is willing to make himself approachable in a form
suitable to humans."[14] He then turns to Ignatius' recipe for *lectio divina*, which
calls the contemplator to throw out old images of the life of Christ and create
new ones by placing herself imaginatively in the scene.[15] He finds a striking
similarity with Antal's insight: the contemplator's very act of imagining the
meeting *in her own way* enables God to meet her.[16] Clooney realizes that MRP
works only if this theology of divine accessibility is true: God has to be willing
to be re-met in multiple traditions in order for us to meet God in them.

Though few in number, these examples already make it abundantly clear
that multiple disciplines reveal multiple attributes of MRP—its logic, its practice, and its theological underpinnings. Thus, we cannot fully understand
MRP *without* using multiple disciplines. Moreover, since MRP serves as just
one example of interreligion, it is clear that we cannot understand interreligion
more generally without multiple disciplines. We in the academy need each
other in order to see interreligion in all its glory. Even our combined force will
be just a start at understanding the huge number of attributes it has available
to explore.[17]

Notes

1 Spinoza wrote: "By attribute I understand what the intellect perceives of a substance, as constituting its essence" (D4 in his *Ethics, part 1*, trans. Curley 1985, 408).

2 Roger Scruton, *Spinoza* (New York: Routledge, 1999), 9–10 (emphasis added).

3 There is an amazing case of a man who *lacked* this sort of imagery knowledge while *having* this sort of color knowledge. It is the case of Dr. P that made for the title of Oliver Sacks' *The Man Who Mistook His Wife for a Hat*. As Dr. Sacks tells part of the story: "I had stopped at a florist on my way to his apartment and bought myself an extravagant red rose for my buttonhole. Now I removed this and handed it to him [Dr. P]. He took it like a botanist or morphologist given a specimen, not like a person given a flower. 'About six inches in length,' he commented. 'A convoluted red form with a linear green attachment.' 'Yes,' I said encouragingly, 'and what do you think it *is*, Dr. P?' 'Not easy to say.' He seemed perplexed. 'It lacks the symmetry of Platonic solids, although it may have a higher symmetry of its own. . . . I think it could be an inflorescence of a flower.' 'Could be?' I queried. 'Could be,' he confirmed. 'Smell it,' I suggested, and he again looked somewhat puzzled, as if I had asked him to smell a higher symmetry. But he complied courteously, and took it to his nose. Now, suddenly, he came to life. 'Beautiful!' he exclaimed. 'An early rose! What a heavenly smell!' . . . Reality, it seemed, might be conveyed by smell, not by sight." Sacks, *The Man Who Mistook His Wife for a Hat* (New York: Harper and Row, 1985), 13–14 (emphasis added).

4 We can formalize the inconsistency with sentential logic thus: 1. Gj; 2. (¬Gj ∧ Pj); 3. (¬Gj ∧ ¬Pj); 4. (Gj ∧ ¬Gj) from 1, 2, 3; 5. (Pj ∧ ¬Pj) from 2, 3. See the inconsistency there twice over, at 4 and at 5.

5 Michelle Voss Roberts, "Religious Belonging and the Multiple," *Journal of Feminist Studies in Religion* 26, no. 1 (2010): 51. The same goes for any combination of the three traditions—i.e., being a Muslim-Jew, a Christian-Muslim, or a Jewish-Christian.

6 The intersection set includes beliefs in, e.g., monotheism, Abraham, etc. and practices such as loving one's neighbor, prayer, and more.

7 Rory McEntee and Adam Bucko, *The New Monasticism: An Interspiritual Manifesto for Contemplative Living* (Maryknoll, N.Y.: Orbis, 2016), xx.

8 McEntee and Bucko, *New Monasticism*, xxvii–xxviii.

9 Francis X. Clooney, "God for Us: Multiple Religious Identities as a Human and Divine Prospect," in *Many Mansions?* ed. Catherine Cornille (Eugene, Ore.: Wipf and Stock, 2002), 44–60.

10 Clooney, "God for Us," in Cornille, *Many Mansions?* 45; quoting from K. R. Govindaraja Muthaliyar, "Antal," in *Alvarkal Varalaru*, part 1 (Madurai: South India Saiva Siddhanta Works Publishing Society, 1975 [1948]), 142–68.

11 Clooney, "God for Us," in Cornille, *Many Mansions?* 45.

12   In *Mutual Tiruvantati*, v. 44, by a Vaisnava saint named Poykai Alvar who lived a generation or two before Antal. See Clooney, "God for Us," in Cornille, *Many Mansions?* 45.

13   "However someone takes refuge in me, in that way do I favor them, Partha!" (*Bhagavad Gita* 4.11; Clooney, "God for Us," in Cornille, *Many Mansions?* 47).

14   Clooney, "God for Us," in Cornille, *Many Mansions?* 52.

15   Clooney, "God for Us," in Cornille, *Many Mansions?* 52.

16   Starting "with a blank canvas and the process of filling it [themselves] provides the opportunity for 'the Father in heaven [to meet] His children and [speak] with them'" (Clooney, "God for Us," in Cornille, *Many Mansions?* 55)—in their own inner language.

17   My sincere thanks to Hans S. Gustafson and Christopher Martin for their helpful comments as this paper took shape.

References

Clooney, Francis X. "God for Us: Multiple Religious Identities as a Human and Divine Prospect." In *Many Mansions?*, edited by Catherine Cornille, 44–60. Eugene, Ore.: Wipf and Stock, 2002.

McEntee, Rory, and Adam Bucko. *The New Monasticism: An Interspiritual Manifesto for Contemplative Living*. Maryknoll, N.Y.: Orbis, 2016.

Muthaliyar, K. R. Govindaraja. "Antal." In *Alvarkal Varalaru*, part 1, 142–68. Madurai: South India Saiva Siddhanta Works Publishing Society, 1975 [1948].

Roberts, Michelle Voss. "Religious Belonging and the Multiple." *Journal of Feminist Studies in Religion* 26, no. 1 (2010): 43–62.

Sacks, Oliver. *The Man Who Mistook His Wife for a Hat*. New York: Harper and Row, 1985.

Scruton, Roger. *Spinoza*. New York: Routledge, 1999.

Spinoza, Benedictus. *The Collected Works of Spinoza*. Vol. 1. Edited and translated by Edwin Curley. Princeton: Princeton University Press, 1985.

8

Interreligious or Transreligious?

Anne Hege Grung

Interreligious studies is conceptualized in various ways. In this chapter I reflect on the term "*trans*religious" as a possible source of critique of interreligious studies. "Transreligious" may challenge the term "*inter*religious" in at least two ways: First, "transreligious" represents a feminist and a postcolonial/ decolonial critique of the stable entities and stable boundaries that might be presupposed by the term "inter."[1] Second, "transreligious" challenges the concept of mono-religious belonging and representation. It is possible to imagine "transreligious" to be used in discourses to conflate religious differences in a way that may be caught up in new versions of patriarchy and colonial thinking. I will discuss this later, but let me first explain how "transreligious" could function as a critical lens within interreligious studies.

Interreligious studies as an emerging field attempts to carve out a space within established academia relating to the fields of theology, philosophy, and religious and social studies—among others. Scholars working within the field use a variety of methods and theories. These scholarly discourses take both historical and contemporary perspectives. In many instances, interreligious studies as an academic field is intimately related to interreligious dialogue and activism. Scholars may do research in the field or be active in interreligious work themselves. Scholars of different religious traditions may also be engaged in academic interreligious dialogues.[2] Participants in interreligious dialogues may use interreligious studies as source, inspiration, and constructive criticism in their own practice. This relation between interreligious studies and interreligious dialogue is important to recognize because they sometimes mutually (re)shape each other. How does "transreligious" challenge the concept of interreligious dialogue?

*Inter*religious or *Trans*religious Dialogues?

When we speak about interreligious dialogue, the term generally refers to an organized activity, processes of encounters, or meetings between people from different religious traditions. The constitutive elements are (1) the presence of people of different religious affiliations and (2) some kind of a conscious relational approach. Otherwise, there are very diverse manifestations of activities that employ the general label of "interreligious dialogue." The concept and the activity of interreligious dialogue is increasingly part of the structures of established religions as well as of social and political scenes in many contexts. This is evident on national, regional, and international levels. A "transreligious" perspective would obviously critically inquire about the role of fixed religious boundaries in a given dialogue, but it would also push questions of representation: How are the participants in the dialogues regarded as representatives, and who decides the accepted parameters of religious representation? Do participants represent official versions of their traditions on behalf of a larger group, are they representing themselves as individual believers, or are they a combination of the two? Lastly, a "transreligious" perspective asks about how human differences other than religious diversity are marked and signified in the dialogues.

What is the purpose of interreligious dialogues? There are specific aims and goals connected to the various dialogues, but they usually share the intention to establish a new "we." Social anthropology understands the establishment of a "we" as always corresponding to the establishment of a "they."[3] The question here is what kind of "we"-groups are established, and how do they shape and correspond to the "they"-groups. A promising way to get at this question is to begin with a study of mechanisms for inclusion and exclusion in dialogues.

Ursula King, Jeannine Hill Fletcher, and others have showed how interreligious dialogues are often modeled and structured after the traditional gender hierarchies within the religious traditions.[4] This has to do with the overwhelmingly male-dominated leadership of these traditions (with some contextual exceptions) as well as with the legitimacy of men's religious representation over women's that is woven into the traditions through divine legitimization of the men's positions as leaders.[5] Not only do these dialogues become male dominated without any women or with very scarce female representation, but gendered and women's perspectives are missing thematically and epistemologically.

This male domination has consequences not only for the way religions are interpreted, presented, and represented, but also for how interreligious dialogues themselves are represented, and how they negotiate and interact with established power structures. What kind of "we's" and "they's" are being created? If the "we" established is multireligious, but "kyriarchic," to borrow Elizabeth Schüssler Fiorenza's term, then what kind of "they" would that shape?[6] The people outside such a kyriarchic "we" would be women, men of less social status, LGBTQ people, and people with a cultural or racial background seen to be less significant. A kyriarchic "we" would establish not one but many "they's." The "they's" share only that they are all defined out of the particular "we," which is formed due to the common bond of their missing the required qualifications (yet in many different ways).

The model of "religion" as a category that includes fixed traditions has been undergoing postcolonial/decolonial criticism as a Western construct. This critique taps into the debate about interreligious in relation to transreligious. If what is regarded as representative religious differences are signified as the most important aspect and even the constitutive element for interreligious dialogues, it means that these differences must be kept and protected. To show mutual respect and to refrain from criticism of other religious traditions could hinder possible transformative elements of the dialogue processes from happening. Such processes may be replaced by establishing a solid "we" of gatekeepers of the traditions represented. This "we" could easily establish a "they" consisting not only of people identifying with secular values or worldviews and the nonreligious, but also people with hybrid religious identities or multiple belonging.

Suggestions for Engaging with Transreligious Perspectives in Interreligious Studies

How could transreligious perspectives be useful both as critique and for suggesting constructive perspectives for the field of interreligious studies? I suggest three possible ways the term "transreligious" could represent a necessary and refreshing challenge: (1) to engage with postcolonial/decolonial and feminist intersectional theories when analyzing interreligious relations, including interreligious dialogue; (2) to engage with other human identity markers when studying the dynamics and relations between religious traditions regarding both texts and people (examples include gender, culture, social class, and ethnic and geographical contexts and backgrounds; these categories should also be treated as complex categories); (3) to focus on establishing "thick narratives" about interreligious relations and interreligious dynamics—this implies moving beyond the "thin narratives" that often are the official, straightforward (re)presentations of religious traditions and often miss the complexity, hybridity, and contradictions needed to establish transreligious perspectives.[7]

The dilemma of operating with categories such as religion, gender, social class, and cultural belonging are obvious. We need categories to understand the world and other people in the everyday, and in research we need them in order to be able to relate and separate things, and to analyze and interpret. The question is how we apprehend the categories and how they relate to one another. It becomes problematic if they are used with an essentialist understanding because it raises the danger of conflating our constructed categories with our other perceptions of the realities. This could result in allowing us to only see and understand what we have already captured and thus not challenge our taken-for-granted perspectives. In interreligious studies the category of religion is particularly challenging regarding this since it interconnects with other categories of human difference, but most importantly the category of religion itself is often treated differently from other categories (e.g., culture). In research, social anthropologists (among others) study how cultures influence, mix, and blend with each other. If you see religion as solely part of culture, then religions could be part of the complexity defined as cultural. Most theologians and religious studies scholars understand religion as a category distinctly different from culture, although most would also acknowledge a close relation between the two, and that religious praxis is always expressed culturally. However, it is uncommon for scholars (and others) to imagine religious traditions blending with one another in the same way cultures mix.[8] Religions are more often seen to be mutually exclusive and are understood by many—scholars and others—as unmixable. Some theologians, interestingly enough, advocate for the establishment of transreligious theology.[9] It will be interesting to follow how this initiative will develop and how it could interact with interreligious studies.

Establishing a transcultural perspective in cultural studies has been criticized for neglecting differences and attempting to recolonize other cultures.[10] A transreligious perspective in interreligious studies could be in danger of trying to assimilate other religions into a majority religion, which, in North America and Europe, would generally mean the Christian Protestant or Catholic traditions. Scholars in interreligious studies mostly reflect the majority by affiliation, so the question for them becomes one of how to avoid the transreligious perspective as a critique of colonialism and patriarchy?

It is possible to use a transreligious perspective in a manner that not only avoids erasing differences between religious traditions but also avoids benefiting only the stronger and most dominant party. If a transreligious perspective is employed as a method to deconstruct with a power-critical lens, and used in a constructive fashion to include other narratives and perspectives from different margins, problems of conflation and assimilation are avoided. To explore material in other ways, ask other questions, and include other perspectives in a way that engages with the three points mentioned above would be part of establishing transreligious perspectives. (1) Engaging with postcolonial/decolonial perspectives and feminist intersectional perspectives not only entails revealing and criticizing power structures, but it also includes women's and LGBTQ people's stories in a way that establishes new interpretations of the past, present, and future expectations. (2) Including other human differences and (3) establishing "thick narratives" are both constructive techniques, although it should also include deconstructive and critical approaches to how knowledge is established and shared, and ask about which perspectives, stories, and analysis ought to be signified over others.

Interreligious studies is constantly in danger of modeling its worldview after a binary model of religions, and/or of religions and secularity, by regarding them as mutually exclusive. Usually interreligious studies does not compartmentalize religions, or religion and secularity, in such a fixed way. There remains the ever-present danger of the widely shared multicultural model, which understands and administrates cultural and religious group identities in parallel universes, acting as a strong influence on how interreligious studies approaches religious differences. A multicultural model of human cultural and religious differences assumes cultures and the relations between them are group-based with fixed identities and have static conceptual boundaries. A transreligious perspective challenges this way of approaching cultures and religions, and it focuses instead more on communication and relations across these boundaries. It also considers individual, and not only group-based, representations of various traditions, which is the shift of perspective required in order to include intrareligious differences within religious traditions. This is seen by many political theorists, such as Ann Phillips, as a necessary step for acknowledging more gender-fair perspectives.[11]

Diasporic Imagination: A Tool for the Present and the Future

The postcolonial feminist theologian Kwok Pui-lan has suggested an epistemological tool useful in constructive transreligious work within interreligious studies: diasporic imagination.[12] Diasporic imagination is a skill where linguistic, cultural, social, and religious knowledge and understanding is translated from one context to another context, or between contexts. This requires knowledge about the involved contexts, communicative skills, and the experience of being multilocated. As such, this can transform a possible "displaced" position into an important place for establishing knowledge. People with hybrid religious identities or those who claim multiple religious belonging are possible examples of those who employ aspects of a diasporic imagination. Appreciating multilocality also entails the propensity to value multiple belonging, hybrid religious identity, and being on the margins.

Challenging the concept of "interreligious" with transreligious perspectives within the academic field, as well as in interreligious dialogues, complicates the concept of religion as such and the nature of religious identity. Embracing this complexity, however, holds promise for equipping scholars working in these fields for the possibility of contributing more relevant and constructive contributions in the present and the future.

Notes

1   Anne Hege Grung, *Gender Justice in Muslim–Christian Readings: Christian and Muslim Women in Norway Making Meaning of Texts from the Bible, the Koran and the Hadith* (Leiden: Brill Rodopi, 2015), 69.

2   Oddbjørn Leirvik, *Interreligious Studies: A Relational Approach to Religious Activism and the Study of Religion* (London: Bloomsbury, 2014), 10.

3   Thomas Hylland Eriksen, "The Meaning of 'We,'" in *The Challenge of Minority Integration*, ed. Peter A. Kraus and Peter Kivisto (Berlin: De Gruter Open, 2015), 1.

4   Ursula King, "Feminism: The Missing Dimension in the Dialogue of Religions," in *Pluralism and the Religions: The Theological and Political Dimensions*, ed. John D'Arcy May (London: Cassell, 1998); and Jeannine Hill Fletcher, "Women in Inter-religious Dialogue," in *The Wiley-Blackwell Companion to Inter-religious Dialogue*, ed. Catherine Cornille (Hoboken, N.J.: Wiley-Blackwell, 2013).

5   Linda Woodhead, "Gender Differences in Religious Practice and Significance," in *The Sage Handbook of the Sociology of Religion*, ed. N. J. Demerath and J. A. Beckford (Los Angeles: Sage, 2007).

6   Elisabeth Schüssler Fiorenza, *But She Said: Feminist Practices of Biblical Interpretation* (Boston: Beacon, 1992).

7   For examples of what this may mean in practice, see the theorizing over the importance of "thick narratives" in counseling, in Carmen Schuhmann, "Stories of Crime, Stories of Suffering: A Narrative Perspective on Ethical Issues in Criminal Justice Counselling," *European Journal of Psychotherapy and Counselling* 17, no. 1 (2015): 21–38, doi:10.1080/13642537.2014.996172.

8   See Manuela Kalsky, "Flexible Believers in the Netherlands: A Paradigm Shift towards Transreligious Multiplicity," in "Multiple Religious Belonging," topical issue, *Open Theology* 3 (2017): 345–59.

9   John J. Thatamanil, "Transreligious Theology as the Quest for Interreligious Wisdom: Defining, Defending and Teaching Transreligious Theology," *Open Theology* 2 (2016): 354–62.

10   Manuela Guilherme and Gunther Dietz, "Difference in Diversity: Multiple Perspectives on Multicultural, Intercultural and Transcultural Conceptual Complexities," *Journal of Multicultural Discourses* 10, no. 1 (2015): 1–21.

11   Ann Phillips and Jose Casanova, "A Debate on the Public Role of Religion and Its Social and Gender Implications," in *Gender and Development*, paper 5, United Nations Research Institute for Social Development, September 2009.

12   Kwok Pui-lan, *Postcolonial Imagination and Feminist Theology* (London: SCM Press, 2005), 44.

References

Eriksen, Thomas Hylland. "The Meaning of 'We.'" In *The Challenge of Minority Integration*, edited by Peter A. Kraus and Peter Kivisto, 2–21. Berlin: De Gruter Open, 2015.

Fiorenza, Elisabeth Schüssler. *But She Said: Feminist Practices of Biblical Interpretation*. Boston: Beacon, 1992.

Fletcher, Jeannine Hill. "Women in Inter-religious Dialogue." In *The Wiley-Blackwell Companion to Inter-religious Dialogue*, edited by Catherine Cornille, 168–83. Hoboken, N.J.: Wiley-Blackwell, 2013.

Grung, Anne Hege. *Gender Justice in Muslim–Christian Readings: Christian and Muslim Women in Norway Making Meaning of Texts from the Bible, the Koran and the Hadith*. Leiden: Brill Rodopi, 2015.

Guilherme, Manuela, and Gunther Dietz. "Difference in Diversity: Multiple Perspectives on Multicultural, Intercultural and Transcultural Conceptual Complexities." *Journal of Multicultural Discourses* 10, no. 1 (2015): 1–21.

Kalsky, Manuela. "Flexible Believers in the Netherlands: A Paradigm Shift towards Transreligious Multiplicity." In "Multiple Religious Belonging," topical issue, *Open Theology* 3 (2017): 345–59.

King, Ursula. "Feminism: The Missing Dimension in the Dialogue of Religions." In *Pluralism and the Religions: The Theological and Political Dimensions*, edited by John D'Arcy May, 40–57. London: Cassell, 1998.

Leirvik, Oddbjørn. *Interreligious Studies: A Relational Approach to Religious Activism and the Study of Religion*. London: Bloomsbury, 2014.

Phillips, Ann, and Jose Casanova. "A Debate on the Public Role of Religion and Its Social and Gender Implications." In *Gender and Development*, paper 5, United Nations Research Institute for Social Development, September 2009.

Pui-lan, Kwok. *Postcolonial Imagination and Feminist Theology*. London: SCM Press, 2005.

Schuhmann, Carmen. "Stories of Crime, Stories of Suffering: A Narrative Perspective on Ethical Issues in Criminal Justice Counselling." *European Journal of Psychotherapy and Counselling* 17, no. 1 (2015): 21–38. doi:10.1080/136425 37.2014.996172.

Thatamanil, John J. "Transreligious Theology as the Quest for Interreligious Wisdom: Defining, Defending and Teaching Transreligious Theology." *Open Theology* 2 (2016): 354–62.

Woodhead, Linda. "Gender Differences in Religious Practice and Significance." In *The Sage Handbook of the Sociology of Religion*, edited by N. J. Demerath and J. A. Beckford, 550–70. Los Angeles: Sage, 2007.

II
HISTORY AND METHOD

9

Historical Precedents

Thomas Albert Howard

A simple Internet search will yield countless interfaith or interreligious "centers," "institutes," "councils," "projects," "initiatives," "forums," "groups," and "alliances." Most of these have been established in the last several decades, and most are committed to some form of "dialogue."

From whence did this phenomenon come? This *historical* question is salient because even as many today practice, theorize, and/or theologize about interreligious dialogue, few have attended carefully to its past. Simply put, the topic is heavily theologized and scantly historicized. Recognition of this reality several years ago led me to undertake an inquiry into the roots and rise of interreligious dialogue.[1] At the outset of my inquiry, I had assumed that the phenomenon was almost exclusively a modern development, perhaps beginning, as many scholars note, with Chicago's well-known Parliament of the World's Religions (1893). In my forthcoming book, I argue that this event represents a major turning point. But "interfaith," albeit avant la lettre, is not altogether without precedent; it has earlier harbingers, in either actual dialogues or literary simulations of dialogue among representatives of different faith traditions. In this chapter, I selectively sketch several of these before suggesting why the history of interreligious dialogue bears significance for contemporary theory and practice. In particular, I cover key persons and instances of dialogue from the medieval Islamic world, Mongolia, Western Europe, and South Asia. Having a sense of this history of interreligious dialogue, and its relation to contemporary theory and practice, can be a significant resource for the scholar of interreligious studies today.

The Islamic World

In the medieval Islamic world, sultans and emirs sometimes convened assemblies (*majālis*; singular, *majlis*) in which theological topics were discussed or debated. Often only Muslim scholars participated, but evidence attests to the participation of Christians, Jews, Manichaeans, and Zoroastrians as well. These conversations sometimes inspired literary works, several written in the form of a dialogue. The anonymous *Risalat al-Kindi* (ca. ninth century) is one such work. Written in dialogue form between a Muslim and Christian, referred to respectively as "Servant of Allah, son of Ishmael" and "Servant of the Messiah, son of Isaac," the work reflects discussions held at the Abbasid court in Baghdad. Also during the Abbasid caliphate, the Jewish scholar Ibn Kammuna produced *Examination of the Three Faiths*, an early instance, we might say, of the comparative study of religion and one based on extensive conversations among Jews, Christians, and Muslims.[2]

Francis of Assisi probably participated in a *majlis* when he traveled to Egypt on a missionary errand during the Fifth Crusade (1217–1221). There, he conversed with the Ayyubid sultan of Egypt, al-Malik al-Kamil (r. 1218–1238), renowned for his wisdom and curiosity. When Francis left, al-Kamil gave him an ivory trumpet, which is still preserved in the crypt of the basilica in Assisi. Giotto rendered the remarkable encounter in a fresco cycle of Francis' life; Bonaventure mentions it in his life of Francis, as does Dante in his *Paradiso*. Although the sources lend themselves to different interpretations of what actually took place between Francis and the sultan, Paul Moses fairly concludes that the encounter nonetheless "endures as a memorable forerunner of peaceful dialogue between Christians and Muslims."[3]

The Mongol Empire

Besides medieval Muslim *majālis*, various Mongol leaders held discussions at court among adherents of different faiths. Given the fearsome reputation of Mongols, this might come as a surprise. But it is well established that Mongol leaders often became curious of the faith traditions among the people that they conquered and, once an area was subdued, they had a political interest in keeping a lid on religious conflict. Staging peaceful discussions at court was one means of doing this.

The Flemish Franciscan mendicant William of Rubruck (ca. 1220–ca. 1293) left a remarkable record of one such discussion in the diary of his travels to the Mongol court at Karakorum in present-day Mongolia.[4] There, the Mongol chief, Möngke Khan (r. 1251–1259) arranged for a conversation (*collatio* is the Latin term Rubruck employs) that included a Latin Christian (Rubruck), Nestorian Christians, Muslims, and Buddhists—the latter being likely from Tibet.[5] (This is the first known formal dialogue between a European Christian and Buddhists in world history.) The actual debate lasted an entire day. At the outset, the great Khan laid down through his secretaries the ground rules, including the directive "that no man should be so bold as to make provocative or insulting remarks to his opponent, and that no one is to cause any commotion that might obstruct these proceedings."[6]

This was not an isolated event. Similar conversations had taken place before and afterward. Kwand Amir, a Persian observer at the court of Khublai Khan, successor of Möngke, recorded the following: "[Khublai Khan would] gather the *ulema* [religious scholars] of Islam, the learned of the Jews, Christian monks, and the wise men of China and hold deliberations, for he enjoyed listening to philosophical and religious debates."[7] Marco Polo also attests to such interactions under Mongol rule.

Europe

Moving to Western Europe, two notable written dialogues exist from the late medieval and Renaissance periods: Ramon Llull's *Book of the Gentile and the Three Wise Men* (ca. 1274–1276) and Nicholas of Cusa's *On the Peace of Faith* (ca. 1453). The former presents an irenic dialogue among Jewish, Christian, and Muslim savants, each attempting to persuade a religiously inquisitive "gentile." Unlike other more polemical dialogues from this period, the conversation that Llull presents is remarkably irenic. At its closing, in fact, each interlocutor "asked forgiveness of the other for any disrespectful word that he might have spoken."[8] While Llull, more implicitly than explicitly, portrays Christianity in a more favorable light than the other two faiths, the work as a whole is surprisingly free from slander, caricature, and accusation. There are no broadsides against Mohammed or the Qur'an, no charges of Jewish deicide or of the blasphemy of the Talmud. "Scrupulous in his use of authentic Jewish and Muslim sources," Llull, sums up the historian John V. Tolan, "presents a remarkably fair and accurate portrayal of each of the three religions. Llull's tract stands out as an irenic island in a sea of tempestuous disputation and polemic."[9]

A redoubtable polymath, Nicholas of Cusa (1401–1461) is a fascinating figure in the Christian intellectual tradition, a notable forerunner of interreligious dialogue, and one of the few Renaissance scholars familiar with the work of Llull. To a fellow theologian, Cusa once complained that the solution to religious conflict should be settled not on the battlefield but through some sort of "dialogue" (*colloquia*).[10] In 1453, Cusa experienced the fall of Constantinople to the Ottoman Empire, an epochal moment in world history. News of Ottoman troops desecrating and looting ancient Christian sites of worship exacerbated long-standing anti-Islamic sentiments. From this point on, "the Turk"—and not just "the Saracen"—became a reviled Other in the Christian imagination, inciting intellectual refutations, eschatological speculation, and successive martial actions to forestall further Ottoman advance.[11]

But for Cusa, the events of 1453 inspired a different kind of thinking. Vexed and saddened by religious divisions, he wrote and published in 1453 *De pace fidei* (On the peace of faith), based on a vision that he claimed to have experienced.[12] In the vision, a heavenly host—comprised of God, the Word (the second person of the Trinity), an archangel, and the apostles Peter and Paul—met in an "assembly" (*coetu*) to converse with seventeen people representing different ethnicities, languages, and faiths. These include representatives from Europe (a Greek, Italian, Frenchman, Spaniard, Englander, German, and Bohemian), from the Middle East (an Arab, Chaldean, Jew, Scythian, Persian, Syrian, Turk, and Armenian), and from farther east (an Indian and a Tatar). Cusa's knowledge of the East was scanty, derived in large part from reading Marco Polo, but that he included figures beyond the "Abrahamic" fold testifies to the breadth of his aim.[13] Written in dialogue form, the conversation takes various twists and turns before all participants conclude that it is mainly different rituals and outward appearances that divide them from one another, for they all, at some level, bear witness to the unity of faith. To be sure, Cusa is finally a Christian, and it should not surprise that the religious truth that they all reflect is most fully expressed in Christianity. But the irenicism that he displays is extraordinary given the times in which he lived. Cusa, James E. Biechler sums up, "set a new record of inclusiveness. It is probably the first Christian work that attempts to come to grips in a concrete way with the problem of world religion using an approach along lines other than conversion or mission."[14] Cusa himself seemed to recognize that his approach to other faiths might at first be met with skepticism; but he held out the hope, in the introduction to *De pace fidei*, that one day his heavenly vision "might come to the knowledge of those who [actually] resolve such important matters."[15]

Mughal India

Finally, permit me to jump to South Asia and the captivating case of the sixteenth-century Islamic Mughal Empire in India, during which Emperor Akbar (1542–1605) organized and presided over conversations among representatives from the Indian subcontinent's vast patchwork of faith traditions.[16] In his imperial city, Fatehpur Sikri, south of Delhi, Akbar built the *Ibadat Khana* (House of Worship). The evening before Friday prayers, he regularly gathered religious leaders there to discuss and compare views. Muslims of differing opinions were his first interlocutors, but soon he included Hindus, Buddhists, Jains, Parsis, Jews, and Christians. The latter, Jesuit missionaries from their mission outpost in Goa, have left extensive records of their encounters at Akbar's court—and there are many other sources as well.[17] Akbar's chief aide, Abu'l-Fazl described the *Ibadat Khana* as a "veritable assemblage of the wise of every religion and sect, where everyone brought forward seriously the assertions and contentions of his belief."[18] Or, as one Sheikh Nur al-Haq described Akbar's interfaith forum:

> Learned men from Khorasan and Iraq and Transoxiania, and India, both doctors and theologians, Shia and Sunnis, Christians, philosophers and Brahmins assembled together. . . . Here they discussed the rational and traditional manners of discourse, travel and histories of each other's prophecies. They widened the circle of debate.[19]

Regrettably, the ethos of the *Ibadat Khana* was largely abandoned by Akbar's successors, particularly by his grandson, Aurangzeb (r. 1658–1707), promoter of a strict interpretation of Islam. But the memory of Akbar has loomed large in more recent Indian history, many seeing Akbar's quest for interreligious understanding reappearing in Gandhi and in India's 1947 Constitution that grants religious freedom. And not least, the *Ibadat Khana* represents a remarkable forerunner of interfaith dialogue.

Conclusion

What, finally, are we to make of these harbingers of interfaith dialogue, and how might they serve contemporary scholars in interreligious studies? Permit two concluding points.

First, the Second Vatican Council (1962–1965) nicely held in tension two theological modus operandi as it went about the business of church reform: (1) *aggiornamento*, attempting to bring the church into conversation with the contemporary world and (2) *ressourcement*, returning to (often neglected aspects of) the past for insight. Too often, I will submit, proponents and practitioners of interfaith dialogue have opted for *aggiornamento* alone, neglecting *ressourcement*. Following theologians such as John Hick or Leonard Swidler, they have argued that interfaith dialogue bespeaks a "Copernican Revolution" in theology. Such declarations come with assumption that little, if anything, is to be learned from previous theological engagement with religious alterity. The past becomes, ipso facto, "Ptolemaic," strictly a repository of benighted inquisitions, crusades, and polemics. These realities exist in the past, to be sure, but they are not all that one finds there.

Second, and related, one simply cannot appraise the significance of a thing without some attention to its genesis and history. In the case of interfaith dialogue, we will discover in fact that while its modern efforts represent significant discontinuity with the past, they also bear witness to continuities. Again, this fact is sometimes lost on practitioners of interreligious dialogue today (whether Christian or otherwise) as well as on diagnosticians of contemporary religious pluralism; both are given to touting the radical novelty of our contemporary situation. Yes, modernity has ushered in distinctive forms of pluralism and dialogue, as I argue in my forthcoming book. But rarely in history is something entirely unprecedented. Assuming otherwise impoverishes historical explanation and burdens present-day interreligious endeavors with amnesia about its own past.

Notes

1 This will be published as the forthcoming *The Faiths of Others: Modern History and the Rise of Interreligious Dialogue* (Yale University Press).

2 On the *majlis* tradition in medieval Islam, see Hava Lazarus-Yafeh et al., eds., *The Majlis: Interreligious Encounters in Medieval Islam* (Wiesbaden: Harrowitz Verlag, 1999).

3 See Paul Moses, *The Saint and the Sultan: The Crusades, Islam, and Francis of Assisi's Mission of Peace* (New York: Doubleday, 2009), 3. Cf. Carol Zaleski and Philip Zaleski, "Saint Francis, the Catholic Church, and Islam," *Nova et Vetera* 13 (2015): 39–55.

4 On Rubruck generally and his travels in the East, see Maria Bonewa-Petrowa, "Rubrucks Reisebeschreibung als soziologische und kulturgeschichtliche Quelle," *Philologus* 115 (1971): 16–31.

5 Benjamin Z. Kedar, "The Multilateral Disputation at the Court of the Gran Qan Möngke, 1254," in Lazarus-Yafeh et al., *Majlis*, 162–83.

6   William of Rubruck, *The Mission of Friar William of Rubruck: His Journey to the Court of the Great Khan Möngke, 1253–1255*, trans. Peter Jackson (London: Hakluyt, 1990), 231.

7   Kwand Amir, *Habib al-siyar*, as quoted in Richard C. Foltz, *Religions of the Silk Road* (New York: St. Martin's Griffin, 2000), 124.

8   Anthony Bonner, ed., *Doctor Illuminatus: A Ramon Llull Reader* (Princeton: Princeton University Press, 1985), 167–69.

9   John V. Tolan, *Saracens: Islam in the Medieval European Imagination* (New York: Columbia University Press, 2002), 266.

10   The scholar to whom Cusa wrote was Juan de Segovia; see Nicholas Rescher, "Nicholas of Cusa: A Fifteenth-Century Encounter with Islam," *Muslim World* 55 (1965): 200. Cf. Anne Marie Wolf, *Juan de Segovia and the Fight for Peace: Christians and Muslims in the Fifteenth Century* (Notre Dame: University of Notre Dame Press, 2014).

11   Robert Schwoebel, *The Shadow of the Crescent: The Renaissance Image of the Turk (1453–1517)* (New York: St. Martin's, 1969).

12   Nicholas of Cusa, *Nicolai de Cusa: Opera Omnia* (Hamburg: F. Meiner, 1959), 7:9–10; and William F. Wetz, ed., *Toward a New Council of Florence: "On the Peace of Faith" and other Works by Nicolaus of Cusa* (Washington, D.C.: Schiller Institute, 1993), 231–35.

13   James E. Biechler, "Interreligious Dialogue," in *Introducing Nicholas of Cusa: A Guide to a Renaissance Man*, ed. Christopher M. Bellitto, Thomas M. Izbicki, and Gerald Christianson (New York: Paulist, 2004), 273.

14   Biechler, "Interreligious Dialogue," in Bellitto, Izbicki, and Christianson, *Introducing Nicholas of Cusa*, 274.

15   Nicholas of Cusa, *Nicolai de Cusa: Opera Omnia*, 7:4.

16   Arnold Hottinger, *Akbar der Grosse: Herrscher über Indien durch Versöhnung der Religionen* (Munich: Wilhelm Fink Verlag, 1998), 80ff. For the ongoing relevance of Akbar in India today, see Amartya Sen, *The Argumentative Indian: Writings on Indian History, Culture, and Identity* (New York: Farrar, Straus and Giroux, 2005), xii, passim.

17   Pierre du Jarric, *Akbar and the Jesuits: An Account of the Jesuit Missions to the Court of Akbar*, trans. C. H. Payne (New Delhi: Tulsi House, 1979); and George Gispert-Sauch, "Antonio de Monserrat, Ambassador in the Court of Emperor Akbar," *Vidyajyoti Journal of Theological Reflection* 76 (2012): 457–71.

18   Quoted in Walter J. Fischel, "Jews and Judaism at the Courts of the Moghul Emperors of Medieval India," *Proceedings of the American Academy for Jewish Research* 18 (1948–1949): 145.

19 Quoted in Jawad Syed, "Akbar's Multiculturalism," *Canadian Journal of Administrative Sciences / Revue canadienne des sciences de l'administration* 28 (2011): 406.

References

Biechler, James E. "Interreligious Dialogue." In *Introducing Nicholas of Cusa: A Guide to a Renaissance Man,* edited by Christopher M. Bellitto, Thomas M. Izbicki, and Gerald Christianson, 270–96. New York: Paulist, 2004.

Bonewa-Petrowa, Maria. "Rubrucks Reisebeschreibung als soziologische und kulturgeschichtliche Quelle." *Philologus* 115 (1971): 16–31.

Bonner, Anthony, ed. *Doctor Illuminatus: A Ramon Llull Reader.* Princeton: Princeton University Press, 1985.

du Jarric, Pierre. *Akbar and the Jesuits: An Account of the Jesuit Missions to the Court of Akbar.* Translated by C. H. Payne. New Delhi: Tulsi House, 1979.

Fischel, Walter J. "Jews and Judaism at the Courts of the Moghul Emperors of Medieval India." *Proceedings of the American Academy for Jewish Research* 18 (1948–1949): 137–77.

Foltz, Richard C. *Religions of the Silk Road.* New York: St. Martin's Griffin, 2000

Gispert-Sauch, George. "Antonio de Monserrat, Ambassador in the Court of Emperor Akbar." *Vidyajyoti Journal of Theological Reflection* 76 (2012): 457–71.

Hottinger, Arnold. *Akbar der Grosse: Herrscher über Indien durch Versöhnung der Religionen.* Munich: Wilhelm Fink Verlag, 1998.

Kedar, Benjamin Z. "The Multilateral Disputation at the Court of the Gran Qan Möngke, 1254." In Lazarus-Yafeh et al., *Majlis,* 162–83.

Lazarus-Yafeh, Hava, Mark R. Cohen, Sasson Somekh, and Sidney H. Griffith, eds. *The Majlis: Interreligious Encounters in Medieval Islam.* Wiesbaden: Harrowitz Verlag, 1999.

Moses, Paul. *The Saint and the Sultan: The Crusades, Islam, and Francis of Assisi's Mission of Peace.* New York: Doubleday, 2009.

Nicholas of Cusa. *Nicolai de Cusa: Opera Omnia.* Vol. 7. Hamburg: F. Meiner, 1959.

Rescher, Nicholas. "Nicholas of Cusa: A Fifteenth-Century Encounter with Islam." *Muslim World* 55 (1965): 195–202.

Schwoebel, Robert. *The Shadow of the Crescent: The Renaissance Image of the Turk (1453–1517).* New York: St. Martin's, 1969.

Sen, Amartya. *The Argumentative Indian: Writings on Indian History, Culture, and Identity.* New York: Farrar, Straus and Giroux, 2005.

Syed, Jawad. "Akbar's Multiculturalism." *Canadian Journal of Administrative Sciences / Revue canadienne des sciences de l'administration* 28 (2011): 402–12.

Tolan, John V. *Saracens: Islam in the Medieval European Imagination.* New York: Columbia University Press, 2002.

Wetz, William F, ed. *Toward a New Council of Florence: "On the Peace of Faith" and Other Works by Nicolaus of Cusa.* Washington, D.C.: Schiller Institute, 1993.

William of Rubruck. *The Mission of Friar William of Rubruck: His Journey to the Court of the Great Khan Möngke, 1253–1255.* Translated by Peter Jackson. London: Hakluyt, 1990.

Wolf, Anne Marie. *Juan de Segovia and the Fight for Peace: Christians and Muslims in the Fifteenth Century.* Notre Dame: University of Notre Dame Press, 2014.

Zaleski, Carol, and Philip Zaleski. "Saint Francis, the Catholic Church, and Islam." *Nova et Vetera* 13 (2015): 39–55.

10

From Comparison to Conversation

Frans Wijsen

When I conducted my doctoral research in East Africa in the early 1980s, Tanzania was referred to as a "haven of peace." Africa's "triple heritage" and "peaceful co-existence of religions" were the guiding concepts of my research. When "seeds of conflict"[1] emerged in the later 1980s, I had to revise my previous work. Had there been issues that I had not noted before? Or had the situation dramatically changed? When I tried to make sense of the "seeds of conflict" in the "haven of peace," I noted that the traditional paradigms of studying religion did not help me further. This is where the shift "from religious studies to interreligious studies" in my work arose.[2]

Conceptual Clarification

When scholars of religion study interreligious relations or conflicts, they go into two directions, broadly defined as "theology" and "science" of religions.[3] Theology of religions first defines what a religion is in itself, its texts and traditions, and then how it relates to others. Science of religions does more or less the same, by first classifying religions and then comparing them.[4] Both approaches reify religion. They distinguish the knowing subject and the known object, and assume that religion "exists."

Based on the assumption that dialogue is constitutive for identity,[5] I started at the other end, not with what religions are in themselves, sui generis, but with factual existing interactions. I assumed that it is in the interaction with the "other" religions that one's "own" religion and religious identity is constructed, negotiated, and manipulated.

Theology of interreligious dialogue was a step forward compared to reifying approaches, such as theology of religions. It took the primacy of practice principle into account and showed that grassroots realities were more complex than the clear-cut categories of "exclusivism," "inclusivism," and "pluralism" that theology of religions had brought forward. The same applied to the "Primal Religion," "Islam," and "Christianity" classification, that the "world religions approach" had brought forward.[6]

But, theology of interreligious dialogue remained an insider's model. It perceived of "the other" religion from the perspective of one's "own" religion. To go beyond the insider's model, the label "interreligious theology" arose, which recognized that the passive objects of study in religious studies had become subjects, and the idea was to theologize together with traditions other than one's own.

In theologizing together, another issue came up. Various theologians that I collaborated with in Africa and Asia worked in departments of religious studies. From a postcolonial perspective, the boundary between "insider" and "outsider" perspectives, "theology" of and "science" of religions, including "philosophy of religion," blurred. Thus, my approach became not only interreligious, but also interdisciplinary. This is where the label "interreligious studies" in my work came from, and this is the label that my cofounders and I used when we started the European Society for Intercultural Theology and Interreligious Studies (ESITIS) in 2005.

Five Shifts in the Study of Religion

In harmony with the findings summarized above, I concluded that there was an urgent need for a new field of study to be taught in faculties of theology and departments of religious studies that went beyond traditional courses such as "World Religions," "Islam in Africa," or "African Traditional Religions," and beyond the classical disciplines of theology, philosophy, and religious studies. From a postmodern perspective, the distinction between these disciplines had become irrelevant anyway.[7] Consequently, I propose five shifts in the study of religion.

First, I move from a "world religions" approach to the study of "interreligious relations," which emphasizes the interconnectedness and interdependence of religions as its material object (research object) and not the religions as they are "in themselves." After all, we do not know what religions are "in themselves," and there has been a plea to do away with the term "religion"[8] and to study religion discursively and how it comes about, not what religion is.[9]

Second, I define interreligious studies not as a new discipline but as an interdisciplinary field of study, which studies interreligious relations in a multi-perspective and poly-methodical way (formal object, research perspective). This approach overcomes the classic distinction between insider and outsider perspectives, and thus it defuses the controversy about "religionist" versus "reductionist" research methods.

Third, I move from a "comparative" to a "conversational" epistemology. This approach does away with essentialist or reified notions of religion.[10] The postcolonial and postmodern view plays a role here in that scholars of religion do not see "the others" in objective ways based on the positivistic attitude, but rather they construct images of the other. Put differently, from a "critical realist" perspective,[11] truth comes about in a conversation between the knowing subject and the known object. Methodologically speaking, I opt for "dialogical research."[12]

Fourth, I move from "disengaged" to "engaged" research. In order to be "objective" or "neutral," classical religious studies wants to be disengaged. Emancipating itself from theology, which is perceived as "biased" and "prejudiced," religious studies strives for "value-free" neutrality. This may have been important during its emancipation from theology in the twentieth century; however, in the twenty-first century this seems naïve.

Fifth, I advocate methodological conversion, in addition to methodological agnosticism.[13] I do not understand why methodological agnosticism is considered to be more scientific than methodological conversion. In my view, methodological agnosticism does not make sense in non-Western contexts anyway. From the Pew Forum on Religion and Public Life, the Gallup Polls, and the World Values Survey scholars of religion, we know that most people in the non-Western world say that they are religious and that they attach a great value to their religion. This applies also to members of departments of religious studies. Western scholars of religion are not taken very seriously by their non-Western colleagues if they take an agnostic view of religion.[14]

Retrospect and Prospect

In conclusion, there have been various shifts in my work: historical (from a world religion approach to interreligious studies), methodological (from disengaged to dialogical research), and epistemological (from comparison to conversation). I label what I am doing now as "practical religious studies."

A final shift is theoretical. In *Seeds of Conflict*,[15] I criticized the social identity theory[16] that reifies "us" and "them" classifications. I proposed Dialogical Self Theory as an alternative theory for better understanding multiple loyalties.[17] In Dialogical Self Theory, "the other" is not only perceived of as a complete stranger and potential enemy but also understood as already a part of "me." As such, Dialogical Self Theory blurs the boundary between self and society, and it conceptualizes the self as a mini-society.

Ever since, my writing has sought to elaborate on the Dialogical Self Theory.[18] Originating from personality psychology, Dialogical Self Theory widened its scope to positioning and counter-positioning in globalizing societies.[19] Recently, Dialogical Self Theory has widened further to focus on the relationship between the dialogical self as democratic self in democratic societies.[20] From the perspective of this theory, I can better explain the "peaceful co-existence of religions" that I started with, and I am better able to articulate where "seeds of conflict" come from. In short, Dialogical Self Theory is a strong theoretical foundation for interreligious studies.[21]

Notes

1   Frans Wijsen and Bernardin Mfumbusa, "Seeds of Conflict: Muslim–Christian Relations in Tanzania," in *Religion, Conflict and Reconciliation: Multifaith Ideals and Realities*, ed. J. Gort, H. Jansen, and H. Vroom (Amsterdam: Rodopi, 2002).

2   Frans Wijsen, *Seeds of Conflict in a Haven of Peace: From Religious Studies to Interreligious Studies in Africa* (Amsterdam: Rodopi, 2007).

3   Wijsen, *Seeds of Conflict*, 41–52.

4   Gavin Flood, *Beyond Phenomenology: Rethinking the Study of Religion* (London: Cassell, 1999), 28–33.

5   Pierre Bourdieu, *Language and Symbolic Power* (Cambridge: Polity, 1991), 220.

6   Tomoko Masuzawa, *The Invention of World Religions; or, How European Universalism Was Preserved in the Language of Pluralism* (Chicago: University of Chicago Press, 2005).

7   Wijsen, *Seeds of Conflict*, 247.

8   Wilfred Cantwell Smith, *The Meaning and End of Religion: A New Approach to the Religious Traditions of Mankind* (New York: New American Library, 1963).

9   Frans Wijsen and Kocku von Stuckrad, eds., *Making Religion: Theory and Practice in the Discursive Study of Religion* (Leiden: Brill, 2016).

10 Jonathan Z. Smith, *Imagining Religion: From Babylon to Jonestown* (Chicago: University of Chicago Press, 1982); Flood, *Beyond Phenomenology*.

11 Norman Fairclough, *Analysing Discourse: Textual Analysis for Social Research* (London: Routledge, 2003), 22.

12 Frans Wijsen, *Religious Discourse, Social Cohesion and Conflict: Studying Muslim–Christian Relations* (Oxford: Peter Lang, 2013), 38

13 James L. Cox, *Rational Ancestors: Scientific Rationality and African Indigenous Religions* (Cardiff: Cardiff Academic, 1998), 93–96.

14 Frans Wijsen, "Are Africans Incurably Religious? Discourse Analysis of a Debate, Direction of a Discipline," *Exchange* 46 (2017): 370–97.

15 Wijsen, *Seeds of Conflict*.

16 Henri Tajfel and John C. Turner, "The Social Identity Theory of Intergroup Behaviour," in *Psychology of Intergroup Relations*, ed. Stephen Worchel and William G. Austin (Chicago: Nelson Hall, 1986).

17 Wijsen, *Seeds of Conflict*, 170–77.

18 Wijsen, *Religious Discourse*, 189.

19 Hubert Hermans and Agnieszka Hermans-Konopka, *Dialogical Self Theory: Positioning and Counter-Positioning in a Globalizing Society* (Cambridge: Cambridge University Press, 2010).

20 Hubert Hermans, *Society in the Self: A Theory of Identity in Democracy* (New York: Oxford University Press, 2018).

21 Frans Wijsen, "Religion, Radicalism, Relativism: Between Social Identity Theory and Dialogical Self Theory," in *Moral and Spiritual Leadership in an Age of Plural Moralities*, ed. H. Alma and I. ter Avest (New York: Routledge, 2019), 48–69.

References

Bourdieu, Pierre. *Language and Symbolic Power*. Cambridge: Polity, 1991.

Cox, James L. *Rational Ancestors: Scientific Rationality and African Indigenous Religions*. Cardiff: Cardiff Academic, 1998.

Fairclough, Norman. *Analysing Discourse: Textual Analysis for Social Research*. London: Routledge, 2003.

Flood, Gavin. *Beyond Phenomenology: Rethinking the Study of Religion*. London: Cassell, 1999.

Hermans, Hubert. *Society in the Self: A Theory of Identity in Democracy*. New York: Oxford University Press, 2018.

Hermans, Hubert, and Agnieszka Hermans-Konopka. *Dialogical Self Theory: Positioning and Counter-Positioning in a Globalizing Society*. Cambridge: Cambridge University Press, 2010.

Masuzawa, Tomoko. *The Invention of World Religions; or, How European Universalism Was Preserved in the Language of Pluralism*. Chicago: University of Chicago Press, 2005.

Smith, Jonathan Z. *Imagining Religion: From Babylon to Jonestown*. Chicago: University of Chicago Press, 1982.

Smith, Wilfred Cantwell. *The Meaning and End of Religion: A New Approach to the Religious Traditions of Mankind.* New York: New American Library, 1963.

Tajfel, Henri, and John C. Turner. "The Social Identity Theory of Intergroup Behaviour." In *Psychology of Intergroup Relations*, edited by Stephen Worchel and William G. Austin, 7–24. Chicago: Nelson Hall, 1986.

Wijsen, Frans. "Are Africans Incurably Religious? Discourse Analysis of a Debate, Direction of a Discipline." *Exchange* 46 (2017): 370–97.

———. "Religion, Radicalism, Relativism: Between Social Identity Theory and Dialogical Self Theory." In *Moral and Spiritual Leadership in an Age of Plural Moralities*, edited by H. Alma and I. ter Avest, 48–69. New York: Routledge, 2019.

———. *Religious Discourse, Social Cohesion and Conflict: Studying Muslim–Christian Relations.* Oxford: Peter Lang, 2013.

———. *Seeds of Conflict in a Haven of Peace: From Religious Studies to Interreligious Studies in Africa.* Amsterdam: Rodopi, 2007.

Wijsen, Frans, and Bernardin Mfumbusa. "Seeds of Conflict: Muslim–Christian Relations in Tanzania." In *Religion, Conflict and Reconciliation: Multifaith Ideals and Realities*, edited by J. Gort, H. Jansen, and H. Vroom, 316–26. Amsterdam: Rodopi, 2002.

Wijsen, Frans, and Kocku von Stuckrad, eds. *Making Religion: Theory and Practice in the Discursive Study of Religion.* Leiden: Brill, 2016.

11

Ethnographic Approaches and Limitations

Nelly van Doorn-Harder

This chapter addresses aspects of interreligious engagement that we as scholars struggle to write about. It focuses on the challenge of transmitting our observations and experiences into "objective" academic language acceptable to our guild. In so doing, we risk writing about people and their faith as if they were fish in a bowl. This chapter is also about the limits we encounter in the process: the expressions and beliefs that we cannot comprehend fully without changing our entire cultural and religious frame of reference.[1]

A Word on Ethnography

My observations come from ethnographic research done within the framework of Religious Studies. Such work requires mindfulness of my position as insider, outsider, or both. Working among the Copts of Egypt and Muslims in Southeast Asia, I cannot escape engaging deeply with the worldviews of the people I study. The line between ethnography and interreligious studies seems thin and easy to cross. The questions that arise, the social and cultural faux pas I have made are akin to both fields.

The Coptic Orthodox Church in Egypt

Technically speaking, studying the Coptic Church in Egypt is an *intra*religious exercise. When my dissertation about women monastics within the Church appeared as a book in 1995, it was the first academic study on contemporary or living Copts.[2] Until then, Coptic Studies focused on history, patristics, art, archeology, linguistics, and liturgy.

Neither my Middle Eastern Studies background nor my experiences as a Christian well versed in theology had prepared me for the degree of "otherness" this community presented. Many of its beliefs and practices were deeply rooted in Egyptian culture and often coincided with those of their Muslim neighbors. However, the main challenge centered on how to adequately convey the core of Coptic belief and practices that focus on the moments when and where heaven and earth meet. These happen during the mysteries of the Eucharistic celebration, and in individuals who are considered saintly, both dead and alive. The Calvinist church of my youth hardly mentioned Saint Mary, let alone saints.

Just analyzing why Copts considered some of the individuals I met to be saintly was not enough. I tried to break down what they offered the community such as powerful prayers of healing, deep psychological insights, and words of comfort or warnings for future events. In the end, I became privy to wisdom and insight only a few selected humans have, and I witnessed events that defied explanation such as healings, prophecies, and exorcisms. The recurring question was how to translate such experiences into "familiar, comfortable, and safe academic language?"[3] How can our Western mindset, which tends to privilege empirical science, process mystical experiences without reducing them to nonsensical babble?

My Calvinist mindset stood in the way. Ever since the era of the Enlightenment, those of us in the West have grappled with a lack of language when confronted with mystical religious expressions. Michel de Certeau blames the divorce between mystical forms of experiencing reality and experimental, scientific modes of thinking on the frame of reference developed since that era. Ideas concerning God, nature, and humanity synthesized into a worldview that celebrated the use of reason.[4]

Scholarly Considerations

During the past years, scholars of religious studies and anthropology have started to theorize about how to articulate phenomena that defy common language or are much more complex than our boiled-down writings convey. Thomas Tweed tried to figure out how we can escape from recreating our observations into static theories.[5] Anthropologists Jean and John Comaroff warned not to skip over what defies explanation by privileging a handful of informants whose ideas and interpretations we "get," which only results in creating "ontologies that give precedence to individuals over contexts."[6]

Mattijs van de Port discusses the same phenomenon in his study on the Brazilian Candomblé community. Specifically, he analyzes the history of how outsiders wrote about them. He concludes that the core of this religion escaped most of the outsiders since it defies articulation and did not fit into their existing frames of scientific explanation. Candomblé priests are acutely aware that an unbridgeable gap exists between two ways of acquiring knowledge: "the way of the words (or world), leading into 'veritable labyrinths', and the way of initiation, leading to 'true knowledge.'"[7] Van de Port observes that we are unable to engage the non-knowing in our academic writing and step away from the conventional methods of producing meaning when facing "mystical" expressions of faith. Fearing it may render our work irrelevant, we dance around the core of such phenomena or retreat into dry descriptions.[8] In the end, van de Port concludes that we cannot cross the threshold dividing those initiated into Candomblé secrets and the researchers who infuse "the truth of their imaginations with a truth that transcends all cultural formulation."[9]

Tweed and van de Port dive into a host of theories to find answers to their questions on how to go about finding and reporting on the "really real." While studying the role of saints within the Catholic religious experience, Robert Orsi suggest we understand religion "as a web not of meanings but of relationships between heaven and earth."[10] This observation serves as a tool that helps scholars of religion find their place within these networks. It also acknowledges our limitations where it concerns knowing another person's inner world.

Using seemingly safe and familiar academic language appears to be the best approach. However, it has its pitfalls and can lead to grave accusations from the groups we study. When more scholars started to study the lived religion of the Copts, a colleague and I decided to publish the core of these new studies in an edited volume called *Between Desert and City: the Coptic Church Today*.[11] The book was well received but the team editing *Le Monde Copte* did not like it one bit. They accused us of "treating the Copts as if they were fish in a bowl." Even though we had discussed the manuscript with several Coptic leaders, they felt we had not managed to convey the essence of their faith. The big lesson was that I simply had to accept that a gap existed that not even deep friendships and a knowledge base of decades could cross.

On Muslim Prophets

An invited lecture on what the Prophet Muhammad meant for Christians opened my eyes to the close connections between the gaps in *intra-* and *inter-* religious studies. In the article "Who is Muhammad for Christians?"[12] I argued that in order to answer this question we need to broaden our base of materials to include poetry, mystical discourses, and other deeply personal faith experiences. Yet, I still managed to dance around the question by hiding behind the opinions of various Christian theologians and by only discussing a limited set of published texts. Reading Shahab Ahmed's *What is Islam? The Importance of Being Islamic*,[13] I realized that he was equally frustrated with the limited collection of materials we tend to rely on when doing religious or interfaith studies. Ahmed's main critique is that "Both Muslim and non-Muslim moderns tend to marginalize the complex modes in which Muslims conceptualized their faith."[14] To Ahmed, getting at the heart of the complex religious system called Islam included taking a closer look at how believers processed and lived the holy message by way of philosophy, mystical practices, poetry, and art. Just using the main body of sacred texts of the Qur'an and Tradition (*Hadith*) does not suffice. This observation pushed me to revisit the question about the Prophet Muhammad.[15]

Two points from these writings warrant reiteration here. One, from a mystical point of view, I argue that many interfaith initiatives ignore the body of text conveying the deep love Muslims feel for their Prophet. Two, we often think we are addressing the same issue but speak from such divergent worldviews that the real differences escape us.

First, non-Muslim scholars often overlook the power of love that Muslims feel for their Prophet. In his novel *How to Be a Muslim: An American Story*, Haroon Moghul explains how love for the Prophet Muhammad made him return to Islam:

> To deny God was merely dishonest. To deny Muhammad was treasonous. When I recalled the favorite stories from Muhammad's life, there would be tears in my eyes. The mere mention of him put me on a watery precipice. If I did not stay in Islam, if I opted out of my faith or all faith altogether, what would happen to this man I loved, to those tears in my eyes, to his effect on the world around him?[16]

Muslims emulate the virtues of the Prophet, and elaborate on them in enormous bodies of writings. For example, Indonesian Sufi scholar Adz-Dzakiey proposes a modern vision of this ideal. Combining psychological research with mystical or Sufi practices, he argues that taking the virtues of the Prophet as example in everything we do, helps us reach our individual potential and fosters deep love for Allah. This wisdom called prophetic intelligence, if practiced correctly, allows the "Light of Muhammad" that derives from God to fill human beings as well.[17] This "Light" inspired Muslim mystics through the ages and moved them to compose poetry and odes of praise.[18]

Second, interfaith research too often overlooks how certain familiar conno-tations can have radically different interpretations within other cultures. For example, George Bristow's study on how Muslims and Christians in Turkey use stories about the prophet Abraham in interreligious dialogue,[19] found that for Turkish Muslims, extra-Qur'anic tales figure prominently in their understand-ing of Abraham. Most Christian participants do not know these stories and miss the point that the two worldviews are different. Abraham's story conveys a different relationship between God and humanity. Christians see a single divine plan running through the Bible, evolving from the Old Testament into the New Testament and concluding in the coming of the Christ.[20] Muslims, on the other hand, see a divine history pointing at the Prophet Muhammad.

Conclusion

Impossibilities in interreligious studies coincide with challenges faced by scholars of religious studies. On the one hand, we do not know how to address the phenomena that we observe in the cloud of unknowing and therefore run the risk of describing fish in a bowl. On the other hand, we often do not know the right questions to ask. Failing to understand the larger frame of reference of certain stories, we end up misunderstanding the way narratives and world-views interconnect, and thus we miss what matters most.[21]

Notes

1   For commentary on a similar topic set within a different context, see Eboo Patel, Jennifer Howe Peace, and Noah J. Silverman, eds., *Interreligious/Inter-faith Studies: Defining a Field* (Boston: Beacon, 2018), part 3, "Challenges and Choices."

2   Pieternella van Doorn-Harder, *Contemporary Coptic Nuns* (Columbia: Uni-versity of South Carolina Press, 1995).

3   Robert A. Orsi, *Between Heaven and Earth: The Religious Worlds People Make and the Scholars Who Study Them* (Princeton: Princeton University Press, 2005), 175.

4   Michel De Certeau, "Mysticism," *Diacritics* 22(2): 11–25.

5   Thomas A. Tweed, *Crossings and Dwellings: A Theory of Religion* (Cambridge, Mass.: Harvard University Press, 2006) 8.

6   John Comaroff and Jean Comaroff, *Ethnography and the Historical Imagina-tion* (Boulder: Westview Press, 1992), 10.

7   Mattijs van de Port, *Ecstatic Encounters: Bahian Candomblé and the Quest for the Really Real* (Amsterdam: Amsterdam University Press, 2011), 14.

8   van de Port, *Ecstatic Encounters*, 23.

9   van de Port, *Ecstatic Encounters*, 258.

10   Orsi, *Between Heaven and Earth*, 5.

11   Nelly van Doorn-Harder, and Kari Vogt, eds., *Between Desert and City: The Coptic Orthodox Church Today* (Oslo: Novus Forlag, 1997; republished: Portland, Ore.: Wipf and Stock, 2004).

12   Nelly van Doorn-Harder, "Who is Muhammad for Christians?" *Studies in Interreligious Dialogue* 26 (2016/1): 57–74.

13   Shahab Ahmed, *What is Islam? The Importance of Being Islamic* (Princeton: Princeton University Press, 2016).

14   Ahmed, *What is Islam?* 82, 83.

15   Nelly van Doorn-Harder, "Thinking about Prophets: Muhammad in the Christian Context," *Bulletin of Ecumenical Theology* 29 (2017): 5–31.

16   Haroon Moghul, *How to Be a Muslim: An American Story* (Boston: Beacon, 2017), 72.

17   Hamdani Bakran Adz-Dzakiey, *Psikologi Kenabian: Menghidupkan Potensi dan Kepribadian Kenabian Dalam Diri* (*Prophetic Psychology: To Revive the Individual Potential and Personality Within Oneself*) (Yogyakarta: Pustaka al-Furqan, 2007), 43–60.

18   For numerous moving examples, see Annemarie Schimmel, *And Muhammad Is His Messenger: The Veneration of the Prophet in Islamic Piety* (Chapel Hill: University of North Carolina Press, 1985); and *Mystical Dimensions of Islam* (Chapel Hill: University of North Carolina Press, 1975).

19   George Bristow, "Abraham in Narrative Worldviews: Doing Comparative Theology through Christian–Muslim Dialogue in Turkey" (PhD diss., Vrije Universiteit, 2015), ch. 7.

20   Colossians 1:17; also see Mattá el Meskīn (Matthew the Poor) *The Communion of Love* (Crestwood, N.Y.: St. Vladimir's Seminary Press, 1984), 47.

21   Bristow, "Abraham in Narrative Worldviews," 357.

References

Adz-Dzakiey, Hamdani Bakran. *Psikologi Kenabian: Menghidupkan Potensi dan Kepribadian Kenabian Dalam Diri* (*Prophetic Psychology: To Revive the Individual Potential and Personality Within Oneself*). Yogyakarta: Pustaka al-Furqan, 2007.

Ahmed, Shahab. *What is Islam? The Importance of Being Islamic.* Princeton: Princeton University Press, 2016.

Bristow, George. "Abraham in Narrative Worldviews: Doing Comparative Theology through Christian–Muslim Dialogue in Turkey." PhD diss., Vrije Universiteit, 2015.

Comaroff, John, and Jean Comaroff. *Ethnography and the Historical Imagination.* Boulder: Westview, 1992.

De Certeau, Michel. "Mysticism." *Diacritics* 22(2): 11–25.

el Meskīn, Mattá (Matthew the Poor). *The Communion of Love*. Crestwood, N.Y.:
St. Vladimir's Seminary Press, 1984).

Moghul, Haroon. *How to Be a Muslim: An American Story*. Boston: Beacon, 2017.

Orsi, Robert A. *Between Heaven and Earth: The Religious Worlds People Make
and the Scholars Who Study Them*. Princeton: Princeton University Press,
2005).

Patel, Eboo, Jennifer Howe Peace, and Noah J. Silverman, eds. *Interreligious/In-
terfaith Studies. Defining a New Field*. Boston: Beacon, 2018.

Schimmel, Annemarie. *And Muhammad Is His Messenger: The Veneration of
the Prophet in Islamic Piety*. Chapel Hill: University of North Carolina Press,
1985.

———. *Mystical Dimensions of Islam*. Chapel Hill: University of North Carolina
Press, 1975.

Tweed, Thomas A. *Crossings and Dwellings: A Theory of Religion*. Cambridge,
Mass.: Harvard University Press, 2006.

van de Port, Mattijs. *Ecstatic Encounters: Bahian Candomblé and the Quest for the
Really Real*. Amsterdam: Amsterdam University Press, 2011.

van Doorn-Harder, Pieternella (Nelly). *Contemporary Coptic Nuns*. Columbia:
University of South Carolina Press, 1995.

———. "Thinking about Prophets: Muhammad in the Christian Context." *Bulletin
of Ecumenical Theology* 29 (2017): 5–31.

———. "Who Is Muhammad for Christians?" *Studies in Interreligious Dialogue* 26
(2016/1): 57–74.

van Doorn-Harder, Nelly, and Kari Vogt, eds. *Between Desert and City: The Coptic Orthodox Church Today*. Oslo: Novus Forlag, 1997. Republished: Portland,
Ore.: Wipf and Stock, 2004.

12

Vitality of Lived Religion Approaches

Hans Gustafson

Raimon Panikkar recounts a story about "a European lady science teacher" in Africa teaching young African children about the cycle of malaria, an awful disease that takes many victims there. After explaining it, she sensed the children did not really understand it. A child protested, "But you didn't explain to us why my grandad died of malaria. That's what I want to know!" Panikkar distinguishes between appealing to the concept and appealing to the heart. In order to truly understand something, beyond the mere concept or scientific explanation, an appeal to the heart is required. In order to grasp a concept at the deepest levels, "it is necessary to use the heart rather than the mind"; it is necessary to "abandon the concept and be 'caught' by the 'thing' that we expect to understand." An appeal to the heart, to the person, to the lived experience, can often go much further and deeper than reliance on appealing to the concept on a theoretical level. Panikkar suggests there is a kind of knowledge "based on participation and experience, a knowledge that is not just rational living but the total intuition of the person who is *con-vinta* by who knows. To know (*co-naître* in French) is to be reborn together with the known thing."[1] Knowing about and researching interreligious encounter (i.e., engaging in interreligious studies at the level of lived religion) is no different.

The lived religion (LR) method within the broad field of the study of religion investigates the many ways people (individuals and communities) live out their religious lives in the concrete rhythms of the everyday. This includes engagement not only with religious communities (synagogue, church, mosque, etc.)

but also with the more mundane daily cycles of family, workplace, and social entanglement.[2] Interreligious studies (IRS), as this book testifies, can proceed under several modes of operation: critical, civic, activist, and others. One aspect they all share is the concern for understanding the complex relations that take place between, among, and within communities and individuals with various religious, worldview, and lifeway identities. As such, IRS is primarily interested in understanding religious people and relations, while understanding religious traditions as such remains perhaps secondary. This chapter argues for LR methodologies as indispensable (vital) for IRS precisely because they expose the overwhelming complexity of interreligious encounters by focusing on individual people and communities. First, I offer a brief working definition of IRS and LR; and second, I propose an argument for why LR is vital to and optimizes IRS. In particular, I focus on what LR offers scholars of IRS and how LR effectively serves IRS pedagogy in the classroom and as a bridge-building technique for practitioners active in the so-called interfaith movement.

Interreligious studies, at its most basic level, refers to the study of the relations and "dynamic encounter between, among, and within religious (and nonreligious) traditions and the space that opens and closes between them."[3] An emerging field, IRS takes several forms. It can mirror the critical approach of "religious studies" privileging description over normativity and prescription. It can also take on very pronounced normative and activist agendas that strive for clearly defined goals such as social cohesion, civic pluralism, leadership, and interfaith understanding. However, many scholars take a blended approach. IRS, at a general level, has four elements: (1) It is *descriptive and critical* in its task to empirically document and analyze the reality of the relations and encounters that take place between, among, and/or within religious (and nonreligious) traditions and people. This includes investigating and demonstrating knowledge of the histories, contexts, and contemporary interreligious encounters. (2) Beyond descriptive data collection and observation, many IRS scholars push for *normative* claims (such as the goal of civic pluralism) with *prescriptive* agendas (such as proposing best practices or ways to achieve normative goals). (3) IRS is often *self-implicating* in that it beckons the scholar to critically reflect "on *one's own position* in the spaces between different traditions. When studying separate religions, it has been commonplace in religious studies to claim that you need not—or should not—be implicated yourself in the object of study."[4] In general, IRS scholars disagree and instead affirm the need to recognize one's place in, and influence on, the examined context. (4) IRS is more often understood as an academic field, not a discipline, and is therefore multi- and interdisciplinary. As such, it does not privilege any one method or approach but rather welcomes several approaches, disciplines, sub-disciplines, and methods to examine interreligious encounter and relations.

Lived religion, also labeled "living religion," refers to "what people actually believe and do" in living out their religious identities. Their lived religion "is real, particular, and often messy—a far cry from safe or neat accounts contained in textbooks."[5] Thus, an LR approach to the study of religion privileges what people actually believe and do in their day-to-day religious lives over what their traditions perhaps teach. LR examines religion as it is lived first, not as it is preached from the pulpit or taught in the textbook or sacred texts. Other approaches, such as vernacular religion or religious folk life ("religion of the people"), share a certain kinship with LR in that while they do not reject so-called "official religions" found in texts, creeds, doctrines, and leaders, they certainly emphasize understanding religion at the street level, on the ground, in the trenches, in the homes, offices, and every place in between. When all spaces are considered legitimate arenas for the enacting of religion ("religion-ing," verb, "to do religion"), religious expression certainly becomes particular, complicated, and messy. The emphasis here is on the particular and the everyday. Nancy Ammerman and Robert Orsi, notable scholars of LR, make this clear. For Ammerman, LR observes the "material, embodied aspects of religion as they occur in everyday life, in addition to listening for how people explain themselves. . . . Finding religion in everyday life means looking wherever and however we find people invoking a sacred presence."[6] Orsi argues that "'religion' cannot be neatly separated from the other practices of everyday life, from the ways that human beings work on the landscape, for example, or dispose of corpses, or arrange for the security of their offspring."[7] All spaces humans occupy and all practices humans engage in, then, become fair game for the study of how people live out their religious identities.

Lived religion optimizes interreligious studies. This assertion rests on three working premises (P_1, P_2, and P_3).

> P_1 assumes that IRS is primarily interested in encounters that take place between people (with various religious identities) and not religious traditions as such. P_1 asserts that IRS, at its most fundamental level, is about people and the relations between, among, and within individuals and communities.

With sociologist Meredith McGuire,

> P_2 asserts that "individual religious commitment is evidenced less by avowed commitment to and participation in the activities of religious

organizations than by the way each person expresses and experiences his or her faith and practice in ordinary places and in everyday moments;"[8] and

P$_3$ asserts that in order to comprehend "modern religious lives, we need to try to grasp the complexity, diversity, and fluidity of real individuals' religion-as-practiced, in the context of their everyday lives."[9]

These premises are not self-evident, nor would all scholars assent to them. With McGuire, I recognize that although "studies of religious organizations and movements are still relevant, they cannot capture the quality of people's everyday religious lives. As messy as these lives may be in practice, individuals' lived religions are what really matters to them."[10] If IRS is primarily interested in people, and LR is hyper-focused on the messiness of religion as lived by people, then IRS logically ought to embrace LR approaches. This seems uncontroversial.

However, the implications (benefits) that follow from embracing LR for IRS may be less obvious and therefore perhaps more controversial. As McGuire points out, "When we no longer assume that individuals' religions can be equated with their religious affiliation or encompassed by their membership in a religious organization, then we realize that we must ask different questions."[11] That is, IRS must ask different and new questions, the findings of which may be welcoming to many while upsetting to others.

There are obvious benefits for IRS in the utilization of LR, especially in the way it complicates religious identity. LR aggressively distinguishes between (a) one's lived religious identity, (b) one's religious tradition(s) as such, and (c) others who identify within their religion. A major obstacle not only for understanding religion, but also for fostering interfaith understanding, is the constant essentialization and oversimplification of the religious other. A strength of LR is its ability to recognize and emphasize vast differences and particularities within religious traditions, which helps overcome the many misconceptions and stereotypes perpetuated due to essentialization. Exposed to the vast internal diversity of religious traditions, one quickly realizes why it is problematic to equate the lived religion of an individual with the "official religion" preached by the textbook, doctrine, or leader. Moreover, LR's emphasis on the individual and the everyday treats people as people, not tokens or official representatives of traditions. LR's focus on particularities of religious practice combats oppressive, violent, and hateful elements of religions by exposing the complexity of religious traditions, practices, and identities for the world to see. Although these elements are often marginal, exposing the world to them helps advance the quest to eliminate them in the various traditions, especially one's own.

LR encourages the self-implication of the scholar in what the scholar studies, which dovetails with the common inclination of IRS scholars that one cannot help but be implicated in that which one studies. Orsi argues, "The study of lived religion risks the exposure of the researcher. His or her most deeply held existential orientations and moral values are on display with an obviousness not found in earlier ethnographic or, especially, historical accounts. . . . The existential implication of the study of lived religion is this: we can no longer constitute the objects of our study as other."[12] LR helpfully exposes the blurry boundary between IRS as an academic field and the "interfaith movement" as a grassroots community-based activism. Many IRS scholars, in addition to publishing first-rate work and teaching at the world's most prestigious universities, are also often energetic interfaith activists. They exemplify Orsi's claim that LR scholars have little choice but to be implicated in their research, also in which their "deeply held existential orientations and moral values are on display."[13]

LR helps to understand power dynamics in interreligious encounter, and in some cases it helps to rebalance power, by focusing on the lived religion of the laity (and not just on religious authorities). This helps to challenge religious authority, especially when authorities exercise abuse of power. Perhaps a consequence of challenging abusive power, and giving more authoritative voice to laity, is the rise in those identifying with no religion (unaffiliated or "none"), multiple religious traditions (dual belonging, multiple religious participation, etc.), and other once-stigmatized religious practices and identities, which, under official religious authority, are often seen as controversial, heretical, and subversive (especially in the West). As such, religious authorities lose much of their authority when the voice of laity is amplified and given equal position on the playing field.

Finally, privileging an LR approach has advantages for those in the interfaith movement striving to foster interreligious understanding. Three advantages stand out from a case study by Martin Stringer, who observed the use of LR in the setting of a six-month small-group interfaith dialogue in Birmingham (U.K.) in 2014.[14] First, Stringer confirmed that having participants focus on their lived religious experience helped them to more easily overcome the tendency to reduce others' religious identity to a monolithic textbook version (or worse, a misunderstood violent version portrayed in some media). Second, employing personal storytelling, focusing on each individual's own lived religious experience, as a primary tool of dialogue freed participants from the unfair pressures to represent the whole of their traditions. Third, the focus on LR demonstrated that, for many, religious language (talk of beliefs, doctrines, creeds, etc.) often fell flat, and instead a focus on friendship-making, based on shared everyday joys and sufferings, contributed to longer and more sustainable relationships among participants.

Notes

1   All quotations in this paragraph are from Raimon Panikkar, "Three Important Intercultural Interpellations," in *Cultures and Religions in Dialogue: Part One, Pluralism and Interculturality*, ed. Milena Carrara Pavan (Maryknoll, N.Y.: Orbis, 2018), 125 (emphasis in original). Originally published as "Tres grandes interpretaciones de la interculturalidad," in *Interculturality, Gender, and Education*, ed. Raul Fornet Betancount (Frankfurt: Iko, 2004), 27–44; this was also the inaugural talk given by Panikkar held at a Congress of Intercultural Philosophy at the Olavide Cultural Center in Carmona in 2004.

2   Martin D. Stringer, "Lived Religion and Difficult Conversations," Birmingham Conversations of the Faith, Neighbors, Changemakers Collaboration, 2015, 4.

3   Oddbjørn Leirvik, "Interreligious Studies: A New Academic Discipline?" in *Contested Spaces, Common Ground: Space and Power Structures in Contemporary Multireligious Societies*, ed. Ulrich Winkler, Lidia Rodriguez, and Oddbjørn Leirvik (Leiden: Brill, 2016), 36.

4   Oddbjørn Leirvik, "Interreligious Studies: A Relational Approach to the Study of Religion," *Journal of Interreligious Studies* 13 (2014): 16 (emphasis in original).

5   Stephen E. Gregg and Lynne Scholefield, *Engaging with Living Religion: A Guide to Fieldwork in the Study of Religion* (London: Routledge, 2015), 7.

6   Nancy T. Ammerman, "2013 Paul Hanly Furfey Lecture: Finding Religion in Everyday Life," *Sociology of Religion* 75, no. 2 (2014): 190–91.

7   Robert Orsi, "Everyday Miracles: The Study of Lived Religion," in *Lived Religion in America: Toward a History of Practice*, ed. David D. Hall (Princeton: Princeton University Press, 1997), 6–7.

8   Meredith B. McGuire, *Lived Religion: Faith and Practice in Everyday Life* (New York: Oxford University Press, 2008), 213.

9   McGuire, *Lived Religion*, 213.

10 McGuire, *Lived Religion*, 213.

11 McGuire, *Lived Religion*, 210.

12 Orsi, "Everyday Miracles," in Hall, *Lived Religion in America*, 18.

13 Orsi, "Everyday Miracles," in Hall, *Lived Religion in America*, 18.

14   Martin D. Stringer, "Lived Religion and Difficult Conversations," Birmingham Conversations of the Faith, Neighbors, Changemakers Collaboration, 2015.

References

Ammerman, Nancy T. "2013 Paul Hanly Furfey Lecture: Finding Religion in Everyday Life." *Sociology of Religion* 75, no. 2 (2014): 189–207.

Gregg, Stephen E., and Lynne Scholefield. *Engaging with Living Religion: A Guide to Fieldwork in the Study of Religion*. London: Routledge, 2015.

Leirvik, Oddbjørn. "Interreligious Studies: A New Academic Discipline?" In *Contested Spaces, Common Ground: Space and Power Structures in Contemporary Multireligious Societies*, edited by Ulrich Winkler, Lidia Rodriguez, and Oddbjørn Leirvik, 33–42. Leiden: Brill, 2016.

———. "Interreligious Studies: A Relational Approach to the Study of Religion." *Journal of Interreligious Studies* 13 (2014): 15–19.

McGuire, Meredith B. *Lived Religion: Faith and Practice in Everyday Life*. New York: Oxford University Press, 2008.

Orsi, Robert. "Everyday Miracles: The Study of Lived Religion." In *Lived Religion in America: Toward a History of Practice*, edited by David D. Hall, 3–21. Princeton: Princeton University Press, 1997.

Panikkar, Raimon. "Three Important Intercultural Interpellations." In *Cultures and Religions in Dialogue: Part One, Pluralism and Interculturality*, edited by Milena Carrara Pavan, 121–31. Maryknoll, N.Y.: Orbis, 2018.

Stringer, Martin D. "Lived Religion and Difficult Conversations." Birmingham Conversations of the Faith, Neighbors, Changemakers Collaboration, 2015, 4.

13

Empirical Approaches to Interreligious Relations

Ånund Brottveit

The field of religious studies is at a crossroads, having embarked for the past two decades on a fundamental reexamination of its most basic ideas and terms, while the world at large has awakened to the enduring public salience of religion and to religion's importance to the everyday lives of much of the planet's population.[1]

Western societies have become more religiously diversified due to demographic processes making people "rub elbows with" other believers belonging to increasingly more "alien" traditions.[2] In my vicinity, the suburban district Grorud in Oslo, the Evangelical-Lutheran majority church lends out a basement room to a charismatic congregation for Ghanaian immigrants. Across the lawn in an industrial building is a Tamil Hindu temple. The Hindu community performs a purification ritual of their gods in the nearby lake, which also serves as the borough's bathing spot. Another church in the same diocese is now permanently rented out to Polish and Vietnamese Roman Catholics. What do local inhabitants, from different religious and worldview groupings, think of this, and how do they adapt? In this chapter, I argue for the benefit of taking into account local experiences and interpretations made by people living together in multireligious contexts. This is a call for an empirical approach to interreligious relations, and as such I point to interreligious dialogue and bridge-building arrangements at the local level as possible fruitful entry points for such studies.

Religious plurality is not new, but the pace of change is experienced as new and challenging for many.[3] It is important to investigate new practices, experiences, and meanings at the actor-level in recently diversified religious landscapes. The focus could be on interreligious encounters at a grassroots level, or it could simply focus on how people from different religious and ethnic groups manage to live together in local communities. A "lived religion" approach may be an expedient strategy in order to grasp the dynamics and meanings of local and personal interreligious encounters. David Hall's edited anthology demonstrates how single case studies can illuminate "lived religion,"[4] while Meredith McGuire has explored "everyday religion as lived"[5] through actor-centered analyses based on personal in-depth interviews.

Religion, or religiosity, may be seen as an aspect of social life and a non-negligible dimension in local community studies. As Robert Orsi declares (in the opening citation above), religion has shown to have an enduring importance for ordinary people's everyday life. The "new religious landscape" is but an aspect of how Western citizens experience "late modernity."[6] The importance of religion may be exaggerated yet given a prominent place in public debates on immigration and integration. A Nordic study of "mediatized religion"[7] discusses how the increased visibility of religion and media representations shape popular images of religions.[8] Islam has come into focus as the proverbial scapegoat in immigration debates because of fear of radical Islamist terror and perceived integration obstacles related to religion. Norwegian scholars on interreligious encounters and integration of immigrants have pointed out that the immigrant or asylum seeker is implicitly perceived as a Muslim, in spite of the fact that only a minority of immigrants to Norway—past or present—are or have been of Muslim background.[9]

Identity Politics and Civil Society Responses

During the last decennia, international conflicts have increasingly changed labels from separatist, Marxist, independence, or liberation movement, and so forth into religious identifications. For instance, Hamas has come to overshadow the PLO (Palestinian Liberation Organization) in Gaza, and terrorist attacks and violent political actions in Western countries are also more often connected to religious identification compared to the 1970s and 1980s. Religion has been more politicized, and, vice versa, politics may also have become more "religionized." Since so many Western societies have simultaneously experienced demographic changes and increasing religious diversity, this polarization on identity or value issues has become ever more distressing and disrupting of basic social trust and solidarity.

Interreligious dialogue, or what I prefer to call "faith and worldview dialogue,"[10] has emerged and been developed in Norway since the late 1980s. The early pioneers were individual activists with a personal motivation but working from within organizations characterized as belonging to civil society. Two prominent examples were a church clergyperson[11] in an eastern Oslo district and a folk high school teacher[12] in Lillehammer. They were initially motivated by the increased cultural diversity and curiosity about differences in religion and beliefs. Later, as the dialogue activity and bridge-building venues developed into the 1990s, prevention of cultural conflicts due to differing worldviews and religious traditions became a strong motivation. The teacher arranged a public conversation between a priest and an atheist on this question: "Secular Humanists and Christians—what divides and what unites them?"[13] The cleric in question, Oddbjørn Leirvik, now a professor in theology at the University of Oslo, was then a priest in a multicultural inner-city district of Oslo. His dialogue initiative started when he made contact with a neighboring mosque in order to achieve "spiritual enrichment" and mutual understanding[14] through face-to-face meetings with the imam. These were still, as Leirvik writes, "innocent times,"[15] preceding both the first Gulf War (1990–1991) and the nearly deadly assault on Salman Rushdie's Norwegian publisher William Nygaard (1993). In the years to follow, faith and worldview dialogue in Norway has been associated with an ideal of peaceful coexistence and efforts to improve social cohesion.

Many dialogue initiatives made by concerned citizens and Norwegian civil society organizations emerged in the 1980 and 1990s. The central and local government entered this field later, often with quite similar goal formulations. Faith and worldview dialogues became official policy in Norway in the second half of the 1990s and might to some extent be viewed as instrumentalized from above (i.e., from the governmental level). Nevertheless, the fact that dialogue and bridge-building projects have become part of the government's religion politics does not impede ever new local and individual initiatives at a grassroots level.[16]

Living Together in Culturally Diverse Societies

In Norway, as in most other Western countries, public debates and political rhetoric on immigration and on Muslim minority groups are becoming more polarized and often tend to demonize Islam as a decisive factor for terrorism, urban criminality, forced marriages, and oppression of women. Therefore, the dialogue initiatives not only aim at reducing common prejudices, misunderstandings, and exaggerations, but the dialogue activists also strive to problematize and reflect upon the "troubling aspects" of the respective religions. There is an ongoing debate—and critique—on the effects of faith and worldview dialogue in Norway. Critics allege the dialogues have been too cozy and avoid the negative sides of religion—for instance, patriarchal traditions and strong social control of women and children. Defenders claim it is necessary to build trust before the most difficult topics can be raised, but they also point to declarations made by religious leaders participating in the dialogues led by the Church of Norway (mentioned above). The declarations assert the principle of freedom of conversion, denounce firmly any kind of violence in family and close relationships, and express a commitment to fight against religious extremism.[17] These public statements are not binding and do not represent all Jewish, Muslim, and Christian communities or individuals, but they may serve as a strong normative message.

A 2015 KIFO study investigated dialogue activities, in three urban regions in Norway, organized by a state-financed dialogue organization called the Council for Religious and Life Stance Communities (STL).[18] The study documented examples of local initiatives to establish dialogue groups and bridge-building arrangements based on the cooperation from local faith and worldview communities.[19] In another study focused on the local district level in Oslo East, KIFO and researchers from the University of Stavanger found several examples of collaborative activities between religious and ethnic groups initiated "from below."[20] The social entrepreneurs behind such initiatives may be a local parish priest, a Hindu temple board member, a youth politician, a youth club leader, a police officer dedicated to improving the relations with minority youth, and so forth. Their initiatives and project proposals have been supported not only by the central government but also by specific municipal or city district programs.

It is an ongoing discussion whether the dialogue and bridge-building activities are initiated and governed from above or from below, and to what extent this may be characterized as a new form of "soft rule," a governance of religious diversity that in reality increases state control over religious life.[21] This may seem, on the one hand, paradoxical since it occurs in a time when the Norwegian state-church arrangement is in a process of gradual dissolution, but on the other hand it could be precisely why the state is looking for alternative ways of governing the religious field.

Nevertheless, there is little reason to doubt the sincerity of the local entre-preneurs and activists when they claim that they are worried about the polar-ization and xenophobia and see themselves as activists for peace and mutual understanding.[22] KIFO found that local initiatives to establish dialogue groups were often counterreactions to international events that raised tensions with, or posed threats against, religious minorities.

The terror acts at the summer camp on the island of Utøya outside Oslo on July 22, 2011, afflicted many local Norwegian communities. Sixty-nine peo-ple, mostly teenagers, were killed. The local majority church in Grorud had already established good relations with the neighboring Tamil Hindu temple. When the Hindus heard that a young church member was killed, the temple invited the congregation to a ritual commemoration of the deceased relatives. This was part of a festival (Tirthutsava) that they organize every summer, but on this occasion they gave special attention to the Utøya massacre. Some days later, the Hindus were invited to attend the memorial service in the church. The priest said, "We came closer, and it felt deeply meaningful to continue our efforts to get to know each other better and to seek unity in diversity."[23] The expressed feeling of solidarity and unity as a means by which to deny the ter-rorists' message of hatred is a common denominator in many similar actions.

After a terrorist attack in Copenhagen in 2015, on a seminar on freedom of speech[24] and a Jewish assembly, a group of young Muslims in Oslo organized a solidarity demonstration as they formed a protective human chain outside the synagogue called "The Ring of Peace."[25]

The Ring of Peace indicated not only that three decades of dialogue have yielded results but also that a new generation is engaged in dialogue and bridge-building efforts.

Conclusion

Empirical interreligious research acknowledges the persistent significance of individual religious or philosophical affiliation and of local organization based on such affiliations. Recent research in Scandinavia has documented that the share of nonbelievers increases simultaneously as religion and religious sym-bols become more visible in the public sphere.[26] Religious diversity is also in-creasing in Scandinavia due to immigration and because of the multitude of religious organizations that serve as channels to teach about minority groups and promote "lived" interreligious encounter with them. An empirical re-search approach may start with organized dialogue and bridge-building work at the local level. However, it is also important to identify spontaneous actions and indirect effects of interreligious communication and cooperation that occur through social networks. And, finally, other indicators of social capital in religiously diverse populations, like associational density, general trust, and altruism, should be considered as well.[27]

Research in Norway has recorded many examples of spontaneous initiatives. Both organized and spontaneous interreligious initiatives may have created lasting personal networks across religions and worldviews that can be mobilized in crises. Dialogue groups have been formed as a response to the polarizing forces that threaten to increase stereotypes, xenophobia, and social conflict. Dialogue activists working at the grassroots level claim their activities reduce conflict, build trust, and demonstrate a better model of coexistence. Whether these claims are true or not is, of course, an empirical question worthy of investigation for scholars working in the multidisciplinary field of interreligious studies.

Notes

1   Robert A. Orsi, introduction to *The Cambridge Companion to Religious Studies*, ed. Robert A. Orsi, 1–13 (Cambridge: Cambridge University Press, 2011), 1.

2   Peter L. Berger, foreword to *Everyday Religion: Observing Modern Religious Lives*, ed. Nancy Tatom Ammerman (New York: Oxford University Press, 2007), vii.

3   Craig Calhoun, foreword to *Religious Complexity in the Public Sphere*, ed. Inger Furseth (Cham, Switzerland: Palgrave Macmillan, 2018), viii–xi.

4   David D. Hall, *Lived Religion in America: Toward a History of Practice* (Princeton: Princeton University Press, 1997).

5   Meredith B. McGuire, *Lived Religion: Faith and Practice in Everyday Life* (Oxford: Oxford University Press, 2008).

6   Anthony Giddens, *Modernity and Self-Identity* (Cambridge: Polity, 1991).

7   "The Role of Religion in the Public Sphere: A Comparative Study of the Five Nordic Countries (NOREL)" was financed by NORDCORP (Nordic Collaborative Research Project) and directed by Inger Furseth, KIFO.

8   Knut Lundby et al., "Religion and the Media: Continuity, Complexity, and Mediatization," in *Religious Complexity in the Public Sphere*, ed. Inger Furseth (Cham, Switzerland: Palgrave Macmillan, 2018).

9   Thomas Hylland Eriksen and Viggo Vestel, "Groruddalen, Alna og det nye Norge," in *Den globale landsbyen: Groruddalen og det nye Norge*, ed. Sharam Alghasi, Elisabeth Eide, and Thomas Hylland Eriksen (Oslo: Cappelen Damm Akademisk, 2012); Anne Hege Grung and Oddbjørn Leirvik,

"Religionsdialog, identitetspolitikk og kompleksitet," *Norsk antropologisk tidsskrift* 23, no. 1 (2012): 76–116.

10 Nonreligious belief has been represented in Norwegian faith and worldview dialogues from the beginning. The Norwegian Humanist Association, which represents agnostic and atheist worldviews, has been a central participant in various dialogue forums.

11 The Lutheran State Church cleric was Oddbjørn Leirvik, now a professor in theology and interreligious dialogue at the University of Oslo and a contributor to this volume.

12 Inge Eidsvåg was a teacher at the private "Folk High School" Norwegian Humanistic Academy (*Nansenskolen*). Folk High School is a Scandinavian school type offering a one-year study without exams or grades for young students that want to develop and mature their personalities.

13 Synnøve O. Stene, Inge Eidsvåg, and Dag Hareide, *Styrke i mangfold? Om svakhet og styrke ved forskjellige typer religions- og livssynsdialoger i Norge de siste 20 år*, report (Lillehammer: Nansenskolen, 2009), 13.

14 Oddbjørn Leirvik, *Interreligious Studies: A Relational Approach to Religious Activism and the Study of Religion* (London: Bloomsbury, 2014), 18.

15 Leirvik, *Interreligious Studies*, 19.

16 Dag Husebø and Øystein Lund Johannessen, "Interreligious Dialogue in Oslo in the Years following the Terror Attacks of 22 July 2011," in *Religion and Dialogue in the City: Case Studies on Interreligious Encounter in Urban Community and Education*, ed. Julia Ipgrave et al. (Münster: Waxmann, 2018); and Grung and Leirvik, "Religionsdialog, identitetspolitikk og kompleksitet."

17 Leirvik, *Interreligious Studies*, appendices 1–3.

18 KIFO (Institute for Church, Religion, and Worldview Research) is a multidisciplinary research institute in Norway that investigates church, religion, and social worldviews, with an emphasis on empirical research (www.kifo.no).

19 Ånund Brottveit, Ann Kristin Gresaker, and Nina Hoel, "Det handler om verdensfreden!" in *Evaluering av Rollen Samarbeidsrådet for Tros- og Livssynssamfunn: Norges Kristne Råd og Islamsk Råd Norge har i Dialogarbeidet* (Oslo: KIFO, 2015).

20 Husebø and Johannessen, "Interreligious Dialogue in Oslo," in Julia Ipgrave et al., *Religion and Dialogue in the City*.

21 Veit Bader, "Governance of Religious Diversity: Theory, Research, and Practice," in *International Migration and the Governance of Religious Diversity*, ed. Paul Bramadat and Matthias Koenig (Kingston: McGill-Queen's University Press, 2009); Tuomas Martikainen, "Multilevel and Pluricentric Network Governance of Religion," in *Religion in the Neoliberal Age: Political Economy and Modes of Governance*, ed. Tuomas Martikainen and Francois Gauthier (Aldershot: Ashgate, 2013).

22 Brottveit, Gresaker, and Hoel, "Det handler om verdensfreden!"

23 Anne Berit Evang, "Two Good Neighbours—Hindus and Christians in Ammerud, Oslo," in *Why Interfaith? Stories, Reflections and Challenges from Recent Engagements in Northern Europe*, ed. Andrew Wingate and Pernilla Myrelid (London: Darton, Longman & Todd, 2016).

24 The seminar "Art, Blasphemy and Freedom of Speech" was organized by the Lars Vilks Committee. The Swedish artist Lars Vilks lives under police protection because of some provocative drawings of the prophet Muhammed. This was shortly after, and probably inspired by, the terrorist attack on the French satirical magazine *Charlie Hebdo*.

25 Henrik Arneberg, "Hun sto bak ringen rundt synagogen," *Aftenposten*, December 4, 2015, 20, Kultur.

26 Inger Furseth, ed., *Religious Complexity in the Public Sphere: Comparing Nordic Countries* (Cham, Switzerland: Palgrave Macmillan, 2018).

27 Simon Szreter and Michael Woolcock, "Health by Association? Social Capital, Social Theory, and the Political Economy of Public Health," *International Journal of Epidemiology* 33 (2004): 650–67.

References

Arneberg, Henrik. "Hun sto bak ringen rundt synagogen." *Aftenposten*, December 4, 2015, 20, Kultur.

Bader, Veit. "Governance of Religious Diversity: Theory, Research, and Practice." In *International Migration and the Governance of Religious Diversity*, edited by Paul Bramadat and Matthias Koenig, 29–58. Kingston: McGill-Queen's University Press, 2009.

Berger, Peter L. Foreword to *Everyday Religion: Observing Modern Religious Lives*, edited by Nancy Tatom Ammerman, v–viii. New York: Oxford University Press, 2007.

Brottveit, Ånund, Ann Kristin Gresaker, and Nina Hoel. "Det handler om verdensfreden!" In *Evaluering av Rollen Samarbeidsrådet for Tros- og Livssynssamfunn: Norges Kristne Råd og Islamsk Råd Norge har i Dialogarbeidet*. Oslo: KIFO, 2015.

Calhoun, Craig. Foreword to *Religious Complexity in the Public Sphere*, edited by Inger Furseth, viii–xi. Cham, Switzerland: Palgrave Macmillan, 2018.

Eriksen, Thomas Hylland, and Viggo Vestel. "Groruddalen, Alna og det nye Norge." In *Den globale landsbyen: Groruddalen og det nye Norge*, edited by Sharam Alghasi, Elisabeth Eide, and Thomas Hylland Eriksen, 15–32. Oslo: Cappelen Damm Akademisk, 2012.

Evang, Anne Berit. "Two Good Neighbours—Hindus and Christians in Ammerud, Oslo." In *Why Interfaith? Stories, Reflections and Challenges from Recent Engagements in Northern Europe*, edited by Andrew Wingate and Pernilla Myrelid, 164–67. London: Darton, Longman & Todd, 2016.

Furseth, Inger, ed. *Religious Complexity in the Public Sphere: Comparing Nordic Countries*. Cham, Switzerland: Palgrave Macmillan, 2018.

Giddens, Anthony. *Modernity and Self-Identity*. Cambridge: Polity, 1991.

Grung, Anne Hege, and Oddbjørn Leirvik. "Religionsdialog, identitetspolitikk og kompleksitet." *Norsk antropologisk tidsskrift* 23, no. 1 (2012): 76–116.

Hall, David D. *Lived Religion in America: Toward a History of Practice*. Princeton: Princeton University Press, 1997.

Husebø, Dag, and Øystein Lund Johannessen. "Interreligious Dialogue in Oslo in the Years following the Terror Attacks of 22 July 2011." In *Religion and Dialogue in the City: Case Studies on Interreligious Encounter in Urban Community and Education*, edited by Julia Ipgrave, Thorsten Knauth, Anna Körs, Dörthe Vieregge, and Marie von der Lippe, 115–40. Münster: Waxmann, 2018.

Leirvik, Oddbjørn. *Interreligious Studies: A Relational Approach to Religious Activism and the Study of Religion*. London: Bloomsbury, 2014.

Lundby, Knut, Henrik Reintoft Christensen, Ann Kristin Gresaker, Mia Lövheim, Kati Niemelä, Sofia Sjö, Marcus Moberg, and Árni Svanur Daníelsson. "Religion and the Media: Continuity, Complexity, and Mediatization." In *Religious Complexity in the Public Sphere*, edited by Inger Furseth, 193–249. Cham, Switzerland: Palgrave Macmillan, 2018.

Martikainen, Tuomas. "Multilevel and Pluricentric Network Governance of Religion." In *Religion in the Neoliberal Age: Political Economy and Modes of Governance*, edited by Tuomas Martikainen and Francois Gauthier, 129–42. Aldershot: Ashgate, 2013.

McGuire, Meredith B. *Lived Religion: Faith and Practice in Everyday Life*. Oxford: Oxford University Press, 2008.

Orsi, Robert A. Introduction to *The Cambridge Companion to Religious Studies*, edited by Robert A. Orsi, 1–13. Cambridge: Cambridge University Press, 2011.

Stene, Synnøve O., Inge Eidsvåg, and Dag Hareide. *Styrke i mangfold? Om svakhet og styrke ved forskjellige typer religions- og livssynsdialoger i Norge de siste 20 år*. Report. Lillehammer: Nansenskolen, 2009.

Szreter, Simon, and Michael Woolcock. "Health by Association? Social Capital, Social Theory, and the Political Economy of Public Health." *International Journal of Epidemiology* 33 (2004): 650–67.

14

Ecumenical and Interreligious

Aaron T. Hollander

At the 2015 Parliament of the World's Religions in Salt Lake City, a recurring recognition could be heard expressed by participants from around the world. In informal conversations, during official sessions, and at mealtimes, Parliament participants described themselves as having more in common and finding it easier to comprehend, communicate, and collaborate with attendees from other religious traditions than they did with so-deemed "conservative" members of their own traditions. How could it be, Parliament attendees pondered aloud, that the differences between themselves and those who shared their tradition but not their evaluation of religious otherness could be experienced as so intractable and hazardous, so exhausting to reckon with, compared with the differences that they were finding so productive and refreshing to celebrate in the company of those who did *not* share their tradition but who were aligned with their appreciation of religious plurality? It may be said that these participants were coming face to face with the tip of a problem that the interfaith movement and the emerging academic field of interreligious studies can struggle to interpret productively, but that has long been a core concern of a related intellectual enterprise: *ecumenical studies*.

This chapter identifies ecumenical studies as a disciplinary forerunner of interreligious studies, with insights and methodology for interpreting the dynamics of religious difference that need to be incorporated if interreligious studies is to engage adequately with what it might (provisionally) identify as "intrareligious difference"—the textures and tensions of which are invariably at work in "interreligious" problems. While an ecumenical framework may in some cases introduce more problems than solutions to interreligious studies (for reasons I hope to make clear), I wager that we will find ecumenical analysis to be a powerful resource—if not an indispensable ingredient—whose liabilities themselves offer whetstones for honing the interpretive capacities of the emerging field.

Existing schematic discussions of interreligious studies have already engaged fruitfully with the slippery relationship between what is conventionally considered the difference "between" religious traditions and the difference "within" religious traditions. For instance, Oddbjørn Leirvik deconstructs oversimplified definitions of interreligious studies by highlighting the multiple interlocking dimensions of religious life that all manifest degrees of difference: textual authorities, social norms and statuses, gender identities, and domains of belonging.[1] Anne Hege Grung levels a feminist critique that explores how "intra" religious differences are easily quelled by institutional power structures, assimilating them within idealized religious boundaries that may not in fact be so fixed—and unwittingly reproducing intrareligious power dynamics in the venues of interreligious dialogue.[2] "Interfaith" definitions such as Eboo Patel's maximally broad "orientation around religion" attempt to avoid the pitfalls of too rigid a distinction,[3] earning the (perhaps puzzling or unproductive but basically correct) recognition that an encounter between two Episcopalians in the same parish is no less an "interfaith" encounter than that between a Taoist and a Sufi, even as the *dynamics* of that encounter and its plausible functions will be decidedly different.[4] And in the introduction to this volume, Hans Gustafson provides a working definition of interreligious studies as a field that scrupulously avoids a hard separation of difference *within* from difference *between* religious traditions, focusing attention instead on the "encounters . . . and relations . . . between, within, and among groups with significant difference in worldview and lifeway"—maximally inclusive of various institutional dynamics and of the range of meanings assigned to this difference by interested parties.[5]

In other words, the spatial language of "within" and "between" (though it has the merit of emic significance, in the sense that people actually relate to their worlds and their own/others' traditions in these terms) reinforces a metaphorical construal of religions as bounded entities, discrete blocs that can "interact." This introduces analytical blind spots that can preemptively obscure or sterilize aspects of the problems we study.[6] For instance, do we classify Protestant-Catholic warfare, Sunni criticisms of Sufi devotion, the integrative practices of Shinto adherents, or the complex trans-Christian belongings of

Friends (Quakers) and Unitarian Universalists as "interreligious" issues? If not, we are overlooking the role played in these arenas by multireligious influences and contrasting understandings of religious otherness. But if we recognize such cases as indeed interreligious, then we are acknowledging that interreligious studies is and must be capable of absorbing the accomplishments of what has traditionally been called ecumenical studies: the scholarly analysis of "intrareligious" divisions and reconciliations in light of their provenance, power, and purpose.[7]

Ecumenical studies has its historical origins in the ecumenical *movement* ("ecumenism") dedicated to the imagination and pursuit of Christian unity, but it must be distinguished from the aims of that movement just as interreligious studies as an analytic framework can be fruitfully distinguished from—and potentially but not necessarily interrelated with—the interfaith movement.[8] Both ecumenical studies as a scholarly activity and ecumenism as a normative pursuit of overcoming divisions within a religious tradition (conventionally but not necessarily Christianity) emerged from an apprehension of global interdependence, of interlocking textures of difference and commonality, toward the turn of the twentieth century.[9] As such, from the earliest manifestations of ecumenics, interreligious studies (*avant la lettre*) was understood, more or less explicitly and enthusiastically, to be intrinsic to the task of ecumenical analysis. Both the research and the activity of the early mission-minded Christian ecumenists took place at interreligious interfaces around the world; the *Journal of Ecumenical Studies* was already including interreligious matters within its regular purview in the 1960s;[10] and, to this day, ecumenical gatherings dedicate sustained and substantial interpretive energy to interreligious affairs.[11] Especially in multireligious societies (where religious others are a fact of everyday life), but also in religious monocultures (where religious others are a fact of imaginative orientation), it has been and remains clear that ecumenical analysis dedicated to intrareligious difference only ever accounts for one dimension of its study subjects' patterns of life.

Although among many traditional ecumenists there has been and remains "a deep-seated suspicion of initiatives that want to approach the non-Christian,"[12] contemporary developments in ecumenical studies in both the English and the German academies (at least) are bringing interreligious studies ever closer to the heart of ecumenics as an intellectual framework. Two of the major centers of ecumenical scholarship—the Irish School of Ecumenics in Dublin and the Catholic Ecumenical Institute in Münster—have reckoned especially well with this mutual inclusivity, the former making interreligious studies a core dimension of its curriculum and the latter recovering elements of the near-abandoned 1970s project of "fundamental ecumenics" (in which the psychosocial processes that undergird and animate interchurch division are inseparable from those at work at interreligious interfaces).[13] In each of these leading ecumenical centers, "intra-" and "inter-"religious relations (and indeed the "trans-"religious tensions and fusions of religious sensibilities with dynamics of economy, politics, ecology, and so forth) can function as interwoven registers of a common enterprise, each rotating into the foreground in any given study of a particular problem without ever being mistaken for separable from the others.

I am suggesting, then, that just as interreligious studies has from the start been a frontier of decreasing danger for ecumenical studies, so too can the methods and resources of ecumenical studies serve the formation of a mature field of interreligious studies that can dexterously incorporate the interpretation of intrareligious difference and division.[14] But ecumenical analysis and ecumenical reconciliation alike *need* interreligious inquiry for their own success. Is the reverse also the case? Does interreligious studies *need* ecumenical studies for its intelligibility and reliability as a framework? Might they even be seen as two registers of a common enterprise (as ecumenics in the Dublin paradigm would have it)? Answering this question depends on whether we place the emphasis in "ecumenical" more on descriptive analysis or more on normative endeavor. To take up the easier conclusion first—if we are referring to a second-order ecumenical studies that specializes in analyzing the interfaces and the dynamics of division between people who identify or act in some manner as belonging to "the same" tradition (though they may view this tradition as having been divided or corroded), the answer is unequivocally *yes*. Even beyond the pragmatic necessity that interreligious studies be capable of incorporating ecumenical insights (as explored above), the interdisciplinary apparatus of ecumenics (providing a well-established, if not necessarily well-known, framework in which ethics, sociology, history, theology, politics, and even ecology can be productively integrated) may offer some solutions to questions that interreligious studies is now in the process of posing.[15]

But insofar as "ecumenical" language also connotes a normative orientation toward a horizon of *unity* (or even the more cautious ideal of *harmony*) between traditions and between the human beings who embody and represent them, the mutual inclusivity of interreligious studies and ecumenical studies is far less clear cut. Where "unity" is on the table as a possible goal (even as the meaning of unity is up for healthy debate and may include an expansive human unity or the ecological unity of the habitable household of life), the status of diversities that have historically been suppressed remains in question. This is the case not only in the heritage of the missionary ecumenists, whose commitment to understand and engage with interreligious difference was grounded in evangelistic endeavor, but also in what we might identify as interreligious gatherings with an ecumenical ambiance, such as the Parliament of the World's Religions—where the celebration of commonalities is readily assumed to outrank the negotiation of differences, and where these commonalities of religions are often imbued with an authenticity that can be denied to differences insofar as the latter can be diagnosed as political entailments, tribal chauvinisms, or illusions to which the minds of those who have not attained to the higher unity are still subject.[16] The normative commitments of ecumenism, in other words—benevolent though they are—risk obscuring the histories of violence, the deep-seated anxieties, and the undertows of reciprocal identification against one another that have shaped how we have arrived to the present moment. These histories can be confronted and renounced, but the freedom to do so is itself asymmetrical and laden with power. It would be a grave error to ignore the privilege of Christian theologians in setting the vocabulary, methods, and pacing of much interfaith engagement (and of academic interreligious studies?), particularly if it is openly framed in "ecumenical" terms as pursuing a human unity that casts, in the eyes of many, the shadow of a Christian inclusivism or universalism.[17]

This is not to suggest that the practitioners of interreligious studies have the option of being nonnormative. The issue, rather, is *what range of normativity* can be agreed upon or at least tolerated within the bounds of academic interreligious studies—and what does this normativity have to do with the ecumenical legacy? Although it is a fair and important question to be asked whether interreligious studies is to be construed more in the paradigm of political science (defined by its attention to certain kinds of subject matter, irrespective of the goals and values of the scholarship) or more in the paradigm of peace and conflict studies (defined by an orientation toward the pursuit of a moral and political purpose), I suspect that few interreligious studies scholars will struggle to embrace a normative position in which interreligious solidarity and peace are preferable to misunderstanding and violence, or to conceive of their scholarship as promoting these aims even when (and I count my own in this category) it is more concerned with analyzing the dynamics of division, suspicion, and antagonism.[18] Since "ecumenical" signifies not solely the ideal of religious unity but also in more general terms a *resistance to sectarianism*, interreligious studies should at the very least be oriented ecumenically in *this* respect, including in studies concerned with impartially assessing the textures and entailments of religious antagonism. Such analyses are gravely needed in a global society experiencing all manner of sectarian polarization today, and interreligious studies is in a position to provide them and promote their public utility.[19] Or is the commitment that drives our tilling of this field just a happenstance interest in understanding these dynamics for our own edification?

So where does this leave us? The perspectives and tools of ecumenical studies are valuable, perhaps indispensable resources for interreligious studies, and they are resources with liabilities. Granted, we are not at liberty to banish the history of our language and to rely solely on sanitized neologisms (otherwise, we would not be studying "religion" at all).[20] Somehow we have to carry on with imperfect terms that reveal upon inspection the wear and tear of their use. But if ecumenical studies is recognized as a bedfellow of interreligious studies—or an alternate side of the same coin, or even an alternate construal of the same comprehensive form of analysis that considers religious difference across, through, and beneath human designations of "inter" and "intra"—it will not be because Christian scholars have asserted that this term, at home in their own history, is universally applicable and acceptable to all. Rather, the contribution of ecumenics to interreligious studies must continue to be negotiated with empathy and self-scrutiny by everyone involved. To the extent that this is realized, we can be confident that the many complexities and difficulties brought to light by the attempt are themselves in the service of a more realistic and mutualistic interpretive enterprise.

Notes

1   See Oddbjørn Leirvik, *Interreligious Studies: A Relational Approach to Religious Activism and the Study of Religion* (London: Bloomsbury, 2014), 8. See also, in this volume, Leirvik, "Area, Field, Discipline"; cf. Anna S. King and Paul Hedges, "What Is Religion? Or, What Is It We Are Talking About?" in *Controversies in Contemporary Religion: Education, Law, Politics, Society, and Spirituality; Volume 1,* ed. Paul Hedges (Santa Barbara: ABC-CLIO, 2014), 13–14, 21–22.

2   See Anne Hege Grung, "Inter-religious or Trans-religious? Exploring the Term 'Inter-religious' in a Feminist Postcolonial Perspective," *Journal of Interreligious Studies* 13 (2014): 11–12. She therefore suggests: "To replace 'inter' with the term 'trans' requires the acknowledgement of a larger fluidity in the encounter between people of different religious affiliation, and opens it up for addressing thematizing *intra-religious* differences. It may also make the relevant contextual power relations influencing the dialogue more visible. On the other hand, the term 'trans' instead of 'inter' may be understood as a challenge or a threat to religious boundaries the participants in the dialogue wish to keep stable in order to feel secured in their own religious identity" (11, emphasis original). See also, in this volume, Grung, "Interreligious or Trans-

religious?"; cf. Hans Gustafson, "Is Transreligious Theology Unavoidable in Interreligious Theology and Dialogue?" *Open Theology* 2 (2016): 251–52.

3   See, for instance, Eboo Patel and Cassie Meyer, "Teaching Interfaith Leadership," in *Teaching Interreligious Encounters*, ed. Marc A. Pugliese and Alexander Y. Hwang (Oxford: Oxford University Press, 2017), 299. See also, in this volume, Patel, "A Civic Approach to Interfaith Studies."

4   That is, such "interfaith" differences and relations among people who identify as belonging somehow to a common community or endeavor (however "complex" those belongings may be—see Leirvik, *Interreligious Studies*, 9) are still meaningfully distinct from those among people who do not.

5   See also, in this volume, Russell C. D. Arnold, "Complicating Religious Identity," which deconstructs "affiliation" as a clear-cut demarcation of who is unambiguously "within" a community; and Peter A. Pettit, "*Kairos Palestine* and Autoimmune Rejection," which offers a compelling case study that makes clearer still the entanglement between interreligious relations and each tradition's internal diversity/division—that is, "the wide disparities in perspectives among co-religionists."

6   For a patient and thorough exploration of such a metaphorical construal and of its liabilities, see Robert Ford Campany, "On the Very Idea of Religions (in the Modern West and in Early Medieval China)," *History of Religions* 42, no. 4 (2003), 288–99.

7   See John Mackay, *Ecumenics: The Science of the Church Universal* (Englewood Cliffs, N.J.: Prentice-Hall, 1964), 18; Michael Hurley, "Ecumenics: What and Why?" *The Furrow* 21, no. 7 (1970): 417–22; and Peter Lengsfeld, "Die Situation als Herausforderung," in *Ökumenische Theologie: Ein Arbeitsbuch*, ed. Peter Lengsfeld (Stuttgart: Kohlhammer, 1980), 23–31. These classic sources (in Christian ecumenics in particular) articulate the shape of a scholarly apparatus for the interdisciplinary investigation and interpretation of the situated diversities that have historically comprised, motivated, and disrupted Christian life in the world.

8   However, as Marianne Moyaert discusses in her chapter for this volume ("The Scholar, the Theologian, and the Activist"), these distinctions can themselves become fetishized and, when they do, can obscure rather than serve the complexity and flexibility of interreligious endeavors that cross between the academy and the wider public.

9   See Andrew Pierce, "Ecumenics as an Intercultural Theology: In Search of Repentant Reconfigurings of Authority, Tradition and Experience," in *Mining Truths: Festschrift in Honour of Geraldine Smyth*, ed. John O'Grady, Cathy Higgins, and Jude Lal Fernando (Sankt Ottilien, Germany: EOS, 2015), 48–51. Cf. Paul Crow, "Ecumenics as Reflections on Models of Christian Unity," in *The Teaching of Ecumenics*, ed. Samuel Amirtham and Cyris H. S. Moon (Geneva: WCC, 1987), 17: "At this historical moment, there is first a *truly global consciousness* . . . the people of the earth now live in an interconnected and interdependent world system which has never before existed." John Mackay too

observes that "technology did in the twentieth century what Greek culture and Roman law had done two thousand years before" ("Ecumenical: The Word and the Concept," *Theology Today* 9, no. 1 [1952]: 1, emphasis original), and that "with the advent of the airplane, groups of people who had lived in regions hitherto virtually inaccessible became part of the human family. All physical boundaries could now be traversed, for the world had become a neighborhood. With the coming of radio, the denizens of the remotest parts of the globe, whether lettered or unlettered, became, through the possession of simple technological devices, the contemporaries of all the inhabitants of the earth. The world neighborhood was also a world auditorium" (*Ecumenics*, 26).

10   See Stefan Höschele, "Defining Ecumenics Fifty Years after Mackay," *Communio Viatorum* 55, no. 2 (2013): 121. Nor was the German ecumenics academy a stranger to this (contested) interreligious inclusivity: see May, "Vom innerchristlichen zum interreligiösen Dialog," in Lengsfeld, *Ökumenische Theologie*, 426–32.

11   Note the consistency with which ecumenical mission gatherings have taken interreligious interfaces seriously as the framework within which their work is intelligible: the 1910 World Missionary Conference in Edinburgh addressed interreligious themes particularly in the course of its Commission 4 ("The Missionary Message in Relation to the Non-Christian Religions"), and its centenary gathering in 2010 took up "Christian Mission among Other Faiths" as its Theme 2 (see David A. Kerr and Kenneth R. Ross, eds., *Edinburgh 2010: Mission Then and Now* [Oxford: Regnum, 2009], 119–51; and see Kirsteen Kim and Andrew Anderson, eds., *Edinburgh 2010: Mission Today and Tomorrow* [Oxford: Regnum, 2011], 127–34, 208–16). So too, in the twenty-first-century convocations of the ecumenical societies Societas Oecumenica and Ecclesiological Investigations, interreligious topics have been decisively (if occasionally controversially) recognized as integral to the nature and purpose of ecumenical endeavor (see, for instance, the conference proceedings included in Andrew Pierce and Oliver Schuegraf, eds., *Den Blick weiten: Wenn Ökumene den Religionen begegnet / Dialogue Inside-Out: Ecumenism Encounters the Religions* [Leipzig: Evangelische Verlagsanstalt, 2014]; and in Gerard Mannion, ed., *Where We Dwell in Common: The Quest for Dialogue in the Twenty-First Century* [New York: Palgrave Macmillan, 2016]). And, in the most recent General Assemblies of the World Council of Churches, interreligious topics have been prominent: see Luis N. Rivera-Pagán, ed., *God, in Your Grace: Official Report of the Ninth Assembly of the World Council of Churches* (Geneva: WCC, 2007), 30–32, 179–93, 369–88; and World Council of Churches, *Ecumenical Conversations: Reports, Affirmations and Challenges from the 10th Assembly* (Geneva: WCC, 2014), 68–76, 115–20.

12   John D'Arcy May, "Ökumene im Zeitalter der Globalisierung," in *Ökumene— Überdacht: Reflexionen und Realitäten im Umbruch*, ed. Thomas Bremer and Maria Wernsmann (Freiburg: Verlag Herder, 2014), 346 (my translation).

13   In future research, I hope to devote substantially expanded attention to the ecumenical paradigms that have emerged at these institutions. See, in the meantime, John F. O'Grady and Peter Scherle, "Ecumenics in the 21st Cen-

tury: Plumbing the Relationships of Theology, Interreligious Dialogue, and Peacebuilding," in *Ecumenics from the Rim: Explorations in Honour of John D'Arcy May*, ed. John F. O'Grady and Peter Scherle (Berlin: Lit Verlag, 2007), 3–20; Andrew Pierce, "New MPhil in Intercultural Theology and Interreligious Studies at ISE, Trinity College Dublin," *Concilium* 1 (2011): 115–18; John D'Arcy May and Linda Hogan, "Visioning Ecumenics as Intercultural, Inter-religious, and Public Theology," *Concilium* 1 (2011): 70–84; Thomas Bremer, "Ökumene und ökumenischen Theologie im Umbruch," in Bremer and Wernsmann, *Ökumene—Überdacht*, 18–36; Maria Wernsmann, "'Überdachte' Ökumene: Überlegungen zu Theorien und Realitäten ökumenischer Prozesse," *Herder-Korrespondenz* 65 (2011): 572–75; Norbert Hintersteiner, "God in Translation: Crosscultural and Interreligious Theologies," *Currents of Encounter* 44 (2012): 9–23; and May, "Ökumene im Zeitalter der Globalisierung," 334–49.

14   This is the case, May suggests, not only among Christian practitioners of interreligious studies but also insofar as the language of "ecumenical studies" is gradually being adopted *by* non-Christians in the course of conceiving and enacting their own much-needed modes of reconciliation (for instance, between Theravada and Mahayana Buddhists and between Sunni and Shi'i Muslims; see May, "Ökumene im Zeitalter der Globalisierung," 346). Though "ecumenical" is doubtless a technical term inextricable from the history of Christianity, it is important to remember that it neither originates with nor belongs to Christians any more than does, say, "theology" or the "sacred."

15   Moreover, ecumenics has the advantage of having its core symbol of *oikoumenē* include the common ground itself on which religious difference takes place—the inhabited, habitable earth itself, the physicality and spatiality of which are indispensable components of sound interreligious analysis as well. See Lisa E. Dahill, "Water, Climate, Stars, and Place: Toward an Interspecies Interfaith Belonging," in *Interreligious/Interfaith Studies: Defining a New Field*, ed. Eboo Patel, Jennifer Howe Peace, and Noah J. Silverman (Boston: Beacon, 2018), 160–70, for a recalibration of human identity (and thus too of interreligious encounter) "within the larger web of creaturely kinship that is our shared biological reality" (160); Konrad Raiser, *Ecumenism in Transition: A Paradigm Shift in the Ecumenical Movement?* (Geneva: WCC, 1991), 79–111, for the construal of ecumenical unity as extending beyond the relations of Christians to involve the whole "household of life"; and Francis I, *Laudato Si': On Care for Our Common Home* (Vatican City: Vatican Press, 2015), throughout, for a vision in which the creaturely kinship of all members of "our common home" both precedes and exceeds the various religious divisions that shape human history.

16   Such an attitude in which difference can be explained away as epiphenomenal to an essential unity of religions has been the case not only in the discourse circulating at contemporary Parliaments since 1993 but also in the interfaith legacy of the original Parliament of 1893, whose paradigm-setting addresses by Swami Vivekananda enacted just such an acclamation of a higher unity that would be recognized by those awakened souls of every religion.

17   See Rachel Mikva, "Six Issues That Complicate Interreligious Studies and Engagement," in Patel, Peace, and Silverman, *Interreligious/Interfaith Studies*, 127–29: "Whether in seminary, college, or community contexts, Christian voices frequently dominate interreligious space, Christian questions shape comparative religious discourse, and Christian experience stands at the center" (128). See also, in this volume, Kevin Minister, "Decolonizing the Study of Religion"; Paul Hedges, "Decolonizing Interreligious Studies"; and Russell C. D. Arnold, "Complicating Religious Identity."

18   Leirvik argues that the normativity of interreligious studies is grounded in the fact that its *relationality* includes the scholar and not only the object of the scholar's study; that is, "interreligious studies can only be meaningfully undertaken in a willingness to reflect critically on one's own position in the spaces between" (*Interreligious Studies*, 10). That position is and must be an *ethical* position, in which the scholar's own attitudes toward religious difference and religious others are entailed. Laurie Patton's recent intervention in the Interreligious and Interfaith Studies Unit at the 2018 American Academy of Religion ("Interreligious/Interfaith Studies: Defining a New Field") served to emphasize, moreover, that this "ethical turn" is taking place throughout religious studies and not only in interreligious studies—even as representatives of the latter should be heartened that they are not in the wilderness regarding so important a development. See also Kate McCarthy's consideration (drawing on the work of Bruce Grelle) of how the *values* of interreligious studies can serve and enhance the secular academy's commitment to "free and open inquiry, respect for multiple perspectives, and evidence-based argumentation": "(Inter)Religious Studies: Making a Home in the Secular Academy," in Patel, Peace, and Silverman, *Interreligious/Interfaith Studies*, 12–14.

19   Here again the robust involvement of interreligious studies in what Laurie Patton calls the "ethical turn" in the religious studies academy is well warranted. See again note 18, and see, in this volume, Navras J. Aafreedi, "Peacebuilding"; Asfa Widiyanto, "Nation Building"; and Jeanine Hill Fletcher, "Scholarship as Activism."

20   This is the thrust of Jacques Derrida's critique in "Faith and Knowledge" in which the word "religion," though asserted to be a neutral umbrella concept of global applicability, appropriates to itself "things which have always been and remain foreign to what this word names and arrests in its history," a colonizing process that Derrida coyly names "globalatinization," in which "no semantic cell can remain alien, I dare not say 'safe and sound,' 'unscathed,' in this apparently borderless process" ("Faith and Knowledge: The Two Sources of 'Religion' at the Limits of Reason Alone," trans. S. Weber, in *Religion*, ed. Jacques Derrida and Gianni Vattimo [Stanford: Stanford University Press, 1998], 29).

References

Bremer, Thomas. "Ökumene und ökumenischen Theologie im Umbruch" [Ecumenism and ecumenical theology in the breach]. In *Ökumene—Überdacht: Reflexionen und Realitäten im Umbruch*, edited by Thomas Bremer and Maria Wernsmann, 18–36. Freiburg: Verlag Herder, 2014.

Campany, Robert Ford. "On the Very Idea of Religions (in the Modern West and in Early Medieval China)." *History of Religions* 42, no. 4 (2003): 289–319.

Crow, Paul A., Jr. "Ecumenics as Reflections on Models of Christian Unity." In *The Teaching of Ecumenics*, edited by Samuel Amirtham and Cyris H. S. Moon, 16–29. Geneva: WCC, 1987.

Dahill, Lisa E. "Water, Climate, Stars, and Place: Toward an Interspecies Interfaith Belonging." In *Interreligious/Interfaith Studies: Defining a New Field*, edited by Eboo Patel, Jennifer Howe Peace, and Noah J. Silverman, 160–70. Boston: Beacon, 2018.

Derrida, Jacques. "Faith and Knowledge: The Two Sources of 'Religion' at the Limits of Reason Alone." Translated by S. Weber. In *Religion*, edited by Jacques Derrida and Gianni Vattimo, 1–78. Stanford: Stanford University Press, 1998.

Francis I. *Laudato Si': On Care for Our Common Home*. Vatican City: Vatican Press, 2015.

Grung, Anne Hege. "Inter-religious or Trans-religious? Exploring the Term 'Inter-religious' in a Feminist Postcolonial Perspective." *Journal of Interreligious Studies* 13 (2014): 11–14.

Gustafson, Hans. "Is Transreligious Theology Unavoidable in Interreligious Theology and Dialogue?" *Open Theology* 2 (2016): 248–60.

Hintersteiner, Norbert. "God in Translation: Crosscultural and Interreligious Theologies." *Currents of Encounter* 44 (2012): 9–23.

Höschele, Stefan. "Defining Ecumenics Fifty Years after Mackay." *Communio Viatorum* 55, no. 2 (2013): 105–36.

Hurley, Michael. "Ecumenics: What and Why?" *The Furrow* 21. no. 7 (1970): 416–27.

Kerr, David A., and Kenneth R. Ross, eds. *Edinburgh 2010: Mission Then and Now*. Oxford: Regnum, 2009.

Kim, Kirsteen, and Andrew Anderson, eds. *Edinburgh 2010: Mission Today and Tomorrow*. Oxford: Regnum, 2011.

King, Anna S., and Paul Hedges. "What Is Religion? Or, What Is It We Are Talking About?" In *Controversies in Contemporary Religion: Education, Law, Politics, Society, and Spirituality; Volume 1*, edited by Paul Hedges, 13–25. Santa Barbara: ABC-CLIO, 2014.

Leirvik, Oddbjørn. *Interreligious Studies: A Relational Approach to Religious Activism and the Study of Religion*. London: Bloomsbury, 2014.

Lengsfeld, Peter. "Die Situation als Herausforderung" [The situation as a provocation]. In *Ökumenische Theologie: Ein Arbeitsbuch*, edited by Peter Lengsfeld, 23–35. Stuttgart: Kohlhammer, 1980.

Mackay, John A. "Ecumenical: The Word and the Concept." *Theology Today* 9, no. 1 (1952): 1–6.

———. *Ecumenics: The Science of the Church Universal*. Englewood Cliffs, N.J.: Prentice-Hall, 1964.

Mannion, Gerard, ed. *Where We Dwell in Common: The Quest for Dialogue in the Twenty-First Century*. New York: Palgrave Macmillan, 2016.

May, John D'Arcy. "Ökumene im Zeitalter der Globalisierung" [Ecumenism in the age of globalization]. In *Ökumene—Überdacht: Reflexionen und Realitäten im Umbruch*, edited by Thomas Bremer and Maria Wernsmann, 334–49. Freiburg: Verlag Herder, 2014.

———. "Vom innerchristlichen zum interreligiösen Dialog" [From intra-Christian to interreligious dialogue]. In *Ökumenische Theologie: Ein Arbeitsbuch*, edited by Peter Lengsfeld, 426–32. Stuttgart: Kohlhammer, 1980.

May, John D'Arcy, and Linda Hogan. "Visioning Ecumenics as Intercultural, Inter-religious, and Public Theology." *Concilium* 1 (2011): 70–84.

McCarthy, Kate. "(Inter)Religious Studies: Making a Home in the Secular Academy." In *Interreligious/Interfaith Studies: Defining a New Field*, edited by Eboo Patel, Jennifer Howe Peace, and Noah J. Silverman, 2–15. Boston: Beacon, 2018.

Mikva, Rachel. "Six Issues That Complicate Interreligious Studies and Engagement." In *Interreligious/Interfaith Studies: Defining a New Field*, edited by Eboo Patel, Jennifer Howe Peace, and Noah J. Silverman, 124–36. Boston: Beacon, 2018.

O'Grady, John F., and Peter Scherle. "Ecumenics in the 21st Century: Plumbing the Relationships of Theology, Interreligious Dialogue, and Peacebuilding." In *Ecumenics from the Rim: Explorations in Honour of John D'Arcy May*, edited by John F. O'Grady and Peter Scherle, 3–20. Berlin: Lit Verlag, 2007.

Patel, Eboo, and Cassie Meyer. "Teaching Interfaith Leadership." In *Teaching Interreligious Encounters*, edited by Marc A. Pugliese and Alexander Y. Hwang, 297–310. Oxford: Oxford University Press, 2017.

Pierce, Andrew. "Ecumenics as an Intercultural Theology: In Search of Repentant Reconfigurings of Authority, Tradition and Experience." In *Mining Truths: Festschrift in Honour of Geraldine Smyth*, edited by John O'Grady, Cathy Higgins, and Jude Lal Fernando, 43–58. Sankt Ottilien, Germany: EOS, 2015.

———. "New MPhil in Intercultural Theology and Inter-religious Studies at ISE, Trinity College Dublin." *Concilium* 1 (2011): 115–18.

Pierce, Andrew, and Oliver Schuegraf, eds. *Den Blick weiten: Wenn Ökumene den Religionen begegnet / Dialogue Inside-Out: Ecumenism Encounters the Religions*. Leipzig: Evangelische Verlagsanstalt, 2014.

Raiser, Konrad. *Ecumenism in Transition: A Paradigm Shift in the Ecumenical Movement?* Geneva: WCC, 1991.

Rivera-Pagán, Luis N., ed. *God, in Your Grace: Official Report of the Ninth Assembly of the World Council of Churches*. Geneva: WCC, 2007.

Wernsmann, Maria. "'Überdachte' Ökumene: Überlegungen zu Theorien und Realitäten ökumenischer Prozesse" ["Reconsidered" ecumenism: Deliberations on the theories and realities of ecumenical processes]. *Herder-Korrespondenz* 65 (2011): 572–75.

World Council of Churches. *Ecumenical Conversations: Reports, Affirmations and Challenges from the 10th Assembly*. Geneva: WCC, 2014.

15

Places and Spaces of Encounter

Timothy Parker

How may attention to interreligious encounters inform the work of an architectural historian or theorist? And how may the perspectives of architectural
history and theory contribute to the field of interreligious studies? Perhaps
these are just two ways to pose the same question: What is (or should, could
be) the relation between interreligious studies and the study of the built environment in which religion occurs? From public liturgies to personal devotions
to struggles over the meaning and control of contested sites, religion happens
somewhere, usually somewhere built. And how do encounters across religious
divides show up in the history and theory of religious architecture?

Interreligious studies may be a nascent or burgeoning field, but religion has
been a major part of architectural history and theory from the beginning. Survey courses and texts routinely feature chief monuments of human endeavor
and have thus, rightly, included many temples, churches, mosques, shrines,
and so on. And while such buildings have often enough been addressed with
emphases on their stylistic, technological, or broadly cultural import, their
roles as places of religious ritual and expression have typically also been acknowledged.

How does this inform our interpretation of the architecture? A common
approach for making sense of religious architecture *as religious* has been to
ask the quintessentially typological question, What type of building is this?
What, essentially, is a church, mosque, temple, and so forth, and how does
its architectural identity relate to the religious phenomena occurring there-

in? As a method for analysis, typology has real value: it enables a synthesis across historical difference to demonstrate developments within a tradition, and it informs comparisons that highlight what remains distinctive. Thus, we can discuss how a given building may fit within a trajectory such as that of house-church to basilica to hall church to meetinghouse to megachurch, and so forth, or among hypostyle, dome-and-minaret, four-iwan, and other types of mosques. Typological particularities of religious buildings as experienced by the faithful can illuminate distinctions that are also theological or institutional or that concern conflicting conceptions of sacrality.[1]

Historically, some architectural situations are clearly relevant to interreligious studies, such as places where sacred spaces are shared or contested. And the very concept of the sacred has at times been seen to bind people together across or despite differences of belief, or itself to be contested within a single tradition. But fuller attention to interreligious perspectives—especially including contemporary or recent interreligious encounters—is instructive: it shows not only the limits of common typological approaches but also the need to consider the interpretive difficulties of modern religious architecture.

For instance, consider interfaith chapels at airports or universities. Spaces designed to serve multiple religious traditions present design and interpretive challenges. Or consider the more ambitious efforts to incorporate multiple religious congregations into the design or the adaptation of a single building or complex that retains each group's distinctiveness yet coheres as a whole. Such cases are important to study and may offer strategies for living together peacefully in and through religious difference. And typologically, they may prompt a reassessment of standard categories. Insofar as such buildings are emphatically many things at once, existing categories are insufficient for their description or analysis. More often they are reduced to a single, quasi-universal thing, as in an evocation of an ineffable sacred through elemental uses of light and/ or pure geometries of form and space, rendering typologies based on use (and thereby on religious identity) less helpful. It is worth noting that typologies are not always based on a building's *use*. They have often been rooted in a building's *form* or its main *idea*.[2] But use-based typologies seem most appropriate for religious buildings given the relevance of ritual activity.

More consequentially, however, and especially insofar as a building's *use* is key, these kinds of buildings are in fact used by only a small and atypical portion of religious people. If interreligious studies involves a broad range of orientations toward religion and not just well-defined religious identities or explicit efforts to cooperate across identities, these cases bypass the vast majority of built environments in which interreligious encounters actually occur. Churches, mosques, and temples may not be interreligious in conception, but they nonetheless provide occasions for interreligious encounters by their public nature and the ways in which (usually inadequate) images or ideas of their use and meaning are taken up by others, including the nonreligious. Some buildings are routinely experienced as sacred even while not being dedicated to a conventionally religious use. However valuable analysis of "interfaith space" is, its exceptional nature rather suggests the unexplored potential of other possibilities for how architecture may relate to interreligious encounter, and this requires a better understanding of modern religious architecture than the standard, largely historical typologies provide. What is needed is an adequate embrace of the complexities of modern architecture and its historiography as they pertain to religion. Symptomatic of larger crises of identity and meaning, this story resists being reduced to a single movement or style. Further, it operates beyond the scale of a building's physical boundaries.

Many Modernisms

If we seek to understand the religious other, it is natural to ask why their sacred spaces are the way they are. But common typologies of religious architecture rarely correspond to the lived experience of our neighbors, a fact the history of modern architecture makes evident. Throughout the nineteenth century, architects were increasingly confronted by an unprecedented array of new construction materials and methods brought by industrialization; entirely new building types required by political, economic, and social changes; and fraying historical traditions relativized by increases in global archaeological and art-historical knowledge. Whether seen as difficulties, opportunities, or something of both, these changes upset the coherence of received architectural tradition. Is history itself to be repudiated in the service of a constantly changing, ever-renewed newness? Is the revival-style historicism of the nineteenth century to be repudiated but some earlier tradition to be recuperated as still promising for the modern age? Is a return to first principles called for, perhaps informed by newly encountered "primitive" arts that appeared abstract to the modern eye? Or are essential traits of classicism to be revived as guiding rules that needed no ornamental elaboration in an age of machine-produced steel and glass? Should the emergent aesthetic of the engineer be the model for an architecture driven by function and efficiency? Out of several such questions, maybe a new style would develop that would be distinctly modern, perhaps drawing from nature or some other unifying source. One way or another, modernism was a response to the conditions of modernity brought about by modernization, and these responses ran the gamut from expression and celebration to resistance and critique.

The historiographical record further complicates the story, for amid such variation certain ideas had outsized influence due to their quick and broad dissemination in an age of growing mass media. While there are variations on this theme, the chief example here was the attempt in 1932 by Henry Russell Hitchcock and Philip Johnson to define modern architecture as a style in purely formal terms. In their book, *The International Style* (and related Museum of Modern Art exhibit), the sociopolitical agendas of the architects featured therein were ignored, and the aesthetic and formal richness and variety of the buildings were misrepresented, but the message prevailed nonetheless.[3] What is more, it helped spur the rapid spread of "international style" buildings during the global building boom after the Second World War, often eclipsing the already existing regional responses to modernization.

But the complications of modern architectural history can also be a prod for better interreligious understanding. When confronted with a modern church, mosque, temple, and so forth, it is natural to ask why it looks the way it does, why the space is arranged as it is, and so on. Relative to any mental images one already possesses for the building type, it is likely to appear strange. The strangeness—and ensuing curiosity—disrupt assumptions about what such buildings are. Seeking to understand the differences evident in a modern religious building will routinely raise questions of how the spaces within are used, valued, and understood—key aspects of understanding religious architecture *as religious*. The inquiry itself will convey how rich and complicated religious sites in fact are, even within one's own tradition. Encounters with modern religious architecture provoke awareness of the differences across and within religions.

So-Called Secularization

Architectural modernism not only takes many forms but also emerges in the midst of a century full of change, including conceptions of religious identity. Arguably the most significant architectural developments have to do with new technologies, new building types, and new forms, but part of the story seems also to be the apparently secularizing nature of modernization. Religious authority is challenged, religious institutional wealth and power are diminished, and people tend less and less to accept the religious traditions of previous generations. Of course, we now see this development from a post-secular perspective, and, architecturally, we see over a century's worth of modern religious architecture that remains relatively unstudied. This is currently a growth field in architectural history and theory. It remains to be seen how it may reconfigure the ways in which religious architecture has been interpreted and considered meaningful.

There are many possibilities here for exploration pertinent to interreligious studies. Typologies may be altogether insufficient to the task of interpreting such an ever-changing landscape of places, spaces, and people. Or more fluid, fine-grained, or subtle typological categories may be needed. Are there analogues to religious experience to be found in the art museum and in the attribution of quasi-religious language to the architecture of these new "sacred" sites? What are the limits of the sacred? How does the growth of the "nones," which includes the religiously unaffiliated and the "spiritual but not religious," and people claiming "multiple religious belonging" affect such projects?[4] Is it time to revisit civil religion, perhaps especially in the American context wherein pragmatism and church-state separation undergird an emphatically pluralist experiment? These questions bring to mind Alasdair MacIntyre's proclamation of a moral philosophy crisis (people remain stuck with fragments of tradition that cannot but undermine consensus) but also Jeffrey Stout's critique of MacIntyre that points to an American pluralist tradition that needs nourishing (and thereby argues against any religious withdrawal from the public sphere).[5] Far beyond any singular notion of "interfaith space," there is substantial potential for interreligious studies and scholarship on the built environment to benefit from each other.

Architecture, the Public Realm, and Material Culture

Architecture does not exist in isolation. Terms like "built environment" or "architectural culture" seek to evoke something broader, and the permutations on "public sphere" (multiple spheres, publics, counter-publics, networks, assemblages) set these into even broader arenas of encounter.[6] Also relevant to religious architectural contexts are the products of allied fields, such as furnishings, graphic design, clothing, memorials, and even print and digital media communication. While interreligious encounters happen somewhere, they also are surely not contained in any definite enclosure. From the mental maps and images that someone may hold about what a mosque is and what happens inside, to how a row of churches dominates a streetscape, to stock caricatures in news reports or derogatory images scrawled on buildings, architecture is the fertile middle ground of an enormous range of venues for interreligious encounter.

How can such an unwieldy and diffuse set of potential sites of interaction be adequately studied, described, analyzed, and understood? Surely it requires multiple methods and collaboration across fields and disciplines. It also requires moving past any single conception of "interfaith space" and toward a conception of spaces of interreligious encounter that are fluid, overlapping, and contested—and marked by particular but typologically complicated forms and expressions of religious identity that cannot be elided. Is it possible to map such spaces or assemblages? One possibility may be found in contemporary and constantly improving mapping technology, which could be informed by the ever-growing world of data that have geo-spatial implications. Such implications are not always obvious and are often merely implicit. Insofar as they pertain to how people orient around religion in material, architectural, and urban terms, the aim would be a fuller, more accurate, and more concrete portrayal of the spaces and places of interreligious encounter. However we may map such a picture, one thing remains certain: the full story is more complicated than we tend to imagine, yet this very complexity offers a fruitful path toward a humble and substantive interreligious understanding.

Notes

1   On sacrality, there is a long history of scholarship in religious studies concerning "the sacred," especially associated with Mircea Eliade's phenomenological approach that would claim a numinous reality to which particular religions point. Critiqued by Jonathan Z. Smith and others on the basis that "the sacred" is at least as much constituted by human activity and attribution as by phenomenal experience, "sacred space" is now best discussed in ways that preserve particularities that distinguish religious practices from each other. A promising redefinition of the idea that seeks to reconcile the phenomenological and the attributive senses of the concept and that incorporates what neurological science can reveal about religious experience is Ann Taves' *Religious Experience Reconsidered: A Building Block Approach to the Study of Religion and Other Special Things* (Princeton: Princeton University Press, 2009). See also Mircea Eliade, *The Sacred and the Profane: The Nature of Religion*, trans. W. R. Trask (New York: Harcourt Brace, 1987 [1957]); and Jonathan Z. Smith, *To Take Place: Toward Theory in Ritual* (Chicago: University of Chicago Press, 1987).

2   On the three common bases of architectural typologies, see Rafael Moneo, "On Typology," *Oppositions* 13 (1978): 36–45. For use-based typology, see Antoine-Chrysostome Quatremère de Quincy, "Type," trans. Anthony Vidler, *Oppositions* 8 (1977): 148–50 (published originally: "Architecture," in *Encyclopédie Méthodique*, vol. 3 [Paris: Panckoucke, 1825]). For idea-based typology, see Giulio Carlo Argan, "On the Typology of Architecture," *Architectural Design* 33, no. 12 (1963): 564–65. For form- or artifact-based (especially urban) typology, see Aldo Rossi, *The Architecture of the City*, trans. Diane Ghirardo and Joan Ockman (Cambridge, Mass.: MIT Press, 1982).

3   Henry Russell Hitchcock and Philip Johnson, *The International Style: Architecture since 1922* (New York: W. W. Norton, 1932).

4 For any project of reconceiving sacred space in ways adequate to modern pluralist societies, the approach developed by Ann Taves is especially promising. See Taves, *Religious Experience Reconsidered*.

5 Alasdair MacIntyre, *After Virtue: A Study in Moral Theory* (Notre Dame: University of Notre Dame Press, 1981); Jeffrey Stout, *Democracy and Tradition* (Princeton: Princeton University Press, 2005).

6 See Jürgen Habermas, *The Structural Transformation of the Public Sphere: An Inquiry into a Category of Bourgeois Society* (Cambridge, Mass.: MIT Press, 1989); Charles Taylor, *Modern Social Imaginaries* (Durham, N.C.: Duke University Press, 2004); Seyla Benhabib, "Toward a Deliberative Model of Democratic Legitimacy," in *Democracy and Difference: Contesting the Boundaries of the Political*, ed. Seyla Benhabib (Princeton: Princeton University Press, 1996).

References

Argan, Giulio Carlo. "On the Typology of Architecture." *Architectural Design* 33, no. 12 (1963): 564–65.

Benhabib, Seyla. "Toward a Deliberative Model of Democratic Legitimacy." In *Democracy and Difference: Contesting the Boundaries of the Political*, edited by Seyla Benhabib, 67–94. Princeton: Princeton University Press, 1996.

de Quincy, Antoine-Chrysostome Quatremère. "Type." Translated by Anthony Vidler. *Oppositions* 8 (1977): 148–50. Published originally: "Architecture." In *Encyclopédie Méthodique*, vol. 3. Paris: Panckoucke, 1825.

Eliade, Mircea. *The Sacred and the Profane: The Nature of Religion*. Translated by W. R. Trask. New York: Harcourt Brace, 1987 [1957].

Habermas, Jürgen. *The Structural Transformation of the Public Sphere: An Inquiry into a Category of Bourgeois Society*. Cambridge, Mass.: MIT Press, 1989.

Hitchcock, Henry Russell, and Philip Johnson. *The International Style: Architecture since 1922*. New York: W. W. Norton, 1932.

MacIntyre, Alasdair. *After Virtue: A Study in Moral Theory*. Notre Dame: University of Notre Dame Press, 1981.

Moneo, Rafael. "On Typology." *Oppositions* 13 (1978): 36–45.

Rossi, Aldo. *The Architecture of the City*. Translated by Diane Ghirardo and Joan Ockman. Cambridge, Mass.: MIT Press, 1982.

Smith, Jonathan Z. *To Take Place: Toward Theory in Ritual*. Chicago: University of Chicago Press, 1987.

Stout, Jeffrey. *Democracy and Tradition*. Princeton: Princeton University Press, 2005.

Taves, Ann. *Religious Experience Reconsidered: A Building Block Approach to the Study of Religion and Other Special Things*. Princeton: Princeton University Press, 2009.

Taylor, Charles. *Modern Social Imaginaries*. Durham, N.C.: Duke University Press, 2004.

III

THEOLOGICAL AND PHILOSOPHICAL CONSIDERATIONS

16

Grist for Theological Mills

J. R. Hustwit

While interreligious dialogue has been occurring for centuries, the past fifteen years have been remarkable. A number of scholars have set out to orient their teaching and scholarship around the moments when religions intersect, in order to reflect the increasing religious diversity present in previously homogenous communities. The growing field of interreligious (or interfaith) studies is developing along several trajectories, guided by different disciplines with different aims. Some interreligious scholars may aim at explaining social behaviors. Others value interreligious studies because it fosters bonhomie among communities. Interreligious studies offers a theological function as well—that is, the analysis of existing religious truth claims and the construction of new religious truth claims. In short, interreligious studies tells us not only about human experience of the sacred but also about the sacred itself. This chapter makes the case for how interreligious studies has helped support, give rise to, and provide valuable data for four important theological subfields: theology of religions, missiology, comparative theology, and transreligious theology.

Those engaged in the interreligious conversation tend to employ either a "religious studies sensibility," which largely aims to describe religious behaviors while withholding judgment about a religion's relationship to truth, or a "theological sensibility," which critically evaluates religious truth claims. It may not be possible to neatly synthesize the two approaches, but there are approaches that include both sets of concerns. In my own view, interreligious studies is best defined as a species of interpretation, à la Ricoeur, that incorporates both critical-explanatory methods (i.e., religious studies) and the theological "naiveté" of the hermeneutically located interpreter.[1] Even while I give a critical analysis of the Vedic caste system, I am only able to see the caste system in light of my own theological perspective (or lack thereof). Interpreting other religions always involves three moments: a projection of prejudice, a critical analysis, and the appropriation of the interpretation into the interpreter's worldview. All this is to say we need not choose between critical comparison of religions and entertaining their truth claims with seriousness. The content produced by theology and religious studies is symbiotic, even while their methods differ.

Theology of Religions

The most obvious fruit born by interreligious studies within confessional Christian theology is the development of the subfield now called "theology of the religions." Both globalization and the Christian missionary activity in the first half of the twentieth century gave rise to a generation of theologians who had lived in fellowship with non-Christians and consequently struggled with the church's rather grim teachings concerning non-Christians. Theology of the religions attempts to determine, from Christian sources, the significance of non-Christian religions. Do these religions offer truth, salvation, or godly values? What are the soteriological prospects of adherents to these other religions? A variety of doctrines have been produced to date: exclusivisms (non-Christians are not saved), inclusivisms (non-Christians are saved by Christianity), and pluralisms (non-Christians are saved by their own traditions). In fact, there is a plurality of pluralisms: differential pluralism, identist pluralism, and complementary pluralism, to name a few.[2] Unlike fifty years ago, it is now unthinkable to pursue a degree in theology without some training in the theology of religions.

Missiology

Other reactions to interreligious studies have caused Christian reflection on the mission and mandate of the church. Many communities have reinterpreted the Great Commission (e.g., in Matthew 28), which calls on the followers of Jesus to "make disciples of all nations, baptizing them in the name of the Father, Son, and the Holy Spirit." Traditionally, Christian mission has focused on evangelism, understood as conversion of non-Christians to the Christian faith. Proselytizers who have detailed and nuanced understanding of other religions may use more strategic rhetoric or establish rapport more easily. A publication by Southern Baptist Theological Seminary recommends "understanding [the non-Christian] for the sake of evangelism" through study and conversation.[3] Although such interviews do not meet most definitions of authentic interreligious dialogue, which is characterized by a mutual openness to transformation and a willingness to give up control in the encounter, interreligious study has been a useful tool to those who are uninterested in or hostile to other religions.

At the same time, interreligious study produces outcomes that undermine the will to convert—for example, revealing the more-or-less moral parity of Christians and non-Christians, nonexclusive religious identities, or multiple religious belonging. One response to these complications is to continue to spread the teachings of Christ without expectation of conversion. Christ's message may be needed by the world but not to the exclusion of the Buddhist Dharma or Qur'anic revelation. Another possible alternative to conversion is to focus missiology and evangelism away from truth claims and toward practice: witnessing through service to others or the pursuit of social justice. Here, identity and doctrine take a backseat to compassionate action.

Comparative Theology

An obvious intersection of interreligious studies and theology occurs in comparative theology—the careful placing side-by-side of two particular expressions from two different religions. There are two types of comparative theology: contextual and synthetic. Contextual comparative theology proceeds with careful "cross-readings" of texts, and it uses the comparison to reframe the theologian's own tradition. Francis Clooney is emblematic of this approach. For example, in *Divine Mother, Blessed Mother*, Clooney cross-reads bhakti hymns to Hindu goddesses and traditional Christian hymns to Mary.[4] Clooney does not adjudicate the texts into a constructive synthesis but reads one in light of the other as a way to disclose features already present in each tradition. Another example is to affirm something like Vedantan absorption into Brahman as a penultimate end within Christian theology, as Mark Heim does.[5] For Heim, this is not a synthesis of two religions—the possibility of *moksha* was always latent in the Christian tradition, but only comparison brings it to light.

Going beyond strict comparison, synthetic theologians compare in order to appropriate religions in service of a more adequate articulation of their own traditions. Jay McDaniel, for example, draws on Whiteheadian philosophy and interreligious studies to provisionally sketch an expansive theology that includes four faces of the divine and three general forms of salvation.[6] In such synthetic projects, religious differences are affirmed and made complementary under one rational scheme. The result is a "Christian theology . . . but not written for Christians alone."[7]

Transreligious Theology

A very recent development has been the rise of scholars who discuss transreligious theology.[8] Like synthetic comparative theologians, transreligious theologians actively appropriate truth claims from other religions. Unlike synthetic comparative theologians, the transreligious theologian does not use coherence with her own tradition as a guiding principle of theological construction. That is, though the transreligious theologian cannot ascend to a place of theological neutrality, she is willing to leave the orthodoxies of her home tradition behind in service to a more complete, inclusive, or liberating theology.

Conclusion

Theology differs from other approaches in religious studies by its preoccupation with questions of human existence, ultimate value, and the nature of reality. Specifically, theology treats these topics as claims to truth, and theological inquiry is truth-directed. Theologians want to do more than report what others claim to be true; they want to settle questions about which beliefs are most likely to be—or certainly are—true. Interreligious studies has been an abundant source of novel grist for theological mills. In theology of religions, missiology, comparative theology, and transreligious theology, religions other than one's own are able to illuminate new avenues for theology by virtue of contrast and to offer new possibilities for theological creativity even by casting critical light on the boundaries of particular religious traditions.

Notes

1   Some models of interpretation allow for a dialectic between belonging-to and criticism-of tradition. See Paul Ricoeur, *Hermeneutics and the Human Sciences*, ed. and trans. John B. Thompson (Cambridge: Cambridge University Press, 1981), 87–100.

2   See David Ray Griffin, ed., *Deep Religious Pluralism* (Louisville: Westminster John Knox, 2005), 1–66.

3   Dan DeWitt, *A Guide to Evangelism* (Southern Baptists Theological Seminary Press, 2013). Excerpted on "Evangelism to World Religions (Part 2)," North American Mission Board, accessed January 21, 2019, https://www.namb.net/apologetics-blog/evangelism-to-world-religions-part-2/.

4   Francis X. Clooney, S.J., *Divine Mother, Blessed Mother: Hindu Goddesses and the Virgin Mary* (Oxford: Oxford University Press, 2005).

5   S. Mark Heim, *The Depth of the Riches: A Trinitarian Theology of Religious Ends* (Grand Rapids: Eerdmans, 2001), 227–30.

6   Jay McDaniel, *Gandhi's Hope: Learning from Other Religions as a Path to Peace* (Maryknoll, N.Y.: Orbis, 2005), 87–97, 112.

7   McDaniel, *Gandhi's Hope*, 5.

8   See Jerry L. Martin, ed., *Theology without Walls: The Transreligious Imperative* (New York: Routledge, 2019).

References

Clooney, Francis X., S.J. *Divine Mother, Blessed Mother: Hindu Goddesses and the Virgin Mary*. Oxford: Oxford University Press, 2005.

DeWitt, Dan. *A Guide to Evangelism*. Louisville: Southern Baptist Theological Seminary Press, 2013.

Griffin, David Ray, ed. *Deep Religious Pluralism*. Louisville: Westminster John Knox, 2005.

Heim, S. Mark. *The Depth of the Riches: A Trinitarian Theology of Religious Ends*. Grand Rapids: Eerdmans, 2001.

Martin, Jerry L., ed. *Theology without Walls: The Transreligious Imperative*. New York: Routledge, 2019.

McDaniel, Jay. *Gandhi's Hope: Learning from Other Religions as a Path to Peace*. Maryknoll, N.Y.: Orbis, 2005.

North American Mission Board. "Evangelism to World Religions (Part 2)." Accessed January 21, 2019. https://www.namb.net/apologetics-blog/evangelism -to-world-religions-part-2/.

Ricoeur, Paul. *Hermeneutics and the Human Sciences*. Edited and translated by John B. Thompson. Cambridge: Cambridge University Press, 1981.

17

Dialogical Theology and Praxis

Wolfram Weisse

Dialogue is central for all levels of interreligious studies. Therefore, a strongly dialogically oriented theology with reference to lived religions is necessary at university. This approach can help to develop a meaningful theology and become a resource for the peaceful coexistence of people with different religions and worldviews. Such an approach, named Dialogical Theology, was developed in recent years (2013–2018) in the context of the research project "ReDi: Religion and Dialogue in Modern Societies" located at the Academy of World Religions of Hamburg University in Germany.[1] In an interdisciplinary and internationally comparative approach including colleagues in Scandinavia, England, and the United States, Dialogical Theology was produced by a team of researchers from different religious traditions. This research was context oriented, which is to say that it observed and studied various forms of interreligious dialogue in real time as they were practiced. To that end, beliefs about and the practice of interreligious dialogue as it exists today were analyzed by methods developed in empirical sociology.

Dialogical Theology

While remaining aware of the potential for conflict and aggression inherent in the relations between religions, Dialogical Theology primarily focuses on the extent to which core elements in the basic theological foundation of all religions substantiate both dialogue and the acceptance and appreciation of people of other religious and cultural affiliation. Over the past decades, the question of interreligious dialogue in theology has been advanced through various approaches.[2] This includes early efforts of a Pluralist Theology of Religions,[3] Intercultural and Interreligious Theology,[4] and Comparative Theology.[5] Dialogue plays a role in these approaches, but it is not the center of their focus. Dialogical Theology, on the other hand, puts dialogue itself at the heart of theology.[6]

Obviously, Christian theology cannot do this alone. It calls for a shared effort with other major religions such as Judaism, Islam, Hinduism, and Buddhism. If dialogue is placed at the center of theological thought, a denominationally limited theology is inadequate for the task.[7] Concrete reference to context plays an important role in Dialogical Theology. Religions and their forms of expression are interpreted within the framework of the social and political parameters they occur in; thus, intercultural and interreligious theology provide important reference points for this effort.[8] As such, Dialogical Theology is tasked with promoting the coexistence of people from different religions and cultures and with analyzing dialogue as it is practiced.[9] It also relates to societal discourses on social engagement and liberation theology.[10] As Reinhold Bernhardt and Perry Schmidt-Leukel point out, "Understood as an attitude and a style, interreligious theological work remains reconnected with concrete dialogue."[11]

Dialogical Theology understands dialogue as a "relationship in mutuality," as opening up to others and "discovering that the opinions and views of the Other are needed or can at least be very helpful for a better understanding of one's own identity and thoughts."[12] Our analyses in ReDi on the question of openness within different religions have shown that significant elements were found in the core texts of all traditions studied that seem to view dialogue with other religions as not only possible and permitted but mandated.[13]

Dialogical Theology not only reflects interreligious dialogue conceptually but also analyses it as a practiced activity. This is a core point of Dialogical Theology; that is, its approach is not only about researching positions of one's own religion (or nonreligious worldview) and other religions from a theoretical perspective, but it is also calls for analyzing dialogues taking place in society, school, and university (e.g., the dialogue between and among researchers of different religious provenance).

In a "Research Laboratory Dialogical Theology," which we established as part of the abovementioned ReDi project at the Academy of World Religions, interreligious dialogues centered on fundamental texts of Christianity, Islam,

Judaism, Hinduism, and Buddhism. We thus created conditions to answer the question about which processes of understanding are possible in a dialogue between researchers of different religious perspectives.[14]

From the analyses of the transcribed conversations carried out in the research laboratory, we were able to develop a dialogical interreligious hermeneutics that showed that "Dialogical Theology develops in the execution and in the reflection of practices; it is and remains dependent on people of different religious and ideological backgrounds coming together and entering into a conversation."[15] Our empirical analyses showed that different religious affiliations of the involved researchers were not an obstacle for shared reflections. Encounters between views whose approaches to understanding basic religious texts and basic religious positions partly differed, but they also partly overlapped. This led to a process that enabled participants to transcend their respective positions and—without abandoning them—to reach new shared insights. This is in line with what Ephraim Meir understands as "transdifference"[16] and what Paul F. Knitter expresses as the "joint searchers."[17]

Dialogical Practice

The second level of our ReDi research approach on "Religion and Dialogue in Modern Societies" focused on Dialogical Practice: the understanding of dialogue in societal and educational developments of the metropolitan areas of London, Oslo, Stockholm, Rhine-Ruhr, and Hamburg. This level of research functioned as a practical counterpart to the level of Dialogical Theology and functioned to develop an analytical understanding of concrete reflections, experiences, and actions in religious communities, societies, and education. Empirical research on the possibilities and limitations of interreligious dialogue was carried out in urban environments, including educational institutions. Given the scope of our findings, here are a few general remarks:[18]

- The great significance of social factors for interreligious dialogue became evident.

- In the evaluation of interreligious relationships as a resource for building social capital, it became clear that interreligious dialogue is a product of growing social capital. On the other hand, existing interreligious activities seemed to stimulate a lasting growth and spread of social capital among their actors. Improvements in their social relationships, however, depended on previously extant ones.

- With regard to education, our research on the possibilities and limitations of dialogical practice showed the great relevance of interreligious dialogue in a plural student body.[19] We analyzed the potential of students to reflect the need and the limits of interreligious dialogue, both for societal and for religious reasons.

Final Remarks

Dialogical Theology as an approach is relevant for the development of an academic theology appropriate for humankind in plural modern societies. It can also serve as a background to legitimize interreligious dialogue in school and society. Dialogical Praxis in society and at school in turn can anchor a context-related Dialogical Theology in reality. Beyond this, we see a potential at the grassroots level—for example, for students to reflect the need and the limits of interreligious dialogue, including reflections that could stimulate academic debates in the fields of intercultural theology and interreligious studies. Dialogical Theology can thus be seen as addressing the theological needs of renewal and the praxis-orientated priorities of improving coexistence, as well as a mode of learning mutual appreciation in spite of, and within, religious and cultural diversity.[20]

Notes

1   Wolfram Weisse, "Ansätze zu einer Dialogischen Theologie vor dem Hintergrund religiöser Pluralisierung und Säkularisierung," in *Christentum und Europa: XVI; Europäischer Kongress für Theologie (10–13 September 2017 in Wien)*, ed. Michael Meyer-Blank (Leipzig: Europäische Verlagsanstalt, 2019), 708–22; Weisse, "The European Research Project ReDi: Religion and Dialogue in Modern Societies; An Overview," *Religion and Education* 46, no. 1 (2019). See also Carola Roloff and Wolfram Weisse, eds., *Dialogue in Buddhism and Hinduism: Public Presentations of the 14th Dalai Lama, Sallie B. King, Anantanand Rambachan, and Samdhong Rinpoche*, Documentation Series of the Academy of World Religions, vol. 2 (Münster: Waxmann, 2015).

2   Wolfram Weisse, Katajun Amirpur, et al., eds., *Religions and Dialogue: International Approaches*, Series of the Academy of World Religions at Hamburg University: Religions in Dialogue 7, (Münster: Waxmann, 2014).

3   Paul F. Knitter, *Horizonte der Befreiung: Auf dem Weg zu einer pluralistischen Theologie der Religionen* (Frankfurt/Main: Lembeck, 1997); Reinhold Bernhardt, "Jesus Christ as a Stumbling Block in Interreligious Dialogue?" in Weisse et al., *Religions and Dialogue*, 139–50.

4   Perry Schmidt-Leukel, "Interkulturelle Theologie als interreligiöse Theologie," *Evangelische Theologie* 71, no. 1 (2011): 4–16; Volker Küster, *Einführung in die Interkulturelle Theologie* (Göttingen: Vandenhoeck & Ruprecht, 2011).

5   Francis X. Clooney, *Comparative Theology: Deep Learning across Religious Borders* (Oxford: Wiley-Blackwell, 2010); Marianne Moyaert, "Ricoeur on the (Im-)possibility of a Global Ethics towards an Ethics of Fragile Interreligious Compromises," *Neue Zeitschrift für Systematische Theologie und Religionsphilosophie* 52, no. 4 (2010): 440–61.

6   Katajun Amirpur, Thorsten Knauth, et al., eds., *Perspektiven Dialogischer Theologie: Offenheit in den Religionen und eine Hermeneutik des interreligiösen Dialogs*, Series of the Academy of World Religions at Hamburg University: Religions in Dialogue 10 (Münster: Waxmann, 2016).

7 Reinhold Bernhardt and Perry Schmidt-Leukel, *Interreligiöse Theologie: Chancen und Probleme* (Zürich: TVZ Theologischer Verlag, 2013); Oddbjørn Leirvik, *Interreligious Studies: A Relational Approach to Religious Activism and the Study of Religion* (London: Bloomsbury, 2014); Ephraim Meir, *Becoming Interreligious: Towards a Dialogical Theology from a Jewish Vantage Point* (Münster: Waxmann, 2017); Wolfram Weisse, Julia Ipgrave, Oddbjørn Leirvik, and Muna Tatari, eds., *Pluralisation of Theologies at European Universities* (Münster and New York: Waxmann, 2020).

8 Schmidt-Leukel, "Interkulturelle Theologie als interreligiöse Theologie"; Küster, *Einführung in die Interkulturelle Theologie*.

9 Katajun Amirpur and Wolfram Weisse, *Religionen-Dialog-Gesellschaft: Analysen zur gegenwärtigen Situation und Impulse für eine dialogische Theologie* (Münster: Waxmann, 2015).

10 Sally B. King, *Socially Engaged Buddhism* (Honolulu: University of Hawai'i Press, 2009); Anantanand Rambachan, *A Hindu Theology of Liberation: Not-Two Is Not One* (Albany: SUNY Press, 2014).

11 Reinhold Bernhardt and Perry Schmidt-Leukel, "Einleitung," in *Interreligiöse Theologie: Chancen und Probleme*, ed. Reinhold Bernhardt and Perry Schmidt-Leukel (Zürich: TVZ Theologischer Verlag, 2013), 7–20 (quote on p. 9).

12 Wolfram Weisse, Carola Roloff, et al., "Einleitung," in *Perspektiven Dialogischer Theologie*, ed. Katajun Amirpur et al. (Münster: Waxmann, 2016), 9–28 (quote on p. 12, author's translation).

13 Amirpur et al., *Perspektiven Dialogischer Theologie*.

14 Thorsten Knauth et al., "Auf dem Weg zu einer dialogisch-interreligiösen Hermeneutik," in Amirpur et al., *Perspektiven Dialogischer Theologie*, 207–324 (quote on p. 299).

15 Knauth et al., "Auf dem Weg zu einer dialogisch-interreligiösen Hermeneutik," in Amirpur et al., *Perspektiven Dialogischer Theologie*, 316.

16 Meir, *Becoming Interreligious*.

17 Paul F. Knitter, "Interreligiöser Dialog: Bleibende Differenz oder kreatives Potenzial? Am Beispiel des christlich-buddhistischen Dialogs," in *Religion und Dialog in modernen Gesellschaften: Dokumentation der öffentlichen Auftaktveranstaltung eines internationalen Forschungsprojektes*, ed. Wolfram Weisse et al. (Münster: Waxmann, 2014), 39–60.

18 Julia Ipgrave et al., *Religion and Dialogue in the City: Case Studies on Interreligious Encounter in Urban Community and Education*, vol. 37, *Religious Diversity and Education in Europe* (Münster: Waxmann, 2018).

19 Ipgrave et al., *Religion and Dialogue in the City*.

20 Paul Ricoeur, *Wege der Anerkennung: Erkennen, Wiedererkennen, Anerkanntsein* (Frankfurt: Suhrkamp Verlag, 2006).

References

Amirpur, Katajun, Thorsten Knauth, Carola Roloff, and Wolfram Weisse, eds. *Perspektiven Dialogischer Theologie: Offenheit in den Religionen und eine Hermeneutik des interreligiösen Dialogs.* Series of the Academy of World Religions at Hamburg University: Religions in Dialogue 10. Münster: Waxmann, 2016.

Amirpur, Katajun, and Wolfram Weisse. *Religionen-Dialog-Gesellschaft: Analysen zur gegenwärtigen Situation und Impulse für eine dialogische Theologie.* Münster: Waxmann, 2015.

Bernhardt, Reinhold. "Jesus Christ as a Stumbling Block in Interreligious Dialogue?" In *Religions and Dialogue: International Approaches,* edited by Wolfram Weisse, Katajun Amirpur, Anna Körs, and Dörthe Vieregge, 139–50. Münster: Waxmann, 2014.

Bernhardt, Reinhold, and Perry Schmidt-Leukel. "Einleitung." In *Interreligiöse Theologie: Chancen und Probleme,* edited by Reinhold Bernhardt and Perry Schmidt-Leukel, 7–20. Zürich: TVZ Theologischer Verlag, 2013.

———. *Interreligiöse Theologie: Chancen und Probleme.* Zürich: TVZ Theologischer Verlag, 2013.

Clooney, Francis X. *Comparative Theology: Deep Learning across Religious Borders.* Oxford: Wiley-Blackwell, 2010.

Ipgrave, Julia, Thorsten Knauth, Anna Körs, Dörthe Vieregge, and Marie von der Lippe, eds. *Religion and Dialogue in the City: Case Studies on Interreligious Encounter in Urban Community and Education.* Vol. 37, *Religious Diversity and Education in Europe.* Münster: Waxmann, 2018.

King, Sally B. *Socially Engaged Buddhism.* Honolulu: University of Hawai'i Press, 2009.

Knauth, Thorsten, Carola Roloff, Katja Drechsler, Florian Jäckel, and Andreas Markowsky. "Auf dem Weg zu einer dialogisch-interreligiösen Hermeneutik." In *Perspektiven Dialogischer Theologie,* edited by Katajun Amirpur, Thorsten Knauth, Carola Roloff, and Wolfram Weisse, 207–324. Münster: Waxmann, 2016.

Knitter, Paul F. *Horizonte der Befreiung: Auf dem Weg zu einer pluralistischen Theologie der Religionen.* Frankfurt/Main: Lembeck, 1997.

———. "Interreligiöser Dialog: Bleibende Differenz oder kreatives Potenzial? Am Beispiel des christlich-buddhistischen Dialogs." In *Religion und Dialog in modernen Gesellschaften: Dokumentation der öffentlichen Auftaktveranstaltung eines internationalen Forschungsprojektes,* edited by Wolfram Weisse, Katajun Amirpur, Anna Körs, and Dörthe Vieregge, 39–60. Münster: Waxmann, 2014.

Küster, Volker. *Einführung in die Interkulturelle Theologie.* Göttingen: Vandenhoeck & Ruprecht, 2011.

Leirvik, Oddbjørn. *Interreligious Studies: A Relational Approach to Religious Activism and the Study of Religion.* London: Bloomsbury, 2014.

Meir, Ephraim. *Becoming Interreligious: Towards a Dialogical Theology from a Jewish Vantage Point.* Münster: Waxmann, 2017.

Moyaert, Marianne. "Ricoeur on the (Im-)possibility of a Global Ethics towards an Ethics of Fragile Interreligious Compromises." *Neue Zeitschrift für Systematische Theologie und Religionsphilosophie* 52, no. 4 (2010): 440–61.

Rambachan, Anantanand. *A Hindu Theology of Liberation: Not-Two Is Not One.* Albany: SUNY Press, 2014.

Ricoeur, Paul. *Wege der Anerkennung: Erkennen, Wiedererkennen, Anerkanntsein.* Frankfurt: Suhrkamp Verlag, 2006.

Roloff, Carola, and Wolfram Weisse, eds. *Dialogue in Buddhism and Hinduism: Public Presentations of the 14th Dalai Lama, Sallie B. King, Anantanand Rambachan, and Samdhong Rinpoche.* Documentation Series of the Academy of World Religions, vol. 2. Münster: Waxmann, 2015.

Schmidt-Leukel, Perry. "Interkulturelle Theologie als interreligiöse Theologie." *Evangelische Theologie* 71, no. 1 (2011): 4–16.

Weisse, Wolfram. "Ansätze zu einer Dialogischen Theologie vor dem Hintergrund religiöser Pluralisierung und Säkularisierung." In *Christentum und Europa: XVI; Europäischer Kongress für Theologie (10–13 September 2017 in Wien),* edited by Michael Meyer-Blank, 708–22. Leipzig: Europäische Verlagsanstalt, 2019.

———. "The European Research Project ReDi: Religion and Dialogue in Modern Societies; An Overview." *Religion & Education* 46, no. 1 (2019): 1–19.

Weisse, Wolfram, Carola Roloff, Thorsten Knauth, and Katajun Amirpur. "Einleitung." In *Perspektiven Dialogischer Theologie,* edited by Katajun Amirpur, Thorsten Knauth, Carola Roloff, and Wolfram Weisse, 9–28. Münster: Waxmann, 2016.

Weisse, Wolfram, Julia Ipgrave, Oddbjørn Leirvik, and Muna Tatari, eds. *Pluralisation of Theologies at European Universities.* Münster and New York: Waxmann, 2020.

Weisse, Wolfram, Katajun Amirpur, Anna Körs, and Dörthe Vieregge, eds. *Religions and Dialogue: International Approaches.* Series of the Academy of World Religions at Hamburg University: Religions in Dialogue 7. Münster: Waxmann, 2014.

18

Interreligious Theology and Truth Seeking

Perry Schmidt-Leukel

Let me state from the outset that I am not keen on labeling or on delineating new demarcations between one label and another. Neither am I keen on establishing a new discipline or subject area at universities in addition to, and distinction from, theology, philosophy of religion, and religious studies. I am also not interested in the question of whether what I call "interreligious theology" is, or is not, regarded (or ought to be regarded) as part of "interreligious studies." Instead, I am interested in something quite different, a question that I take to be important and urgent but not new. It is the age-old question of religious truth. What is, at least to some extent, new is the idea to pursue this question through a multireligious, interreligious, transreligious, or whatever it may be called (again, I am not into labels), collaborative effort that is not confined to the source material of one single religious tradition. Will such collaborative effort need its own distinct institutional space? Presumably this would be helpful, but it is not a necessary condition. My guess is rather that in the future, the theology (and its analogues) in every religious tradition will increasingly become interreligious.

Religious studies has largely abandoned questions of religious truth and focuses on finding the truth about religions (at least as long as it has not yet replaced the concept of "religion" by the concept of "culture," which—being also a concept of Western origin—might be the next candidate for which a replacement will be sought). But can we ever tell the truth *about* religion (at least hypothetically) without inquiring into the truth *of* religion? If someone sees a UFO with a crew of aliens, does it not make a world of difference whether there actually was or was not a UFO to be seen? It is the difference between cognition and hallucination, possibly between sanity and insanity. Or, to give another example, if we perceive ourselves as free agents (although within limits), does it not make a world of difference if this is a veridical cognition or an illusion created by a causally determined electrochemical machine? And if religion, as Schleiermacher famously held in the second of his speeches, is the "sense and taste for the Infinite" and "the immediate consciousness of the universal existence of all finite things, in and through the Infinite" (J. Oman's translation), does it not make a whole world of difference whether this "Infinite" is merely a chimera of the human mind or whether it is a reality to which the human mind is indeed open?[1]

There is a long tradition in European atheism or naturalism to regard religious diversity as evidence against the veracity of religion. Whether such atheism appears in the cynical (mentally hurt) and vulgar form of de Sade's essay *Dialogue between a Priest and a Dying Man*, in the noble words of d'Holbach's *System of Nature*, or in Hume's sophisticated *Enquiry concerning Human Understanding*, the argument remains the same: Religions are all at variance with each other. Hence they cannot all be true. Moreover, they all accuse each other as false, and thus it is most likely that all of them are right only in this respect; that is, they are all false. Today, the diversity of religions has become a tangible reality in many societies around the world. This, as the late Peter Berger emphasized in his last monograph, "undermines many of the certainties by which human beings used to live." It deprives "religion of its taken-for-granted quality," and "thus the management of doubt becomes a problem for every religious tradition."[2] Such doubt, however, springs from the premise that, as David Hume put it, "in matters of religion, whatever is different is contrary."[3] It is therefore an irrefutable and vital task for each religious tradition to manage such doubts by checking the accuracy of the doubt-producing premises. In other words, it is in the best interest of each religion to find out if their deepest hopes and convictions are really irreconcilable and hence mutually refuting, or if religious diversity can be, at least to a significant extent, explained as a diversity of compatible differences.[4] This is, by its own nature, a task that can be carried out only through a collaborative inquiry by means of an open-minded and serious theological dialogue or colloquy. This is what I call "interreligious theology."

Yet there is more to interreligious theology than this apologetic necessity. Finding out whether their differences are ultimately incompatible or compatible carries the promise for each among the religious traditions to arrive at a deeper understanding of the nature of its own faith and thereby of the faith of all of them. As early as 1971, Wilfred Cantwell Smith pointed out the need for a "world theology" in that sense:

> Theology is critical intellectualization of (and for) faith, and of the world as known in faith; and what we seek is a theology that will interpret the history of our race in a way that will give intellectual expression to our faith, the faith of all of us, and to our modern perception of the world.[5]

This, says Smith, has to be a "theology of religions" in which the religions are not the object (which is "the faith of all of us") but the subject.[6] Such joint theology or interreligious theology, I suggest, rests on *four principles* and should follow *four methodological guidelines*.[7]

First of all, it presupposes a *hermeneutics of trust* instead of suspicion, a theological principle of charity assuming that the ultimate reality that grounds and ensures the proper orientation and genuine well-being of human life is also known to other religious tradition although in different forms and different ways. This principle is affirmed by the inclusivist and pluralist approaches within the different traditions, while their exclusivist positions walk right into the trap of the atheist critique. A second principle is derived from intuition and affirms the *unity of reality*. This principle warrants that all genuine insights into reality will be compatible. It is foundational to the attempt of figuring out whether doctrinal differences must be read as ultimately incompatible or not. According to the third principle, interreligious theology should be seen as a process that is intrinsically *tied to interreligious discourse*. It is neither a theological "no-man's-land" nor something above or beyond the actual religions: it is their joint enterprise. And fourthly, it will be an *open process*, unfinished as a matter of principle, a new style of doing theology. Otherwise, its findings would become the dogmatics of a new religion, as in Whitehead's famous phrase: "the many become one, and are increased by one."[8]

Methodologically, interreligious theology should be *perspectival, imaginative, comparative*, and *constructive*. It is *perspectival* in that anyone involved is aware of his or her background assumptions and is not pretending to start from a neutral vantage point. One's background assumptions ought to be brought into the dialogue and kept open to change in the face of other perspectives. The latter happens through the *imaginative* effort of looking at the world, as much as possible, through the eyes of the other. In order to understand the other, it is not necessary to convert to the other's convictions. Rather, it is necessary to understand the reasons that motivate the other in his or her views, so that looking through the other's eyes becomes a genuine challenge. In looking through the other's eyes, one will gain a new perspective not only on the world but also on oneself. This may at times be painful, yet also all the more rewarding. Interreligious theology ought to be *comparative* in this sense. It should not assume the seemingly distanced attitude of phenomenological comparison but make one's own views part of the comparison, exposing them to possible challenges. In this way, interreligious comparison carries the promise of reciprocal illumination. Finally, interreligious theology needs to be *constructive* in pursuing mutual transformation. Its comparative efforts are not an end in itself. Reciprocal illumination implies reciprocal transformation. In gaining a better understanding of religious diversity, the self-understanding of one's own religious tradition will be affected. Diversity is a web of real and potential relations. An altered self-understanding will be the inevitable outcome of a clearer perception of interconnectedness. To quote Smith again: the "we-they" mode in understanding religious diversity will be transformed first into a "we-you" and finally into a "we-us" paradigm, "where we human beings learn, through critical analysis, empirical enquiry, and collaborative discourse, to conceptualise a world in which some of us are Christians, some of us are Muslims, some of us are Hindus."[9] This vision is in line with the pluralist approaches as they have begun to emerge within the various religious traditions.[10]

In gaining a better understanding of ourselves by means of a better understanding of our interrelatedness, we most likely also arrive at a better understanding of the structures in this web of relations. In following the discoveries of some early scholars in comparative religion, and some recent observations in intercultural philosophy and interreligious theology, I suggest that religious diversity is not entirely random and chaotic but displays, to a significant extent, fractal patterns.[11] That is, typological differences discerned between the major religious traditions reappear in the intrareligious diversity found within each of the traditions and can, *in nuce*, even be identified at the still-smaller level of the religious individual. Individuals often undergo different types of religiosity successively, in the course of their lifetime, or exhibit them simultaneously in various forms of religious hybridity. In the end, the typical patterns replicating in *inter*religious, *intra*religious, and *intra*subjective diversity may be rooted in the transcendental structures of the human mind as had already been speculated by Rudolf Otto. One implication of such a fractal perspective on religious diversity is that other religious traditions are never exactly the same nor ever completely different. Religions resemble each other in their internal diversity. Interreligious theology, in trying to make sense of interreligious diversity, is therefore continuous with ecumenical theology, which tries to make sense of intrareligious diversity. On closer investigation, it may be found that many of the fractal patterns are composed of compatible and necessary differences. Thus, Hume's premise that "in matters of religion, whatever is different is contrary," may very well turn out to be premature—and religious diversity may turn out as a rich, multifaceted, and powerful testimony to the basic veracity of faith.

Notes

1   John Hick, *An Interpretation of Religion: Human Responses to the Transcendent* (Basingstoke: Macmillan, 1989), 204–8.

2   Peter L. Berger, *The Many Altars of Modernity: Toward a Paradigm for Religion in a Pluralist Age* (Boston: De Gruyter, 2014), 9, 20, 32.

3   David Hume, *Enquiry concerning Human Understanding*, sect. 10, part 2.

4   Hick, *Interpretation of Religion*, 210–30.

5   Wilfred Cantwell Smith, *Towards a World Theology: Faith and the Comparative History of Religion* (Maryknoll, N.Y.: Orbis, 1989), 125. The book is based on a lecture series given in Birmingham in 1971 (1st ed., 1981).

6   Smith, *Towards a World Theology*, 124.

7   Perry Schmidt-Leukel, *Religious Pluralism and Interreligious Theology: The Gifford Lectures—An Extended Edition* (Maryknoll, N.Y.: Orbis, 2017), 130–46.

8   Alfred North Whitehead, *Process and Reality: An Essay in Cosmology*, corrected ed., ed. David Ray Griffin and Donald W. Sherburne (New York: Free Press, 1978), 21.

9   Smith, *Towards a World Theology*, 101.

10 On pluralist approaches within Judaism, Islam, Hinduism, Buddhism, and Chinese religions, see Schmidt-Leukel, *Religious Pluralism and Interreligious Theology*, 32–106; on the presuppositions and advantages of a pluralist approach within Christianity see Perry Schmidt-Leukel, *God beyond Boundaries: A Christian and Pluralist Theology of Religions* (Münster: Waxmann, 2017).

11 See Schmidt-Leukel, *Religious Pluralism and Interreligious Theology*, 222–45. For a multireligious and multidisciplinary discussion of this theory, see Paul F. Knitter and Alan Race, eds., *New Paths for Interreligious Theology: Perry Schmidt-Leukel's Fractal Interpretation of Religious Diversity* (Maryknoll, N.Y.: Orbis, 2019).

References

Berger, Peter L. *The Many Altars of Modernity: Toward a Paradigm for Religion in a Pluralist Age*. Boston: De Gruyter, 2014.

Hick, John. *An Interpretation of Religion: Human Responses to the Transcendent*. Basingstoke: Macmillan, 1989.

Knitter, Paul F., and Alan Race, eds. *New Paths for Interreligious Theology: Perry Schmidt-Leukel's Fractal Interpretation of Religious Diversity*. Maryknoll, N.Y.: Orbis, 2019.

Schmidt-Leukel, Perry. *God beyond Boundaries: A Christian and Pluralist Theology of Religions*. Münster: Waxmann, 2017.

———. *Religious Pluralism and Interreligious Theology: The Gifford Lectures—An Extended Edition*. Maryknoll, N.Y.: Orbis, 2017.

Smith, Wilfred Cantwell. *Towards a World Theology: Faith and the Comparative History of Religion*. Maryknoll, N.Y.: Orbis, 1989.

Whitehead, Alfred North. *Process and Reality: An Essay in Cosmology*. Corrected ed. Edited by David Ray Griffin and Donald W. Sherburne. New York: Free Press, 1978.

19

Vivekananda's Vision

Jeffery D. Long

In this chapter, I aim to contribute to the growing body of work in interreligious studies by briefly exploring Swami Vivekananda's philosophy of religion and its implications for interreligious, or interfaith, dialogue. Swami Vivekananda (1863–1902) is best known as the first Hindu spiritual teacher to gather a considerable following in the Western world, establishing the first Vedanta Society in New York in 1894, and as a major contributor to the early interfaith movement, through his celebrated lectures at the first Parliament of the World's Religions in Chicago in 1893. He is also known as the preeminent disciple of the nineteenth-century Bengali sage Sri Ramakrishna Paramahansa (1836–1886). Ramakrishna himself is known for his multireligious spiritual practices, by means of which he attained experiences of meditative absorption, or *samadhi*, through devoted contemplation not only of the varied Hindu deities and the impersonal Brahman of the Advaita Vedanta system of Hindu thought, but also through Islamic and Christian practices.[1]

Swami Vivekananda's philosophy of religion is deeply indebted to that of his teacher.[2] In fact, Vivekananda describes his own teaching as "my own interpretation of our ancient books, in the light which my Master shed upon them."[3] Vivekananda's teaching is not simply a restatement, though, of the teachings of Ramakrishna. Vivekananda had a highly creative and original mind, and he was also more conversant with Western thought than his master was. Ramakrishna emphasized the salvific efficacy of the world's religions, affirming that many paths could lead to the realization of the potential divinity within all beings. He can thus be characterized quite easily as a religious pluralist. Vivekananda does not part company with his master in this regard but gives a greater emphasis to the differences among religions and displays a leaning toward a Hindu inclusivism.

In brief, the implications of Swami Vivekananda's philosophy of religion for interreligious dialogue—and for dialogue across worldviews in general, for he also had a keen interest in science and in harmonizing the claims of religion and science—are that this philosophy gives a strong basis for such dialogue. This basis is twofold. It includes the ethical or moral imperative that one often finds presented as a rationale for interreligious dialogue. But it also includes an epistemic imperative rooted in the search for truth, and in the understanding that no religion is exhaustive in its conception of truth. There is always more to learn, always more to be gained from listening to the views of others. Ultimately, Vivekananda's vision is one of creative cross-fertilization, in which each religion, without losing its particular uniqueness, or the particular richness that it contributes to human consciousness, will nevertheless be positively transformed by absorbing truths and values from the others. Given Swami Vivekananda's prominence in the Western world and his celebrated influence at the inaugural Parliament of the World's Religions in Chicago in 1893, a scholarly grasp of his all-inclusive vision, with its moral and epistemic implications, belongs in a volume such as this one, which is dedicated to carving out the nature of interreligious studies for scholarship and research.

The Moral Imperative: Overcoming Sectarianism, Bigotry, and Fanaticism

Swami Vivekananda's first welcome address at the 1893 Chicago Parliament of the World's Religions, delivered on September 11 of that year, can be seen as a manifesto for the interfaith movement. He expresses pride in his native Hindu tradition. But this is not a pride born of a sense of inherent superiority or derived from an exclusivist theology that sees Hinduism as somehow necessary for human salvation. This pride is rooted, rather, in the ancient values of hospitality and acceptance that this tradition, at its best, has exhibited:

> I am proud to belong to a religion which has taught the world both tolerance and universal acceptance. We believe not only in universal toleration, but we accept all religions as true. I am proud to belong to a nation which has sheltered the persecuted and the refugees of all religions and all nations of the earth.[4]

Elsewhere, Vivekananda points out the insufficiency of the concept of "tolerance," indicating that the ideal to which humanity ought to aspire is not merely one of tolerance but one of acceptance:

> For so-called toleration is often blasphemy, and I do not believe in it. I believe in acceptance. Why should I tolerate? Toleration means that I think you are wrong and I am just allowing you to live. Is it not blasphemy to think that you and I are allowing others to live? I accept all religions that were in the past, and worship with them all . . . [and] I shall keep my heart open for all that may come in the future.[5]

The basis of this acceptance is the idea, found in the life and teaching of Ramakrishna, but also having precedent in numerous Hindu scriptures, that all religions lead to the highest goal:

> As the different streams having their sources in different places all mingle their water in the sea, so, O Lord, the different paths which men take through different tendencies, various though they appear, crooked or straight, all lead to Thee.[6]

Vivekananda is here quoting from an ancient text of the Shaiva tradition of Hinduism, the *Śiva Mahimna Stotra*. He then quotes from the *Bhagavad Gītā*:

> Whosoever comes to Me, through whatsoever form, I reach him; all men are struggling through paths which in the end lead to me.[7]

At the conclusion of his welcome address, he diagnoses what he takes to be the fundamental problem of interreligious relations, to which he takes his philosophy of universal acceptance to be a solution:

> Sectarianism, bigotry, and its horrible descendant, fanaticism, have long possessed this beautiful earth. They have filled the earth with violence, drenched it often and often with human blood, destroyed civilization and sent whole nations to despair. Had it not been for these horrible demons, human society would be far more advanced than it is now. But their time is come; and I fervently hope that the bell that tolled this morning in honour of this convention may be the death-knell of all fanaticism, of all persecutions with the sword or with the pen, and of all uncharitable feelings between persons wending their way to the same goal.[8]

Interreligious dialogue is thus a moral imperative. Mutual understanding, appreciation, and acceptance are essential, according to Vivekananda, for overcoming sectarianism, bigotry, and fanaticism, and thus enabling the evolution of society to a level "far more advanced than it is now."

The Epistemic Imperative: Interreligious Dialogue and the Search for Truth

Vivekananda, as a Hindu, views the Vedas as the highest source of truth, much as a Christian and a Muslim, respectively, would view the Bible and the Qur'an as the word of God. There is an important distinction, though, according to Vivekananda, between the "eternal Veda" affirmed by the Hindu tradition and set of books that go by this name. As Vivekananda elaborates:

> The whole body of supersensuous truths, having no beginning or end, and called by the name of the Vedas, is ever-existent. The Creator Himself is creating, preserving, and destroying the universe with the help of these truths. . . . But by the Vedas no books are meant. They mean the accumulated treasury of spiritual laws discovered by different persons in different times. Just as the law of gravitation existed before its discovery, and would exist if all humanity forgot it, so it is with the laws that govern the spiritual world.[9]

What is the relationship of the set of texts known as the Vedas and "the whole body of supersensuous truths" to which Vivekananda refers by this name? What is the relationship of this "eternal Veda" to actual texts? Vivekananda explains:

> The Hindus found their creed upon the ancient Vedas, a word derived from Vid, "to know." These are a series of books which, to our minds, contain the essence of all religion; but we do not think they alone contain the truths. They teach us the immortality of the soul. In every country and every human breast there is a natural desire to find a stable equilibrium— something that does not change.[10]

All knowledge, according to Swami Vivekananda, is Veda. It can be found in the Vedas but also in the texts of religions from every part of the world and every period of human history, as well as in the discoveries of modern science. Indeed, religion itself is seen by Vivekananda as a kind of "spiritual science."

No particular textual manifestation of eternal wisdom is complete, and, indeed, both Swami Vivekananda and Sri Ramakrishna repeatedly enjoin their followers to aim for a direct experience of ultimate reality rather than to content themselves with the deliverances of sacred books.

The imperfection of knowledge that can be captured in words and taught in texts is another motive, according to Vivekananda's thought, for interreligious dialogue. We can each learn from the vision of the other, for each of our individual visions are incomplete. Ramakrishna illustrates this with the popular Indian story of the blind men and the elephant:

Once some blind men chanced to come near an animal that someone told them was an elephant. They were asked what the elephant was like. The blind men began to feel its body. One of them said the elephant was like a pillar; he had touched only its leg. Another said it was like a winnowing-fan; he had touched only its ear. In this way the others, having touched its tail or belly, gave their different versions of the elephant. Just so, a man who has seen only one aspect of God limits God to that alone. It is his conviction that God cannot be anything else.[11]

Because each vision of God, offered by a different world religion, is incomplete, if we wish to advance in our understanding of truth, we need to listen to one another, incorporating insights from one another's traditions into our own, distinctive understanding. The idea is not that we will all convert to one another's religion, or that one religion will emerge triumphant over the rest, but that we will all be transformed through dialogue with one another. As Vivekananda explains:

Do I wish that the Christian would become Hindu? God forbid. Do I wish that the Hindu or Buddhist would become Christian? God forbid. The seed is put in the ground, and earth and air and water are placed around it. Does the seed become the earth, or the air, or the water? No. It becomes a plant, it develops after the law of its own growth, assimilates the air, the earth, and the water, converts them into plant substance, and grows into a plant. Similar is the case with religion. The Christian is not to become a Hindu or a Buddhist, nor a Hindu or a Buddhist to become a Christian. But each must assimilate the spirit of the others and yet preserve his individuality and grow according to his own law of growth.[12]

Conclusion

Such is Swami Vivekananda's organic vision for interreligious dialogue. Each of the world's religions captures some portion of the truth. Each is true, but each is only a portion. In order to have a more complete vision of truth, we must each study and learn from the others and assimilate the insights of the others into the matrix of our own understanding, constantly expanding our own vision of truth.

This vision has already been tremendously influential in both India and in the Western world. Vivekananda was a hero to the Mahatma, Mohandas K. Gandhi, who, like Vivekananda, famously affirmed:

Religions are different roads converging upon the same point. What does it matter that we take different roads so long as we reach the same goal? In reality there are as many religions as there are individuals. I believe in the fundamental truth of all great religions of the world. I believe that they are all God-given, and I believe that they were necessary for the people to whom these religions were revealed. And I believe that, if only we could all of us read the scriptures of different faiths from the standpoint of the followers of those faiths we should find that they were at bottom all one and were all helpful to one another.[13]

This vision informed Gandhi's resistance, and that of his subsequent followers in India, to the emergence of Hindu nationalism: a resistance that led to Gandhi's tragic assassination on January 30, 1948.

In the West, Vivekananda's vision shaped such approaches to religious diversity as that of Aldous Huxley, found in his famous work *The Perennial Philosophy*, as well as those of religion scholar Huston Smith and philosopher of religion John Hick. The pluralistic turn in the philosophy of religion and in Christian theology, as well as the movements for greater inclusion and welcome to the religious other by which this turn has been informed—and that it has, itself, also informed—certainly includes within its genealogy the Hindu monk who stood on the stage at the Chicago parliament and welcomed his audience with the words, "Sisters and Brothers of America."

Notes

1   Ramakrishna's pluralistic spiritual path has been documented in numerous works, probably the best known of which, in English, are Swami Nikhilananda's *The Gospel of Sri Ramakrishna* (New York: Ramakrishna-Vivekananda Center, 1942), which is a translation of the Bengali *Śrīśrīrāmakṛṣṇakathāmṛta*, by Mahendranath Gupta; and Christopher Isherwood's *Sri Ramakrishna and His Disciples* (Hollywood: Vedanta, 1965). Certainly, the most detailed source on his life is the Bengali *Śrīśrīrāmakṛṣṇalīlāprasaṅga*, by Swami Saradananda, recently translated into English by Swami Chetanananda as *Sri Ramakrishna and His Divine Play* (St. Louis: Vedanta Society of St. Louis, 2003).

2   Sri Ramakrishna's own philosophy is most fully elaborated by Ayon Maharaj in his work *Infinite Paths to Infinite Reality: Sri Ramakrishna and Cross-Cultural Philosophy of Religion* (Oxford: Oxford University Press, 2018).

3   Swami Vivekananda, *Complete Works* (Mayavati, India: Advaita Ashrama, 1979), 5:186.

4   Vivekananda, *Complete Works*, 1:3.

5   Vivekananda, *Complete Works*, 2:374.

6   Vivekananda, *Complete Works*, 1:4.

7   Vivekananda, *Complete Works*, 1:4.

8   Vivekananda, *Complete Works*, 1:4.

9   Vivekananda, *Complete Works*, 6:181.

10   Vivekananda, *Complete Works* 1:338.

11   Nikhilananda, *Gospel of Sri Ramakrishna*, 191.

12   Vivekananda, *Complete Works*, 1:24.

13   Mohandas K. Gandhi, cited in Glyn Richards, *A Sourcebook of Modern Hinduism* (London: Curzon, 1985), 156, 157.

References

Isherwood, Christopher. *Sri Ramakrishna and His Disciples*. Hollywood: Vedanta, 1965.

Maharaj, Ayon. *Infinite Paths to Infinite Reality: Sri Ramakrishna and Cross-Cultural Philosophy of Religion*. Oxford: Oxford University Press, 2018.

Nikhilananda, Swami. *The Gospel of Sri Ramakrishna*. New York: Ramakrishna-Vivekananda Center, 1942.

Richards, Glyn. *A Sourcebook of Modern Hinduism*. London: Curzon, 1985.

Saradananda, Swami. *Sri Ramakrishna and His Divine Play*. Translated by Swami Chetanananda. St. Louis: Vedanta Society of St. Louis, 2003.

Vivekananda, Swami. *Complete Works*. Mayavati, India: Advaita Ashrama, 1979.

IV

CONTEMPORARY CHALLENGES

20

Decolonizing the Study of Religion

Kevin Minister

The emergence of the field of interreligious studies could be read as a subfield of the study of religion focused on discrete moments in which persons orienting around religion differently interact and on the implications of those interactions.[1] Rather than read the emergence of interreligious studies in this way, I would like to suggest that interreligious studies represents a broader shift in religious studies and how we theorize the nature of religion. In particular, interreligious studies emerges in contrast to the world religions paradigm that has dominated and continues to dominate religious studies. The theorization of religion in interreligious studies has the potential to redress the failures and coloniality of world religions as the dominant model of making sense of religious ways of being. In this short chapter, I contend that the *inter*active, *inter*sectional, and *inter*personal approaches of interreligious studies have wide-ranging implications for redressing the colonial legacy of the study of religion when interreligious studies is grounded in a commitment to liberation.

In *The Invention of World Religions*, Tomoko Masuzawa demonstrates that the world religions framework for conceptualizing the nature of religion and religious difference assumes, first, the ability to identify, extract, and prioritize religious beliefs and practices over against other social and cultural ways of being and, second, the ability to essentialize universal forms of religion that can be compared and contrasted. On the basis of these assumptions, Masuzawa argues that world religions has been from its origins "a discourse of secularization; at the same time, it was clearly a discourse of othering."[2] The very framework of world religions, according to Masuzawa, perpetuates the colonial project by submitting the world to European ways of knowing and normalizing the identity of "the West."[3] The concept of "multiple religious belonging" emerged as an attempt to shore up the failures of the world religions framework to accurately represent the complicated reality of religious identities outside of "Western religions." But scholars now recognize that the category of "multiple religious belonging" is itself redundant because all religious ways of being are contextually constituted through the interaction of multiple ways of being that can never be reduced to a conceptual whole.[4] In the same way, Jonathan Z. Smith's critique that the study of religion has had "an ideological emphasis on purity of lineage" highlights the colonial essence of the world religions framework that continues to obscure the intermingling of religious ways of being in the world.[5] Yet, even as critiques of the failures and coloniality of theorizing religion through the world religions framework seem ubiquitous today, world religions remains the dominant framework for structuring curricula, departments, and publishing in religious studies, making world religions still the de facto theoretical model for the study of religion. Decolonizing the study of religion requires addressing the flows of power and inequalities created by the construction of religious difference that separates religion from ecological contexts, the signification of bodies, and human encounters. In what follows, I argue that interreligious studies marks a theoretical intervention in the study of religion capable of working toward the decolonization of the study of religion in three ways, namely through *inter*active, *inter*sectional, and *inter*personal approaches.

First, interreligious approaches emphasize the *inter*active nature of lived religion as emerging from the dynamic encounters of religious persons with their environments.[6] The focus on the interactive nature of lived religion perceives religious ways of being as emerging from material environments, connecting interreligious studies to new materialist understandings of religion. As William Connolly argues, religious ways of being have always been marked out over against other ways of being in the world—the interaction of different ways of being religious is fundamental to the nature of religion.[7] But religious ways of being emerge not only in relation to the social, human context but as a part of ecological environments. As Robin Wall Kimmerer demonstrates in relation to indigenous traditions,[8] and David Haberman shows in Krishna worship in Northern India,[9] religious ways of being emerge through interactions with trees, waters, and rocks. Religious ways of being are, therefore, shaped by the particular ecological contexts in which they are lived out and shape the environmental context. All religious ways of being emerge in these dynamic and unpredictable interactions with communities both human and more than human (though some traditions are more self-reflective about these interactions than others). Acknowledging the emergent nature of religious ways of being through interaction with other ways of being, ecological places, and events is essential to undermining the colonial emphasis on purity of lineage in the field that tends to give priority to white, Western modes of religiosity. Emphasizing the interactive nature of lived religion creates openings for serious engagement with the multiplicity of (particularly nonwhite and non-Western) traditions that have been historically relegated to areas of specialization as impure, derivative, or local. Moreover, the interactive nature of lived religion requires reengagement with white, "Western" traditions to highlight how they include a diversity of traditions that are all products of a process of emergence shaped by other ways of being, ecologies, and events. Once we locate lived religion as part of an interactive ecology, we can attend to the ways power flows in these embodied encounters.

Second, approaching the study of religion in interreligious ways allows us to take the embodied nature of religion seriously with *inter*sectional analyses.[10] In her examination of the identification of a Sikh man as a "terrorist fag" in the wake of 9/11, Jasbir Puar demonstrates that raced, gendered, and sexed bodies bear the signification of religious difference and interrelation.[11] In this way, religion, race, gender, and sexuality are always already mutually constituted as a complex and even contradictory assemblage of bodily markers that affect both the experience of bodies and how those bodies are experienced. As Puar makes clear, this is never as simple as locating a positionality of an identity as the stable addition of identity markers, because such identity-based approaches to intersectionality box people in as a way to make them visible and eligible for inclusion. Instead, intersectional approaches to religious ways of being must attend the complex and contradictory ways that identity markers collude to affect bodies within specific times and spaces with openness to how these assemblages of identity change and to movements that seek to affect such change. Understanding the implications of how people who orient around religion differently interact requires intersectional analyses of how power flows through religious identities, practices, and significations because the racing, gendering, sexing, and nationalizing of religious embodiment both is socially affective of how others perceive, feel about, and interact with religious people and affects the way that individuals experience being a religious person. The world religions model relegates the racing, gendering, sexing, and nationalizing of religious embodiment as a subcategory of the study of religion to a form of religious particularity, making these categories *theoretically* optional to address, obscuring the ways they are integral to the constitution of religious ways of being, and evading the constructions of power they deploy. Interreligious studies opens up the possibility of recognizing that intersectional analysis is integral to any theorization of religion because religious ways of being and the embodied experience of religious persons is constituted through these assemblages of difference.

Third, in awareness of the emergent and embodied nature of religion, we must take seriously the role of *inter*personal encounters in humanizing interreligious approaches to the study of religion by recognizing the (limited but real) agency of religious persons in determining how they live out their religious ways of being in the world. Tyler Roberts' humanistic method for the study of religion sets a helpful trajectory here as he draws on the works of Robert Orsi and Saba Mahmood to exemplify how to study religion as an encounter.[12] Treating the study of religion as a genuine encounter requires openness to being surprised and necessitates resisting reducing the religious ways of being to either simple social formation or ideology. Similarly, engaging the study of religion as an encounter leaves a valuable indeterminacy about whether or not certain religious ways of being might still be important to how persons who do not identify as religious live in the world. Attending to interpersonal encounter allows us to attend to interreligious experiences of fitting and misfitting, which the disability theory of Rosemary Garland-Thompson points out are encounters of body-subjects and the built environment, shaped by social organization, context, and physical matter.[13] Only by attending to the experiences of fitting and misfitting can we engage the ways that colonial legacies have built communities and societies around certain (religious) ways of being, and how this designs power differentials into our built social environment (including the structuring of time, labor and professionalism, public space and citizenship, etc). Furthermore, by acknowledging the material emergence of religion in context and the agency of religious subjects, interreligious studies demonstrates greater honesty and (dis)comfort in negotiating the interaction of scholars with religious persons and communities. Religious studies scholars cannot help but affect the persons and communities they study and be affected by them. By rejecting a sharp distinction between academics and activists, interreligious studies remains open to and self-reflective about the transformative encounters that can and do occur in the study of religion. Openness to and reflexivity about such encounters is essential to subverting the coloniality of the world religions paradigm that presumed the ability of scholars to operate as objective interpreters of religious ways of being.

Interreligious studies addresses the coloniality of the world religions paradigm with the potential to transform the discipline of religious studies through
theoretical interventions that illuminate the interactive, intersectional, and interpersonal nature of religion. But the capacity of interreligious studies to live
up to this potential depends on how liberatory interreligious studies can be.[14]
Because interreligious studies is immediately relevant to navigating religious
diversity by cultivating the knowledge and skills to understand and collaborate
with those who orient around religion differently, it is vital to the exchange of
ideas, goods, and services in the wake of globalization in a postcolonial era.
While this makes interreligious studies valuable and justifiable in an increasingly professionalized academy, interreligious studies must resist cooptation
by global capitalism's drive to maximize the inclusion of difference through
incorporation into the free market system to avoid perpetuating the colonial
legacy of religious studies in a postcolonial context. It is not a bad thing that
interreligious competence has become a vital professional skill. But a fundamental commitment to cultivating liberatory engagements must permeate every dimension of interreligious studies if it hopes to transform the coloniality
of world religions and most accurately represent the multiplicity of ways of being religious. For this reason, the extent to which the theoretical interventions
of interreligious studies transform the field of religious studies will all depend
on how liberatory interreligious studies can be.

Notes

1   This is one of the most commonly used definitions of the field, drawing on
    Eboo Patel, "Towards a Field of Interfaith Studies," *Liberal Education* 99
    (2013): 38.

2   Tomoko Masuzawa, *The Invention of World Religions* (Chicago: University of
    Chicago Press, 2005), 20.

3   Through a genealogical critique of the field, she argues that these two gener-
    ative assumptions of the nature of world religions "conjointly enable this dis-
    course to do the vital work of churning the stuff of Europe's ever-expanding
    epistemic domain, and of forging from that ferment an enormous apparition:
    the essential identity of the West" (Masuzawa, *Invention of World Religions*,
    20).

4   See for example, Paul Hedges, "Multiple Religious Belonging after Religion:
    Theorising Strategic Religious Participation in a Shared Religious Landscape
    as a Chinese Mode," *Open Theology* 3 (2017): 48–72; Devaka Premawardhana,
    "The Unremarkable Hybrid: Aloysius Pieris and the Redundancy of Multiple
    Religious Belonging," *Journal of Ecumenical Studies* 46, no. 1 (2011); Jeannine
    Hill Fletcher, "We Are All Hybrids," *Monopoly on Salvation? A Feminist Ap-
    proach to Religious Pluralism* (New York: Continuum, 2005); and Michelle

Voss Roberts, "Religious Belonging and the Multiple," *Journal of Feminist Studies in Religion* 26, no. 1 (2010): 43–62.

5   Jonathan Z. Smith, *Relating Religion: Essays in the Study of Religion* (Chicago: University of Chicago Press, 2004), 171.

6   See chapters in this volume by Gustafson and Brottveit on lived religion and empirical approaches to the field.

7   William Connolly, *Pluralism* (Durham, N.C.: Duke University Press, 2005), 27.

8   Robin Wall Kimmerer, *Braiding Sweetgrass: Indigenous Wisdom, Scientific Knowledge, and the Teachings of Plants* (Minneapolis: Milkweed Editions, 2013).

9   David Haberman, *Journey through the Twelve Forests: An Encounter with Krishna* (Oxford: Oxford University Press, 1994); and *River of Love in an Age of Pollution: The Yamuna River of Northern India* (Berkeley: University of California Press, 2006).

10 Kimberle Crenshaw, "Mapping the Margins: Intersectionality, Identity Politics, and Violence against Women of Color," *Stanford Law Review* 43, no. 6 (1991): 1241–99.

11 Jasbir Puar, *Terrorist Assemblages: Homonationalism in Queer Times*, tenth anniversary ed. (Durham, N.C.: Duke University Press, 2007), 195–96.

12 Tyler Roberts, *Encountering Religion: Responsibility and Criticism after Secularism* (New York: Columbia University Press, 2013), 114–18.

13 Rosemary Garland-Thompson, "Misfits: A Feminist Materialist Disability Concept," *Hypatia* 26, no. 3 (2011): 592–95.

14 I am drawing on a question posed by Lori Patton at a session of the book *Interreligious/Interfaith Studies: Defining a New Field* in the Interreligious and Interfaith Studies Unit at the 2018 American Academy of Religion: "How liberatory can interreligious studies be?" (Lori Patton, respondent to *Interreligious/Interfaith Studies: Defining a New Field*, session at the annual meeting of the American Academy of Religion, Denver, November 19, 2018).

References

Connolly, William. *Pluralism*. Durham, N.C.: Duke University Press, 2005.
Crenshaw, Kimberle. "Mapping the Margins: Intersectionality, Identity Politics, and Violence against Women of Color." *Stanford Law Review* 43, no. 6 (1991): 1241–99.
Fletcher, Jeannine Hill. "We Are All Hybrids." In *Monopoly on Salvation? A Feminist Approach to Religious Pluralism*. New York: Continuum, 2005.
Garland-Thompson, Rosemary. "Misfits: A Feminist Materialist Disability Concept." *Hypatia* 26, no. 3 (2011): 592–95.
Haberman, David. *Journey through the Twelve Forests: An Encounter with Krishna*. Oxford: Oxford University Press, 1994.

———. *River of Love in an Age of Pollution: The Yamuna River of Northern India.* Berkeley: University of California Press, 2006.

Hedges, Paul. "Multiple Religious Belonging after Religion: Theorising Strategic Religious Participation in a Shared Religious Landscape as a Chinese Mode." *Open Theology* 3 (2017): 48–72.

Kimmerer, Robin Wall. *Braiding Sweetgrass: Indigenous Wisdom, Scientific Knowledge, and the Teachings of Plants.* Minneapolis: Milkweed Editions, 2013.

Masuzawa, Tomoko. *The Invention of World Religions.* Chicago: University of Chicago Press, 2005.

Patton, Lori. Respondent to *Interreligious/Interfaith Studies: Defining a New Field.* Session at the annual meeting of the American Academy of Religion, Denver, November 19, 2018.

Premawardhana, Devaka. "The Unremarkable Hybrid: Aloysius Pieris and the Redundancy of Multiple Religious Belonging." *Journal of Ecumenical Studies* 46, no. 1 (2011).

Puar, Jasbir. *Terrorist Assemblages: Homonationalism in Queer Times.* Tenth anniversary ed. Durham, N.C.: Duke University Press, 2007.

Roberts, Michelle Voss. "Religious Belonging and the Multiple." *Journal of Feminist Studies in Religion* 26, no. 1 (2010): 43–62.

Roberts, Tyler. *Encountering Religion: Responsibility and Criticism after Secularism.* New York: Columbia University Press, 2013.

Smith, Jonathan Z. *Relating Religion: Essays in the Study of Religion.* Chicago: University of Chicago Press, 2004.

21

Decolonizing Interreligious Studies

Paul Hedges

Although a new field of study, and still in the process of being defined (with this volume being a notable contribution to this),[1] it is imperative that, in this foundational period, interreligious studies (hereafter IRS) grapples with questions of colonialism, postcolonialism, neocolonialism, decolonization, and orientalism. I will shortly define my use of these terms, but first I will state the reasons for the importance of this. Academia as a whole, including especially the academic study of religion, has been embroiled—if not complicit—in the shaping of the world from a Western perspective. From defining what we mean by "religion," to determining which areas of study or culture are given priority or valorized, the academic study of religion has often been part of the orientalist project. Within this, Western norms, values, experiences, cultural perspectives, and agendas have been placed upon the rest of the world in terms of how it is studied, interpreted, understood, and explained. The imperial regimes of power (economic, cultural, and military) have underlain this project, and they explain the dominance that in recent centuries has accompanied Western hegemony in many areas. Today, academics are increasingly aware of this problem, and many disciplines are grappling with the issues raised by this. As a relatively young academic field, IRS has the possibility to seek to define its terms of study, and its modes of operation, in opposition to previous orientalist practices. This is not to say that there is any one way to do this or a single way to escape this heritage. Indeed, given the problems raised, and their nature, it may not be possible to ever be entirely successful in decolonizing academic studies. Nevertheless, the attempt is itself worth pursuing.

Defining the Terms: Postcolonialism, Decolonization, and More

For the purposes of this chapter, I offer working definitions of a range of terms that may be employed in this context. As a first note, and following Walter Mignolo,[2] I would note that I do not see postcolonialism and decolonization as distinct or conflicting perspectives. Though some have drawn this distinction, following Mignolo I would note that they refer to similar practices but ones that have arisen in different contexts: "postcolonialism" has often named this agenda in Asia, and "decolonization" has been the term used in Latin America as well as in indigenous studies. Here, though, I use them in two distinct ways. I employ "postcolonialism" as a generic term that defines the broad field of attempts to resist, or offer an alternative to, orientalism. "Decolonization" I will use to refer to the ways in which we attempt to make strategic moves to change modes of study. As such, we may wish to decolonize our curricula as part of a postcolonial agenda to ensure our ways and areas of study are not entirely Western.

"Orientalism," I employ here, following Edward Said's groundbreaking work, as the way that generations of Western scholarship—as an exercise of power/politics—have been complicit in enforcing Western agendas upon the way the world is understood.[3] Importantly, though, I am critical of aspects of Said's work and especially of some of his interpreters, who have problematical-ly sought to tar all (Western) academics as entirely orientalist or to enhance the dichotomy of "East" and "West" as distinct and discrete spheres.[4] Space does not allow me to expand on this at length; however, it is worth noting some key points raised by a variety of postcolonial scholars among others. One, Said's work seems to disempower the Orient as always subject to Western control, which neglects periods when it has itself been in power. Two, some (Western) academics have not simply distorted or misrepresented the Orient to enhance the West—indeed, it is in part because some academic work is more accurate than others that we can determine that others have misinterpreted the data.[5] Third, it potentially reinforces the binary of East and West, making it, in Richard King's terms, a "hyper-reality."[6]

We should also consider "colonialism" and "neocolonialism." Colonialism refers here to situations where an outside group exerts direct power and control (normally via some form of military occupation or coercion) over another group. Neocolonialism refers here to situations—often after colonial rule—

where the situation of dependency on the previous colonial power is maintained through various forms of hegemonic control, which may be cultural influence, economic dominance, or even potential military exertion. Often this is depicted or portrayed simply as related to the period and context of European (then American) colonialism; however, we must be aware that it is far more than this. Colonial powers have operated throughout history, while, as postcolonial scholars in India have noted, the situation of dominance can be perpetuated by an elite group within one country against others, the subalterns, of that country. Akin to Marxist critiques of the control of capital, certain groups dominate the means of production broadly construed (they control, inter alia, the definition of law, access to education, the generation of finance, the control of the military and police) and so exert control over others.

Decolonizing the Study of Religion

Within this context, a large number of factors need to be considered in the study of religion. As mentioned, the terminology of "religion" and how it is conceptualized has been associated with the colonial legacy. As is well known, the modern meaning of religion and religions developed from around the sixteenth century as Europeans "discovered" for themselves (they had, of course, been discovered by others in their own contexts already) the religious worlds around them. Therefore, we came to speak of "religion"—and most especially "the world religions"—through a lens shaped by a modern, Western, and (Protestant) Christian perspective. It was imagined that around the world various things like Christianity existed, each defined by a particular "scripture," with a "church"-like organization, sets of "beliefs," and a hierarchy of "priests" as leaders. Critiques of the so-called world religions paradigm have shown that this particular set of characterizations is quite false and misrepresents the way that religious behavior, practice, and institutions occur in other places.[7] An even more radical critique suggests that even my language here is problematic, because it presumes that we can identify this common ground of the "religious." As such, we do not simply replace the world religions paradigm to describe religious aspects of culture but more radically suggest that the very terms "religion," "religions," and "religious" are meaningless or simply Western scholarly imaginaries.[8] However, this seems to rely upon a deeply problematic understanding both of the nature and use of language and of the problem at stake in defining "religion." Yes, to speak of religion in the ways we do is to use language developed within a colonial context that is both English-language speaking, modern, and Christian; however, so is almost anything meaningful we can say. These critiques apply equally to the terms "culture," "society," "philosophy," "art," "human," "politics," "economics," and so forth. However, extreme critics of religion tend to assume it is some unique problem with this one word, when it quite simply is not.[9] We can employ "religion" and many other terms as what have been termed "essentially contested concepts." However, the way we speak about "religion" must be done carefully in ways that avoid the world religions paradigm model, a point that leads us to a number of other issues.

When we speak about a religion we often ask what the beliefs are. This prioritizes a predominantly (but not uniquely) Christian paradigm, that a tradition or religious worldview is defined by beliefs, creedal statements, and so forth. In many contexts, this is at best a secondary consideration. Again, to ask about texts—often assumed to be foundational/originary—as the "scriptural foundation" is a very Protestant dynamic, as the belief that tradition changes, and that oral teachings, or bodily practices are equally or even more significant abounds in many traditions. Attention also needs to be paid to traditions beyond Christianity, and beyond the so-called Abrahamic monotheisms (Judaism, Christianity, and Islam), to include not just other "great" traditions but also smaller (numerically) or lesser-known traditions, including indigenous traditions. We could continue, but within the current limits of space this outlines the way that studies of religion need to be decolonized.[10]

Interreligious Studies and Decolonization

While not only developing from the academic study of religion, the kinds of tropes discussed above—about what "religion" is—are predominant in many fields of study. As a distinct field, IRS should therefore seek to work in ways that counter such orientalist projections. Rather than developing any particular issue in detail, I will outline a range of issues that scholars of IRS should be alert to.

First, religion is not a sui generis category but a culturally determined one that can be spoken of as an essentially contested concept. Its nature is determined not by Western and Christian presuppositions but by attention to a wider global range of manifestations of what we may analytically define as religious.

Second, developing a point related to the problematic world religions paradigm, to imagine religions as distinct and clearly bounded territories of belonging, identity, and belief is to do conceptual violence to the nature of religious phenomena in many parts of the globe. It may fit a predominantly Protestant paradigm (and a wider Christian/Abrahamic paradigm—though even here it is not the only possible paradigm), but it certainly does not speak to, for instance, the Chinese cultural world where what has been termed "strategic religious participation" (SRP) in a "shared religious landscape" (SRL) is more normal.[11] That is to say, people may naturally cross and live between what we often imagine as fixed or solid boundaries of religious identities/traditions. Certainly, in studies on what is often termed "multiple religious belonging" (MRB), IRS has challenged this. However, in envisaging MRB, too many studies assume Western/Christian norms, and understanding contexts such as SRP in an SRL is imperative to decolonizing perspectives.[12]

Third, our methods and modes of study should not be limited only to a strict Western "canon" of accepted scholarship. Method and theory can come from beyond this context and must. This is a point we have not directly stressed above. However, it is an area that perhaps IRS can help develop. Being inherently interdisciplinary, and/or multidisciplinary, IRS is already open to methodological polymorphism, and so maybe it provides an opening for this. However, work remains to be done developing such perspectives.

Conclusion

Being embedded in Western academia, IRS starts with many existing orientalist notions; however, many scholars in this field are alert to postcolonial concerns. Certainly, as IRS develops, if it is to successfully decolonize, it must be aware that many basic terms and concepts from which it builds do have a colonial or very Western (Protestant) Christian heritage that may be challenged and/or complemented by perspectives from elsewhere. It is the author's hope that IRS may develop as an exemplary site of decolonized academic study.

Notes

1   Two of the standard definitions of the field include those found in Oddbjørn Leirvik, *Interreligious Studies: A Relational Approach to Religious Activism and the Study of Religion* (London: Bloomsbury, 2014); and Paul Hedges, "Interreligious Studies," in *Encyclopedia of Sciences and Religions*, ed. Anne Runehov and Lluis Oviedo (New York: Springer, 2013), 1176–80. More recently, see Eboo Patel, Jennifer Howe Peace, and Noah Silverman, eds., *Interreligious/Interfaith Studies: Defining a New Field* (Boston: Beacon, 2018).

2   Walter Mignolo, "On Subaltern and Other Agencies," *Postcolonial Studies* 8, no. 4 (2005): 381–407.

3   Edward W. Said, *Orientalism* (New York: Pantheon, 1978).

4   See on this a variety of works, including J. J. Clark, *Oriental Enlightenment: The Encounter between Asian and Western Thought* (London: Routledge, 2006); and Paul Hedges, *Understanding Religion: Theories and Methods for Studying Religiously Diverse Societies* (Berkeley: University of California Press, 2021).

5   Relativist theories that suggest everything is only interpretation, and that as such we cannot speak of any interpretations being "better" than any others because we all manifest various biases, are simply incoherent. It is only because we would "know" that such biases exist that we can make such claims, which itself is claiming that one's own interpretation (in this case of relativism) is a "better" interpretation than others (in this case non-relativism).

6   Richard King, *Orientalism and Religion: Postcolonial Theory, India and "The Mystic East"* (London: Routledge, 1999).

7   See Christopher R. Cotter and David G. Robertson, *After World Religions: Reconstructing Religious Studies* (London: Routledge, 2016); and Hedges, *Understanding Religion*.

8   The standard statement is often seen as being Jonathan Z. Smith's "Religion, Religions, Religious," in *Relating Religion: Essays in the Study of Religion* (Chicago: University of Chicago Press, 1994), 179–96. Although there he suggests that the adjective "religious" remains useful even if "religion" as a noun is not. For a discussion of one argument against any use of religion and a rebuttal of it, see Paul Hedges, "Discourse on Discourses: Why We Still Need the Terminology of 'Religion' and 'Religions,'" *Journal of Religious History* 38, no.1 (2013): 132–48.

9   See Kevin Schilbrack, "A Realist Social Ontology of Religion," *Religion* 47, no. 2 (2017): 161–78; and Paul Hedges, "Deconstructing Religion: Some Thoughts on Where We Go from Here—a Hermeneutical Proposal," *Exchange* 64, no. 3 (2018): 5–24. Further elucidation can be found in Hedges, *Understanding Religion*.

10 For a discussion of some of these problems, see Paul Hedges, "Decolonising the Study of Religion (in Relation to the Social and Human Sciences)," *Logosdao*, March 12, 2018, https://logosdao.wordpress.com/2018/03/12/decolonising-the-study-of-religion-in-relation-to-the-social-and-human-sciences/; and Malory Nye, "Some Thoughts on the Decolonization of Religious Studies," *Religion Bites*, October 14, 2017, https://medium.com/religion-bites/decolonisation-of-religious-studies-993727c6d1bc. See also Hedges, *Understanding Religion*.

11 Paul Hedges, "Multiple Religious Belonging after Religion: Theorising Strategic Religious Participation in a Shared Religious Landscape as a Chinese Model," *Open Theology* 3 (2017): 48–72.

12 See also Paul Hedges, "Strategic Religious Participation in a Shared Religious Landscape: A Model for Westerners?" in *Theology without Walls: The Transreligious Imperative*, ed. Jerry Martin (London: Routledge, 2020), 165–71.

References

Clark, J. J. *Oriental Enlightenment: The Encounter between Asian and Western Thought*. London: Routledge, 2006.
Cotter, Christopher R., and David G. Robertson. *After World Religions: Reconstructing Religious Studies*. London: Routledge, 2016.

Hedges, Paul. "Decolonising the Study of Religion (in Relation to the Social and Human Sciences)." *Logosdao*, March 12, 2018. https://logosdao.wordpress .com/2018/03/12/decolonising-the-study-of-religion-in-relation-to-the-social -and-human-sciences/.

———. "Deconstructing Religion: Some Thoughts on Where We Go from Here—a Hermeneutical Proposal." *Exchange* 64, no. 3 (2018): 5–24.

———. "Discourse on Discourses: Why We Still Need the Terminology of 'Religion' and 'Religions.'" *Journal of Religious History* 38, no. 1 (2013): 132–48.

———. "Interreligious Studies." In *Encyclopedia of Sciences and Religions*, edited by Anne Runehov and Lluis Oviedo, 1176–80. New York: Springer, 2013.

———. "Multiple Religious Belonging after Religion: Theorising Strategic Religious Participation in a Shared Religious Landscape as a Chinese Model." *Open Theology* 3 (2017): 48–72.

———. "Strategic Religious Participation in a Shared Religious Landscape: A Model for Westerners?" In *Theology without Walls: the Transreligious Imperative*, edited by Jerry Martin, 165–71. London: Routledge, 2020.

———. *Understanding Religion: Theories and Methods for Studying Religiously Diverse Societies*. Berkeley: University of California Press, 2021.

King, Richard. *Orientalism and Religion: Postcolonial Theory, India and "The Mystic East."* London: Routledge, 1999.

Leirvik, Oddbjørn. *Interreligious Studies: A Relational Approach to Religious Activism and the Study of Religion*. New York: Bloomsbury, 2014.

Mignolo, Walter. "On Subaltern and Other Agencies." *Postcolonial Studies* 8, no. 4 (2005): 381–407.

Patel, Eboo, Jennifer Howe Peace, and Noah Silverman, eds. *Interreligious/Interfaith Studies: Defining a New Field*. Boston: Beacon, 2018.

Said, Edward W. *Orientalism*. New York: Pantheon, 1978.

Schilbrack, Kevin. "A Realist Social Ontology of Religion." *Religion* 47, no. 2 (2017): 161–78.

Smith, Jonathan Z. "Religion, Religions, Religious." In *Relating Religion: Essays in the Study of Religion*, 179–96. Chicago: University of Chicago Press, 1994.

22

Secular Imperatives

Kate McCarthy

New academic disciplines are born out of the imposition of new circumstances—the presence of new data or the demands of new voices—on old frameworks. Interreligious studies is developing with a remarkable level of intentionality and self-reflection about this process. Contemporary patterns of religious affiliation, unaffiliation, and interaction reflect a landscape dramatically different from the stable sets of belief and practice that shaped the formation of both the interfaith movement and the academic discipline of religious studies. At the center of this shift are questions of secularity. Can interreligious studies, rooted in normative and faith-based visions of interreligious harmony, find a place in a secular academy deeply suspicious of such efforts? What is the place of nonreligious actors in the analysis of interreligious relations? And what does the secularized "immanent frame" of the contemporary West mean for the subject and methods of the academic study of religion itself? If it centers these questions, interreligious studies stands to make critical contributions to the discipline and to the urgent demands of pluralist societies.

The reality of religious difference is of course nothing new, and scholars have long worked to map and theorize the interactions of groups and individuals with different religious identities. But that work has mostly been contained within two separate academic worlds: social science disciplines including sociology, psychology, anthropology, and political science, usually employing "outsider" approaches; and theology and philosophy of religion, often guided by doctrinal and ethical "insider" frameworks and located in religiously affiliated institutions. Religious studies has navigated an ambiguous space between these worlds. In the 1950s and 1960s, American college and university programs historically devoted to the development of Christian ministers responded to the social and political urgencies of their day by developing curricula and degrees that emphasized the historical and global study of religion, clearly distancing themselves from their confessional antecedents. The effort to establish itself in the modern academy required religious studies to cultivate an assiduously dispassionate approach to its subject, famously expressed in Russell McCutcheon's insistence that religion scholars are to be "critics, not caretakers" of the material they study.[1] But this is an unfinished conversation. Underlying normative commitments persist in religious studies, no longer confessional but aligned, for better or worse, with "liberal pluralist democratic polities."[2]

Separately, interreligious studies has grown in the past several decades from deep roots in the faith-based interfaith movement, with its normative vision of religious pluralism as a social good, its confidence in the possibility of harmonizing if not reconciling conflicting religious truth claims, and the deference it offers to religion itself. This movement, now more than a century old, has itself been fed by a long tradition of Christian theologizing about religious pluralism. So to locate interreligious studies within a secular discipline like religious studies is not as axiomatic as it might appear to those outside this field. For many religious studies scholars, who for at least two generations now have fought for the legitimacy of their field in an often suspicious academy, the lineage and embedded assumptions of interfaith work run counter to the evidence and, more importantly, to the method of the academic study of religion. Interreligious studies, if it is to find a home in this field, will require a more expansive view of the subject, a broader set of scholarly tools, and more distance from religious institutions and normative constructions of pluralism than has characterized the interfaith movement. This is not to say that interreligious studies must adopt a pretense of scientific neutrality; such neutrality is impossible in any case. But it must frame its values and goals in terms appropriate to the secular academy, aimed at the cultivation of civic rather than religious dispositions, and leaving the outcomes of its investigations radically open.

Importantly, a secular orientation to interreligious studies must enable the interrogation of the very terms used by prominent interfaith initiatives. In particular, the concept of religious pluralism itself, widely promoted as a public good by interfaith initiatives like the Harvard Pluralism Project and the Interfaith Youth Core, relies on a particular vision of multiculturalism that critics argue restrains its most disruptive elements. By universalizing an abstract notion of religion, critics argue, and elevating a pluralist approach to religious diversity that celebrates it as an expression of American exceptionalism, this version of interreligious studies risks narrowing the conversation unnecessarily and unhelpfully. Unwelcome at this pluralist table, Lucia Hulsether has argued, are those for whom religion is a source of radical cultural criticism as well as those unwilling to allow an individualized vision of interreligious harmony to supersede critical conversations centered on race. Tracing the emergence of the "rhetoric of pluralism" at Harvard Divinity School in the late 1960s, she writes that it "undercut radical critiques by translating them as the particular perspectives of individuals, whose voices were welcome to join the dialogue but not to alter its terms."[3] The foundation of religious literacy that interreligious studies promotes must include attention to those aspects of religion, now and in the past, that have served highly partisan and unpluralist agendas as much as the irenic visions of interfaith harmonizers.[4] As interreligious studies develops more fully in nonsectarian and public institutions, it will also need to engage more scholars and students of color, connect more deeply with race and gender studies, and guard against ideals of interreligious cooperation that elide other forms of difference.[5]

In addition to locating itself in the secular discipline of religious studies, with its attendant purposes and methods, interreligious studies also faces a secular imperative to widen its field of scope to include the study of atheism, agnosticism, and other forms of nonreligiousness as key constituents of interreligious relations. With nearly a quarter of Americans now identifying as religiously unaffiliated,[6] understanding religious diversity and building professional and civic capacities for working across lines of religious difference will require significant attention to the complex identities and behaviors of those in this diverse group. The name of the field is important in this context. "Interfaith," with its focus on a personal spiritual disposition, calls to mind efforts at mutual understanding among those who are nonetheless united in having one sort of faith commitment or another, while "interreligious," pointing more toward observable social phenomena, can potentially open to a broader diversity. Joseph Baker and Buster Smith sort the nonreligious into four basic classifications: atheists, agnostics, nonaffiliated believers, and the culturally religious who claim affiliation but have no public or private religious practice.[7] Other analyses point to the solidity of these apparently transitory categories. Drawing on multiple sets of survey data, Lim, McGregor, and Putnam show that there are religious identities between the religious and nonreligious that appear to be enduring in their liminal status, not on their way to becoming more religious or thoroughly unreligious.[8]

Few American departments of religious studies currently include courses on atheism or the complex hybrid forms of religion and nonreligion that increasingly characterize our students and our societies. By centering the analysis of religious *difference* and *interaction*, interreligious studies has the potential to help academic departments still usually organized around "world religions" frameworks to reckon more fully with the contemporary instability and complexity of religious identity within and across these traditions, and also to build more substantive collaborations with other disciplines. While religious studies is already a multidisciplinary field, bringing the systematic study of religious diversity into the work of the discipline promises to incorporate newer approaches, from cognitive science to evolutionary biology to more quantitative forms of sociology than typically characterize the work of the religious studies scholar.

Finally, these subjects, objects, and methods of interreligious studies must be understood in relation to the demands of a wider secular society. Beyond the simple sense of the secular as the absence of religion, secularity refers to the condition of pluralist societies in which multiple religious and nonreligious ways of being interact and vie for attention. Secularity in this sense is "the (correct) response of the democratic state to diversity."[9] Secularity is also the setting of daily "entanglements" of religious and nonreligious people, where shared constructions of meaning can emerge between and around the symbols and structures of specific groups.[10] But these conditions are volatile in their promise. These are the compelling circumstances driving the development of interreligious studies. In the United States, workplaces, schools, and civic and commercial spaces are increasingly religiously diverse; religion-related hate crimes are occurring more frequently;[11] and the rights and roles of religious people and institutions are increasingly contested as those groups experience the loss of majority status.

Bringing increased scholarly analysis to bear on the ways that religiously diverse people think about and interact with each other is critically important to the work of building and sustaining secular pluralist societies. Such societies also demand the religious literacy that can inoculate against stereotypes and bigotry—a knowledge base not well formed in U.S. primary and secondary schools—and the development of civic and professional skills for life and work in religiously diverse societies. These proficiencies require a kind of experiential learning about religious difference that has not typically characterized most preprofessional degree programs. At a time when religious studies is caught between defending its legitimacy by renouncing interest in anything but the most rigorous scholarship, on the one hand, and making the case for its value to a public increasingly demanding capitalist valuations of education, on the other, interreligious studies can be a powerful asset to the larger field of religious studies.

With these considerations in mind, I have suggested that interreligious studies be understood as

> a subdiscipline of religious studies that engages in the scholarly and religiously neutral description, multidisciplinary analysis, and theoretical framing of the interactions of religiously different people and groups, including the intersections of religion and secularity. It examines these interactions in historical and contemporary contexts, and in relation to other social systems and forces.[12]

Implicitly most religious studies faculty hope that their students will be transformed by their courses into more curious, tolerant, and engaged members of diverse societies. Interreligious studies, as an applied subfield, offers a site for the development of these civic capacities by focusing precisely on those differences that make religion a critical subject to engage. With all of higher education giving greater attention to real-world, problem-based learning, the case study and field-based learning characteristic of this emerging discipline open a valuable new space in the secular study of religion.

The methods and scope—not to mention the name—of this emergent subdiscipline are not yet settled matters. As the emergence of women's studies and ethnic studies in the 1960s and 1970s demonstrated, the pressure to establish academic legitimacy involves a difficult relationship with the social urgencies that give rise to the field. The bargain such disciplines make to secure their place in the academy often involves accepting a somewhat marginalized position in order to protect the normative or activist aims of the field. It is not yet clear whether or not interreligious studies, to preserve its pluralist agenda, will need to settle for a peripheral place in the university, more closely allied with the work of student affairs than traditional scholarship, or, alternatively, that it will need to sacrifice that agenda for a more secure disciplinary footing. But by centering critical scholarly methods and framing its purpose in relation to the needs of secular (which is not to say nonreligious) societies, interreligious studies stands to redefine the field of religious studies in a way that might make such dilemmas obsolete.

Notes

1   Russell T. McCutcheon, *Critics Not Caretakers: Redescribing the Public Study of Religion* (Albany: SUNY Press, 2001).

2   Bruce Grelle, "Promoting Religious and Civic Literacy in Public Schools: The California 3 Rs Project," in *Religion in the Public Schools: Negotiating the New Commons*, ed. Michael D. Waggoner (Lanham, Md.: Rowman and Littlefield, 2013), 103.

3   Lucia Hulsether, "The Grammar of Racism: Religious Pluralism and the Birth of the Interdisciplines," *Journal of the American Academy of Religion* 86, no. 1 (2018): 22.

4   Matthew Taylor makes this point in relation to the dissolution of another sub-field in "A Cautionary Tale for Interreligious Studies from Comparative Fundamentalism: Who Is at the Table?" *Journal of Interreligious Studies* 21 (2017): 45–58.

5   See, in this volume, chapter 20, "Decolonizing the Study of Religion," by Kevin Minister; and chapter 21, "Decolonizing Interreligious Studies," by Paul Hedges.

6   Daniel Cox and Robert P. Jones, "America's Changing Religious Identity," Public Religion Research Institute, September 6, 2017, https://www.prri.org/research/american-religious-landscape-christian-religiously-unaffiliated/. See also "America's Changing Religious Landscape," Pew Research Center, May 12, 2015, https://www.pewforum.org/2015/05/12/americas-changing-religious-landscape/.

7   Joseph O. Baker and Buster G. Smith, *American Secularism: Cultural Contours of Nonreligious Belief Systems* (New York: New York University Press, 2015), 13.

8   Chaeyoon Lim, Carol Ann MacGregor, and Robert D. Putnam, "Secular and Liminal: Discovering Heterogeneity among Religious Nones," *Journal for the Scientific Study of Religion* 49, no. 4 (2020): 598.

9   Charles Taylor, "The Meaning of Secularism," *Hedgehog Review* 12, no. 3 (2010): 24.

10 David Cheetham, "Ritualising the Secular? Inter-religious Meetings in the 'Immanent Frame,'" *Heythrop Journal*, February 15, 2017, 12, https://doi.org/10.1111/heyj.12491.

11 Liz Hayes, "Religion-Based Hate Crimes on the Rise," *Wall of Separation Blog*, November 15, 2018, American United for Separation of Church and State, https://www.au.org/blogs/wall-of-separation/religion-based-hate-crimes-on-the-rise.

12 Kate McCarthy, "(Inter)Religious Studies: Making a Home in the Secular Academy," in *Interreligious/Interfaith Studies: Defining a New Field*, ed. Eboo Patel, Jennifer Howe Peace, and Noah J. Silverman (Boston: Beacon, 2018), 12.

References

Baker, Joseph O., and Buster G. Smith. *American Secularism: Cultural Contours of Nonreligious Belief Systems*. New York: New York University Press, 2015.

Cheetham, David. "Ritualising the Secular? Inter-religious Meetings in the 'Immanent Frame.'" *Heythrop Journal*, February 15, 2017. https://doi.org/10.1111/heyj.12491.

Cox, Daniel, and Robert P. Jones. "America's Changing Religious Identity." Public Religion Research Institute. September 6, 2017. https://www.prri.org/research/american-religious-landscape-christian-religiously-unaffiliated/.

Grelle, Bruce. "Promoting Religious and Civic Literacy in Public Schools: The California 3 Rs Project." In *Religion in the Public Schools: Negotiating the New Commons*, edited by Michael D. Waggoner, 91–110. Lanham, Md.: Rowman and Littlefield, 2013.

Hayes, Liz. "Religion-Based Hate Crimes on the Rise." *Wall of Separation Blog*, November 15, 2018. Americans United for Separation of Church and State. https://www.au.org/blogs/wall-of-separation/religion-based-hate-crimes-on-the-rise.

Hulsether, Lucia. "The Grammar of Racism: Religious Pluralism and the Birth of the Interdisciplines." *Journal of the American Academy of Religion* 86, no. 1 (2018): 1–41.

Lim, Chaeyoon, Carol Ann MacGregor, and Robert D. Putnam. "Secular and Liminal: Discovering Heterogeneity among Religious Nones." *Journal for the Scientific Study of Religion* 49, no. 4 (2010): 596–618.

McCarthy, Kate. "(Inter)Religious Studies: Making a Home in the Secular Academy." In *Interreligious/Interfaith Studies: Defining a New Field*, edited by Eboo Patel, Jennifer Howe Peace, and Noah J. Silverman, 2–15. Boston: Beacon, 2018.

McCutcheon, Russell T. *Critics Not Caretakers: Redescribing the Public Study of Religion*. Albany: SUNY Press, 2001.

Pew Research Center. "America's Changing Religious Landscape." May 12, 2015. https://www.pewforum.org/2015/05/12/americas-changing-religious-landscape/.

Taylor, Charles. "The Meaning of Secularism." *Hedgehog Review* 12, no. 3 (2010): 23–34.

Taylor, Matthew D. "A Cautionary Tale for Interreligious Studies from Comparative Fundamentalism: Who Is at the Table?" *Journal of Interreligious Studies* 21 (2017): 45–58.

23

(Neo)Liberal Challenges

Brian K. Pennington

Initially hailed by university administrators as an awakening to the importance of educating students for global citizenship, the national interfaith movement on college campuses in the United States has encountered resistance in recent years. Some of that criticism has been directed at the emergent field called variously "interfaith studies," "interreligious studies," and "interfaith leadership studies" (hereafter "interreligious studies"). These developments in higher education have been both derided as sites for the production of racialized power[1] and critiqued for the re-inscription of the modernist episteme and the nation-state it produced.[2] In ongoing debates about the contours of this new field, it will be important to distinguish interreligious studies from non-curricular interfaith initiatives now so common on U.S. college campuses and to defend *critique* as a central concern of interreligious studies.

The genealogical links between interreligious studies and campus interfaith initiatives have been seldom acknowledged by the field's early advocates and supporters. Their relationship can be observed at two levels. At an ideological level, they are mutually supported by classically liberal notions of personhood and society and the logic of global capitalism, both of which, not coincidentally, also significantly shape university curricula and governance. The distinction between interreligious studies and non-curricular interfaith campus activity can be difficult to maintain because of a much more proximate relation: at an organizational level, the same foundations, nonprofits, and scholars have played formative roles in both. Campus interfaith initiatives are very recent compared to what some identify as a global interfaith movement, whose genesis is often credited to the 1893 Parliament of the World's Religions.[3] The college interfaith movement can be dated to the entry of philanthropical organizations and the Interfaith Youth Core (IFYC) into program development on college campuses late in the last decade. The funding that those foundations provided IFYC and other nonprofits has made the rapid and widespread implementation of sophisticated curricular and non-curricular programs possible.[4] These tangled and often obscured relationships on both levels pose serious challenges to the legitimacy and longevity of the nascent field of study.

Early statements about the scope and methods of interreligious studies programs give evidence of its various sources and influences. Established in 2013, the American Academy of Religion's unit dedicated to "interfaith and interreligious studies" says that the field "examines the many modes of response to the reality of religious pluralism (theological, philosophical, historical, scriptural, ethical, praxiological, and institutional)."[5] In the parenthetical list, one can discern stances that fall in different places along a spectrum from the purely intellectual (philosophical, historical) to the applied (theological, praxiological). Hedges employs a similarly expansive understanding of the new field, as does Patel, who, in addition, in this volume and elsewhere, identifies its objectives with the production of "civic goods" that include the strengthening and consolidation of minority communities.[6]

It is notable that these characterizations of the field of inquiry by those scholars who associate themselves and one another with fostering its birth bear the strong imprint of the classical liberalism of the West. In their valuation of the individual as the locus of knowledge and experience; in their understanding of the social order as a compact; in their belief in the value of free association; and in their representation of collectives such as religious and ethnic groups as subjects with rights, desires, and intentions, these statements and a survey of titles produced in the field reveal interreligious studies to be a true Enlightenment project.

We might question the place that both theology and activism occupy in these early formulations of interreligious studies. Indeed, proponents of the field, invoking the postmodern rebuke of the positionless observer, often make an explicit case for their inclusion that merits our careful assessment. In this volume Marianne Moyaert, Kate McCarthy, and Jeannine Hill Fletcher offer various perspectives on these issues. In this short piece, however, I want especially to point to the convergence of interreligious studies with the neoliberal trajectory of the contemporary university and argue that *critique* must remain at the heart of any school of inquiry that expresses an interest in social change and an opposition to the sociopolitical factors that give rise to urgent calls for interfaith cooperation. I see these convergences in the following three ways:

1. *The configuration of interreligious studies as a professionalizing discipline.* Several advocates for the field argue for its legitimacy on the basis of its capacity for training students to be leaders in a world troubled by religious conflict.[7] The IFYC emphasized the potential for the field to produce supremely employable graduates in an uncertain global environment and changing global economy in its report on a conference it held in 2016.[8] That same conference corresponded with a series of grants awarded by IFYC to faculty to develop some of the first interreligious studies degree programs in the United States (including one at my own institution, which I help to administer). A similar rationale can be seen in the shape of the country's first college major in the field at Elizabethtown College (Pa.), where it is called "Interfaith Leadership Studies."[9]

2. *The elevation of cooperation for collective social action.* A nearly universal interest across interreligious studies programs and articulations of the field is in the reduction of conflict and the promotion of understanding.[10] Social and political crises animated by religious identity, global and local, are invoked to lend an urgency to the institutionalization of interreligious studies and affiliated discourses of religious pluralism, belonging, and inclusion. In the words of one of the early advocates of interreligious studies, "Religious difference is hitting the world hard now."[11] A strong influence in this praxiological element in interreligious studies is the work of a pioneer in the field, Paul Knitter, who argued for the inseparability of interreligious dialogue from cooperative social action as mutually reinforcing and transformative undertakings.[12] This emphasis on what is often called "cooperation across lines of difference" locates the sources of interreligious conflict among people and groups rather than in the imperialism of global markets or highly militarized nation-states.

3. *The alliance with the post-9/11 project to contain the threat of difference.* One often hears that the central paradox of neoliberalism is that the market actually requires the state, whose role neoliberal ideology professes to disdain.[13] When we examine how market logics have transformed our institutions of higher education, however, we can see the deep contradictions that plague us as well as our own complicity in the market/state/academy nexus.[14] Oparah has observed how important the "moral capital" that we and our students supply the state is for its legitimization.[15] The university provides "the support of a liberal class that is always critical for the maintenance of a 'benevolent empire'" by reproducing the ideas that religious pluralism and grassroots

democratic processes are central values of civilized society that demand the state's protection.[16] Indeed, there is substantial evidence from across the globe of state-supported and state-funded multi-faith efforts in the wake of 9/11 as means for countering religious extremism and promoting state security.[17]

Interreligious studies has appeared at nearly the same moment that a literature providing a cogent account of the academy's relationship to global capitalism and the nation-state that facilitates and sanctifies that economic order is developing. Some of that literature laments the subjection of higher education to the logic of the market and calls for universities to intervene in state policy with programs for social innovation.[18] Interreligious studies as it is often currently conceived may well be positioned to do just that. Others, however, see the inextricability of the state from global markets and the corporatized university.[19] One could read this literature as an indictment of both the conditions that inspire the interfaith movement itself and the scholarly discourses like interreligious studies that lionize it. As a nascent field that has proposed, among other things, to examine the ramifications of the movements, intersections, and collisions of people, practices, and discourses, interreligious studies could develop as a space for the interrogation of the (neo)liberal imaginaire that has so thoroughly infiltrated our understanding of social relations and social change, just as it has colonized our academic institutions. Until we can clearly perceive both of those realities, we will, as Hulsether so aptly puts it, "twist in its impossible grip."[20]

Notes

1   Lucia Hulsether, "The Grammar of Racism: Religious Pluralism and the Birth of the Interdisciplines," *Journal of the American Academy of Religion* 86, no. 1 (2018): 1–41, https://doi.org/10.1093/jaarel/lfx049.

2   Amy L. Allocco, Geoffrey D. Claussen, and Brian K. Pennington, "Constructing Interreligious Studies: Thinking Critically about Interfaith Studies and the Interfaith Movement," in *Interfaith/Interreligious Studies: Defining a New Field*, ed. Eboo Patel, Jennifer Howe Peace, and Noah Silverman, 36–48 (Boston: Beacon, 2018).

3   Kusumita P. Pederson, "The Interfaith Movement: An Incomplete Assessment," *Journal of Ecumenical Studies* 41, no. 1 (2004): 74–94; Patrice Brodeur, "From the Margins to the Center of Power: The Increasing Relevance of the Global Interfaith Movement," *Cross Currents* 55, no. 1 (2005): 42–53.

4   Eboo Patel and Cassie Meyer, "Introduction to 'Interfaith Cooperation on Campus': Interfaith Cooperation as an Institution-Wide Priority," *Journal of College and Character* 12, no. 2 (2011), https://doi.org/10.2202/1940-1639 .1794; J. M. Conway, "Interfaith Capacity Building," *Journal of College and*

Character 19, no. 3 (2018): 236–42, https://doi.org/10.1080/2194587X.2018 .1481102.

5   "Interreligious and Interfaith Studies Unit," American Academy of Religion, accessed February 14, 2019, https://papers.aarweb.org/content/interreligious -and-interfaith-studies-unit.

6   Paul Hedges, "Interreligious Studies: A New Direction in the Study of Religion?" *Bulletin for the British Association for the Study of Religion* 125 (2014): 13–14; Patel, Peace, and Silverman, *Interfaith/Interreligious Studies*.

7   Chapters in this volume that take some version of this stance include Patel and McGraw.

8   Interfaith Youth Core, "Interfaith Studies: Curricular Programs and Core Competencies," report, 2016, accessed March 31, 2019, https://www.ifyc.org/ resources/interfaith-studies-curricular-programs-and-core-competencies2.

9   Elizabethtown College, "Interfaith Leadership Studies Major," accessed February 15, 2019, https://www.etown.edu/depts/religious-studies/interfaith -leadership-studies-major.aspx.

10   Long and Mikva offer two examples of such interests in this book.

11   Jeanine Diller et al., "Toward a Field of Interfaith Studies: Emerging Questions and Considerations," *Journal of Interreligious Studies* 16 (2015): 5–13.

12   Paul F. Knitter, "Inter-religious Dialogue and Social Action," in *The Wiley-Blackwell Companion to Inter-religious Dialogue*, edited by Catherine Cornille (Chichester: John Wiley & Sons, 2013), 134–48.

13   Ray Kiely, *The Neoliberal Paradox* (Cheltenham, U.K.: Edward Elgar, 2018).

14   In this volume, Minister and Widiyanto provide contrasting insights on this dilemma, with Minister arguing that interreligious studies can dismantle lingering effects of colonialism and Widiyanto promoting the discipline as a tool for nation building.

15   Julia C. Oparah, "Challenging Complicity: The Neoliberal University and the Prison-Industrial Complex," in *The Imperial University: Academic Repression and Scholarly Dissent*, ed. Piya Chatterjee and Sunaina Maira, 99–122 (Minneapolis: University of Minnesota Press, 2014), 100–101.

16   Piya Chatterjee and Sunaina Maira, "The Imperial University: Race, War, and the Nation-State," in Chatterjee and Maira, *Imperial University*, 7.

17   Anna Halafoff, "Countering Islamophobia: Muslim Participation in Multifaith Networks," *Islam and Christian–Muslim Relations* 22, no. 4 (2011): 451–67, https://doi.org/10.1080/09596410.2011.606191.

18   Michael Rustin, "The Neoliberal University and Its Alternatives," *Soundings* 63 (2016): 147–76. https://doi.org/10.3898/136266216819377057.

19   Kiely, *Neoliberal Paradox*; Oparah, "Challenging Complicity."

20   Hulsether, "Grammar of Racism," 32.

References

Allocco, Amy L., Geoffrey D. Claussen, and Brian K. Pennington. "Constructing Interreligious Studies: Thinking Critically about Interfaith Studies and the Interfaith Movement." In Patel, Peace, and Silverman, *Interfaith/Interreligious Studies*, 36–48.

American Academy of Religion. "Interreligious and Interfaith Studies Unit." Accessed February 14, 2019. https://papers.aarweb.org/content/interreligious -and-interfaith-studies-unit.

Brodeur, Patrice. "From the Margins to the Center of Power: The Increasing Relevance of the Global Interfaith Movement." *Cross Currents* 55, no. 1 (2005): 42–53.

Chatterjee, Piya, and Sunaina Maira. "The Imperial University: Race, War, and the Nation-State." In *The Imperial University: Academic Repression and Scholarly Dissent*, edited by Piya Chatterjee and Sunaina Maira, 1–50. Minneapolis: University of Minnesota Press, 2014.

Conway, J. M. "Interfaith Capacity Building." *Journal of College and Character* 19, no. 3 (2018): 236–42. https://doi.org/10.1080/2194587X.2018.1481102.

Diller, Jeanine, Eboo Patel, Jennifer Howe Peace, and Colleen Windham-Hughes. "Toward a Field of Interfaith Studies: Emerging Questions and Considerations." *Journal of Interreligious Studies* 16 (2015): 5–13.

Elizabethtown College. "Interfaith Leadership Studies Major." Accessed February 15, 2019. https://www.etown.edu/depts/religious-studies/interfaith-leadership -studies-major.aspx.

Halafoff, Anna. "Countering Islamophobia: Muslim Participation in Multifaith Networks." *Islam and Christian–Muslim Relations* 22, no. 4 (2011): 451–67. https://doi.org/10.1080/09596410.2011.606191.

Hedges, Paul. "Interreligious Studies: A New Direction in the Study of Religion?" *Bulletin for the British Association for the Study of Religion* 125 (2014): 13–14.

Hulsether, Lucia. "The Grammar of Racism: Religious Pluralism and the Birth of the Interdisciplines." *Journal of the American Academy of Religion* 86, no. 1 (2018): 1–41. https://doi.org/10.1093/jaarel/lfx049.

Interfaith Youth Core. "Interfaith Studies: Curricular Programs and Core Competencies." Report. 2016. Accessed March 31, 2019. https://www.ifyc.org/ resources/interfaith-studies-curricular-programs-and-core-competencies2.

Kiely, Ray. *The Neoliberal Paradox*. Cheltenham, U.K.: Edward Elgar, 2018.

Knitter, Paul F. "Inter-religious Dialogue and Social Action." In *The Wiley-Blackwell Companion to Inter-religious Dialogue*, edited by Catherine Cornille, 134–48. Chichester: John Wiley & Sons, 2013.

Oparah, Julia C. "Challenging Complicity: The Neoliberal University and the Prison-Industrial Complex." In *The Imperial University: Academic Repression and Scholarly Dissent*, edited by Piya Chatterjee and Sunaina Maira, 99–122. Minneapolis: University of Minnesota Press, 2014.

Patel, Eboo, and Cassie Meyer. "Introduction to 'Interfaith Cooperation on Campus': Interfaith Cooperation as an Institution-Wide Priority." *Journal of College and Character* 12, no. 2 (2011). https://doi.org/10.2202/1940-1639.1794.

Patel, Eboo, Jennifer Howe Peace, and Noah Silverman, eds. *Interfaith/Interreli-gious Studies: Defining a New Field*. Boston: Beacon, 2018.
Pederson, Kusumita P. "The Interfaith Movement: An Incomplete Assessment." *Journal of Ecumenical Studies* 41, no. 1 (2004): 74–94.
Rustin, Michael. "The Neoliberal University and Its Alternatives." *Soundings* 63 (2016): 147–76. https://doi.org/10.3898/136266216819377057.

24

Complicating Religious Identity

Russell C. D. Arnold

For many years, sociologists of religion have wrestled with how to measure religiosity in individuals and in society. While religious affiliation is certainly the easiest and most common measure to obtain, its value has been steadily decreasing in the last few decades. The data from the Pew Forum's 2014 Religious Landscape Survey show that the percentage of the population in the United States that is unaffiliated continues to rise, measured at 22.8 percent.[1] Within these data, the largest group of unaffiliated (15.8 percent of the total) are those who select "nothing in particular" as their preferred affiliation. Although these are often called "nones," the data show that nearly half of these also say that religion is important to them (44 percent), most of them report belief in God (74 percent), and 40 percent report praying at least weekly.[2] It is clear that religious affiliation is no longer the best measure and that we must change the paradigms we use to understand the real lives of those around us.

The article by Terry Shoemaker and James Edmonds titled "The Limits of Interfaith? Interfaith Identities, Emerging Potentialities, and Exclusivity" shows that this is a problem not just for sociologists but also for interfaith leaders.[3] The authors found that interfaith engagement that foregrounded religious identity labels systematically disenfranchised participants whose self-understanding did not fit neatly into the accepted identity labels, or for whom religious identity was not a primary defining characteristic. In their experience as participant-observers, Shoemaker and Edwards found that often the questions that framed the encounters "focused on adherents explicating their subjective religiosity and how the religiosity is practiced, lived and epistemologically informative."[4] Those participants who were not strongly attached to an identity label were unable to effectively engage with the questionnaire because it assumed a strong connection between one's religious or nonreligious identity and one's lived experience in the world. All of this is to say that we need to develop better ways (1) to understand and describe people's lived experiences and (2) to frame and facilitate real encounters between people that are truly inclusive of those for whom religious affiliation and identity is not primary to their self-understanding.

In an effort to challenge the influence of Western, Christian bias, scholars need to continue to challenge common, essentialist definitions of religion. Cluster definitions, which identify a set of qualities that, taken together in different configurations, contribute to something being identified as religion or religious, can allow us to decenter beliefs about god(s) as the sole or dominant religious category.[5] Cluster definitions allow us to better account for diversity of experience without requiring uniformity. These definitions allow people to express their religious lives in different ways and to different degrees.

Like cluster definitions, discussions of intersectional identities developing in other academic fields can help us to think about the complex ways that different aspects of our lives work together, sometimes in tension, to make us who we are. These approaches pay attention to the connections and interactions of identity categories such as race, class, gender, sexual orientation, age, religion, ability, and so forth. They challenge each of us to pay closer attention to the dynamic interplay of these dimensions of our lives within the structures of power and privilege in our society.

Within this context, it is incumbent upon us as interfaith studies scholars, in our practice and in our scholarship, to break free from the overly representational religious identity paradigm and adopt an intersectional approach that invites all of us to engage our whole lives with integrity and authenticity. This tool, which I call the Way of Life Wheel (fig. 24.1), is designed to foster deep reflection and dialogue about the complex constellation of experiences that shape how we live in the world. I propose that something like it can be useful both in our practice of interfaith engagement and dialogue and in interfaith studies scholarship seeking to understand the complexity of religious and other identities within encounters across lines of difference.

The wheel is made up of twelve spokes, each one identifying a different category of beliefs, practices, and commitments that are part of our lives. The categories include: (1) Beliefs about God(s), (2) Justice / Social Action, (3) Beauty / Wonder, (4) Beliefs about Human Nature, (5) Peoplehood / Ethnic Ties, (6) "Sacred" Spaces, (7) Sexuality / Gender, (8) Beliefs about Death /

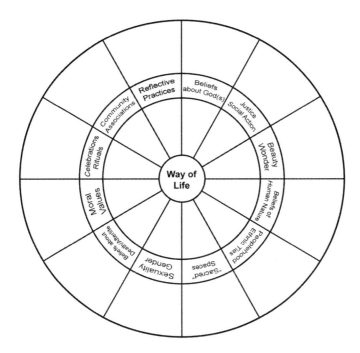

Figure 24.1 The Way of Life Wheel

Afterlife, (9) Moral Values or Principles, (10) Celebrations and Ritual Practices, (11) Community Associations, and (12) Reflective Practices.[6] Participants are invited to take some time with each category, reflecting on experiences, ideas, texts, or other sources that shape their relationship with that category. If the story or idea that arises is particularly salient or important for their self-understanding, they are invited to write a few notes about that story in the inner ring of the wheel. If what arises in connection with the category is not particularly salient to their way of living in the world, the notes can be written in the outer ring of the wheel. After this time of personal reflection, participants are invited to engage with others, beginning with whichever categories are particularly salient to them.

This tool has a number of significant advantages. First, the tool gives participants the opportunity to identify for themselves what aspects of their way of life are most important to them and to introduce themselves to others from that central place. The space created by this approach no longer privileges traditional religious identity labels. By starting with our way of life, instead of our religious identity labels, we avoid the false and dismissive notion that some of us are "nones." Because it focuses on specific experiences, the space becomes equally welcoming to those with complex religious identities—what has variously been described as multiple religious belonging, hybridity, bricolage, syncretism, or spiritual fluidity. The narrative approach also provides those with clearly identifiable religious affiliations a way to speak appreciatively about the ways their lives have been influenced by their encounters with those outside their community or tradition.

Second, the tool reinforces the dynamic nature of our religious and spiritual lives. Participants are asked to pay attention to what seems particularly salient for them at this time, and in this space, recognizing that some aspects of our lives will be more salient in some settings than in others. For example, my ritual practice of covering my head during prayer and in sacred spaces is more salient for me in my work at a Jesuit, Catholic university than it had been in a secular university. Reflecting on the wheel at different points in time—for example, at the beginning and end of a series of gatherings—also yields interesting insights into the ways our lives, identities, and practices change as we are influenced by the people and experiences we encounter.

Finally, reframing the interfaith encounter with emphasis on our "way of life" invites us to meet each other closer to the heart of our lives. Participants have reported that the tool allows them to enter quickly into deep dialogue with others, even those who were strangers to them just minutes before. Having identified for themselves those beliefs, practices, and commitments that are most important to them, participants are able to introduce themselves to their potential dialogue partners more honestly and directly. A constructive and intersectional approach like the one described here will not only allow us to break free from the religious identity paradigm and create interfaith spaces that are truly inviting to all but also guide our scholarship to better appreciate the complexity of identities in research that examines encounters across lines of religious, spiritual, and worldview difference.

Appendix

Way of Life Wheel categories: stories, narratives, or texts that contribute to your understanding of each of the following:

- Beliefs about God(s)
  Is there a god? Are there many divine manifestations? Can we know god(s)? Or know something about Ultimate Reality? How have you experienced god(s)?

- Justice / Social Action
  What experiences help you understand what justice is? What are you working for? What are you committed to? Why?

- Beauty / Wonder
  What experiences awaken awe and wonder in you? When have you experienced transcendence and beauty in nature, in others, etc.?

- Beliefs about Human Nature
  Are people basically good or bad? Can people change? Are humans essentially material, spiritual, or both? What is the relationship between humans and nature? What experiences shape these views for you?

- Peoplehood / Ethnic Ties
  Who are your people? To what people do you belong? Where do you (or your people) come from? How do these ethnic ties shape you?

- "Sacred" Spaces
  What places or spaces (constructed or natural) are special for you? Where do you go for solace, comfort, inspiration, hope, etc.?

- Sexuality / Gender
  How do you understand yourself as a sexual being? As a woman/man/ nonbinary? What stories or experiences have shaped this understanding for you?

- Beliefs about Death / Afterlife
  What happens when a person dies? Does any part of you live on after death? In what form? What stories do you tell about encounters with mortality?

- Moral Values or Principles
  What is the basis of your morality? What makes a person moral? What principles are most important? What experiences have solidified or challenged these moral commitments?

- Celebrations and Ritual Practices
  What days/events are special to you? How do you mark such days? What practices do you engage in that bring order, consistency, and/or meaning to your life? What symbols, objects, or language are important within these actions?

- Community Associations
  What communities or groups have you chosen to be a part of? What are your memberships?

- Reflective Practices (prayer / meditation etc.)
  What do you do when you want to think? How do you reflect or contemplate your life or place in the world?

Notes

1 "America's Changing Religious Landscape," Pew Research Center, May 12, 2015, 4, http://assets.pewresearch.org/wp-content/uploads/sites/11/2015/05/RLS-08-26-full-report.pdf.

2 "'Nones' on the Rise," Pew Research Center, October 9, 2012, http://www.pewforum.org/2012/10/09/nones-on-the-rise/.

3 Terry Shoemaker and James Edmonds, "The Limits of Interfaith? Interfaith Identities, Emerging Potentialities, and Exclusivity," *Culture and Religion* 17, no. 2 (2016): 200–212.

4 Shoemaker and Edmonds, "Limits of Interfaith?" 207.

5 A model cluster definition can be found in William P. Alston, "Religion," in *The Encyclopedia of Philosophy*, ed. Paul Edwards (New York: Macmillan, 1967), 7:141–42. It includes the following nine characteristics: (1) belief in supernatural beings; (2) a distinction between sacred and profane objects; (3) ritual acts focused on sacred objects; (4) a moral code believed to be sanctioned by the gods; (5) characteristically religious feelings (awe, sense of mystery, sense of guilt, adoration), which tend to be aroused in the presence of sacred objects and during the practice of ritual and which are connected in idea with the gods; (6) prayer and other forms of communication with gods; (7) a worldview or a general picture of the world as a whole and the place of the individual therein (this picture contains some specification of an overall purpose or point of the world and an indication of how the individual fits into it); (8) a more or less total organization of one's life based on the worldview; (9) a social group bound together by the above.

6 The appendix includes questions that could be used to elicit connections to each of the categories.

References

Alston, William P. "Religion." In *The Encyclopedia of Philosophy*, edited by Paul Edwards, 7:141–42. New York: Macmillan, 1967.

Pew Research Center. "America's Changing Religious Landscape." May 12, 2015. http://assets.pewresearch.org/wp-content/uploads/sites/11/2015/05/RLS-08-26-full-report.pdf.

———. "'Nones' on the Rise." October 9, 2012. http://www.pewforum.org/2012/10/09/nones-on-the-rise/.

Shoemaker, Terry, and James Edmonds. "The Limits of Interfaith? Interfaith Identities, Emerging Potentialities, and Exclusivity." *Culture and Religion* 17, no. 2 (2016): 200–212.

25

In Reactionary Times

Rachel S. Mikva

Academic research, for all the "ivory tower" aspersions cast at it, cannot be isolated from the world in which it unfolds. In a field like interreligious studies that focuses on the dynamic encounter of people and traditions with differing lifestances, the two realms are particularly interrelated. Thus, the politicization of religious difference and the racialization of religion that imbue our public discourse press for ongoing scholarly attention.

Politicization of Religious Difference

Some work has been done on the contemporary characterization of Muslims and Islam that illuminates the politicization of religious difference. Although Islamophobia began long before 9/11 and it is a global phenomenon,[1] this discussion focuses on the United States after 2001. Beginning on the first anniversary of the September 11 attacks, the United States authorized "special registration" of men over the age of sixteen who were visiting from selected Muslim-majority countries.[2] They were required to be fingerprinted, photographed, and interviewed under oath about their beliefs and their politics, with the information entered into a national database. It was not an effective antiterrorism policy (especially since the majority of attacks on American soil are committed by native-born, white, Christian, right-wing extremists), but it had the political benefit of looking like the George W. Bush administration was doing something to keep its citizens safe. It was a critical step in politicizing and marginalizing Muslim identity.[3]

In the years since, a substantial Islamophobia industry has flourished by selling fear of Muslims, with hundreds of millions of dollars distributed to misinformation centers and activists. Their voices are amplified in an echo chamber of right-wing politicians, media, religious leaders, and grassroots organizations. Its messages infect the general public discourse, so that schools, landlords, Hollywood, law enforcement agencies, and the rest of us become witting or unwitting accomplices.[4] The driving force of this campaign is not religious; it is political, designed to consolidate power.

Donald Trump's repeated efforts to impose a "travel ban" represent one iteration of this agenda. Intended primarily to prevent citizens of Muslim-majority countries from entering the United States, the policy played to his political base. Amid a global refugee crisis, he also sought to severely restrict granting entrance to refugees, and he complained, "Why are we having all these people from shithole countries coming here?" His slogan, "Make America Great Again," bespeaks a reactionary politics designed to resist the social and political liberalization that has been haltingly but doggedly unfolding in American society and around the world. Reactionary politics deploy difference—religious, racial, sexual, gender, ethnic—as a persistent and pernicious threat.

Another strategy of this political movement is anti-sharia legislation. Even though it serves no legal purpose, over two hundred bills have been introduced in state legislatures, and at least twenty have been enacted.[5] The U.S. Constitution already denies the authority of foreign law, and no Muslim group has tried to impose sharia in this country. Nonetheless, as a means of perpetuating the idea of Islam as dangerous, the effort has proven useful for gathering funding and political support. It is largely partisan as well, cultivated as part of conservative Republican identity. Yet there is also anti-Muslim bias on the left, especially as it relates to women's issues—making even the wearing of *hijab* a political act.

Contemporary dynamics of Islamophobia invite investigation of the manifold ways that differences in lifestance have been politicized over time, from polemicizing against the Canaanites in the Hebrew Bible to enshrining religious freedom in the U.S. Bill of Rights. Each instance has shaped the historical encounters of peoples and traditions.

Racialization of Religion

Some scholars and activists have challenged the term "Islamophobia," since it has little to do with the religion of Islam. Learning about the Five Pillars does not generally diminish animosity. In addition, calling it a phobia suggests that the problem is interpersonal, which obscures its systemic dimensions.[6] Anti-Muslim bias is an ideology similar in structure and purpose to racism, fashioning a conceptual map to preserve white, Christian hegemony. American politics deploys religion to create race.

The racialization of religion is not a new phenomenon. It was evident in early twentieth-century U.S. court cases assessing whether certain Asian and Middle Eastern immigrants were "free white persons" and thus eligible for naturalized citizenship. In most instances where the answer was yes, the petitioner was Christian. In *U.S. v. Cartozian* (1925), the court maintained that skin color does not provide an adequate guide for whiteness, so it decided to rely "largely on religion (and assimilation) in its determination."[7] In cases like these, it could be argued that religion stood in for culture as a performance of whiteness, with the presumption that Christian culture equaled white culture.

Religion is more evidently "raced" when otherness is defined not by religious praxis or conviction—or even culture—but by some innate, unalterable quality. Assimilation is not possible. For example, historian Katherine Mayo argued in her controversial 1927 book, *Mother India*, that India was incapable of self-governance due to Hindus' sexual and general depravity. Or, reflecting on the racialization of religion evident long before the twentieth century, George Fredrickson considers the case of the Jews:

> Anti-Judaism became anti-Semitism whenever it turned into a consuming hatred that made getting rid of Jews seem preferable to trying to convert them, and anti-Semitism became racism when the belief took hold that Jews were intrinsically and organically evil rather than merely having false beliefs and wrong dispositions.[8]

We have generally understood this polemical strategy as the essential accessory of religious bias—as justification for discrimination, domination, exclusion, and extermination of the "Other." Yet here, too, the conflation of race and religion has political purposes.

Consider the man who walked into the Tree of Life Synagogue in Pittsburgh and mowed down eleven Jews on a Shabbat morning in October 2018. He hated Jews, clearly, but his motivation was political. Committed to an ideology of white supremacy, he believed Jews were enabling migrant "invaders." His final social media post read, "I can't sit by and watch my people get slaughtered. Screw your optics, I'm going in."[9] It was a flammable mix of religious, national, and racial prejudice, ignited by a culture of violence and manufactured sense of peril.

The Transformative Potential of Interreligious Studies

What are the implications for interreligious studies in these reactionary times? Analysis in the field is intersectional and thus must address the ways that religious identities get raced and gendered and classed. It is also necessarily interdisciplinary, since one cannot analyze the encounter of people and traditions of different lifestances without considering the variety of forces that shape engagement. Consequently, scholarship requires deep conversation with the social sciences in order to analyze constructions of the "other" in the politicization and racialization of religious difference. Although the field currently tends to be sequestered as a subdivision of religious studies, its interrelationship with politics, history, media, science, and other arenas demands interdisciplinary rigor, and it needs to be integrated more effectively throughout the curriculum. Such an approach can also disrupt the colonialist study of "world religions," which has treated religion as a separable category of culture that can be universalized into essential forms for comparison.[10]

It is also important to recognize that interreligious studies has developed chronologically parallel to and, at least partially, as a result of perceived escalation in religious conflicts around the world. This has several consequences that have the potential to distort research and teaching. The most obvious example is the tragic disfigurement of Islam; even in supportive spaces, too much energy is devoted to its teachings about violence. Political authorities are becoming increasingly engaged in distinguishing between "good" and "bad" religions and establishing research priorities, especially as they relate to "combating violent extremism" (CVE in current parlance).[11] Interreligious dimensions of geopolitical conflict can be misrepresented, since religious factors are frequently secondary—although they may provide a transformative ultimacy for opposing worldviews.

When I was a congregational rabbi, I used to complain that almost all Jewish literature written for young adults was about the Shoah; as compelling a topic as it is, the emphasis impedes a thick understanding of Jewish life. Similarly, there is too much being written and taught about interreligious conflict. The books do not necessarily come from scholars who identify interreligious studies as a primary field, but they still dominate the storehouse of resources and shape the agenda.[12]

The corollary, of course, is that examples of similarity and solidarity also receive a great deal of attention. This combination creates a false binary, a caricature of multi-faith encounters that accidentally replicates the reactionary idea of difference as a threat. In addressing the more complex layers of interaction—

reckoning with mutual influence, impact, and interdependence among people and traditions who orient around religion differently—scholarship can articulate the ongoing co-formation of religious identities.

This too is political: according to Edward Said, "The construction of identity is bound up with the disposition of power and powerlessness in each society."[13] At the same time, theories of the other do not serve merely to erect cultural boundaries and establish hierarchies. They are also the means by which we explore internal ambiguities, experiment with alternative values, and comprehend our individual and collective selves.[14] Self and other are mutually constituted. Research in interreligious studies can illuminate this interdependence in fresh and compelling ways.

Notes

1   See, e.g., Commission on British Muslims and Islamophobia, *Islamophobia: A Challenge for Us All* (London: Runnymede Trust, 1997), available at www .runnymedetrust.org/companies/17/74/%20Islamophobia-A-Challenge-for -Us-All.html.

2   Special registration applied to nationals from twenty-five countries, almost all with a Muslim majority: Afghanistan, Algeria, Bahrain, Bangladesh, Egypt, Eritrea, Indonesia, Iran, Iraq, Jordan, Kuwait, Lebanon, Libya, Morocco, North Korea, Oman, Pakistan, Qatar, Saudi Arabia, Somalia, Sudan, Syria, Tunisia, United Arab Emirates, and Yemen. It was cancelled in 2011. See Maia Jachimowicz and Ramah McKay, "'Special Registration' Program," April 1, 2003, Migration Policy Institute, accessed December 6, 2019, https://www .migrationpolicy.org/article/special-registration-program.

3   See Moustafa Bayoumi, "Racing Religion," *CR: The New Centennial Review* 6, no. 2 (2006): 267–93.

4   Matthew Duss et al., "Fear Inc. 2.0: The Islamophobia Network's Efforts to Manufacture Hate in America," Center for American Progress, 2015, available at https://cdn.americanprogress.org/wp-content/uploads/2015/02/FearInc -report2.11.pdf. See also https://islamophobianetwork.com; Todd H. Green, *The Fear of Islam: An Introduction to Islamophobia in the West* (Minneapolis: Fortress, 2015).

5   See "New Database Exposes Anti-Muslim Legislation across the US: Searchable Tool Names Bills' Backers," press release, April 25, 2018, Haas Institute for a Fair and Inclusive Society at the University of California–Berkeley, accessed February 27, 2019, https://haasinstitute.berkeley.edu/new-database -exposes-anti-muslim-legislation-across-us.

6   Su'ad Khabeer et al., "Islamophobia Is Racism: Resource for Teaching & Learning About Anti-Muslim Racism in the United States," public syllabus, accessed December 11, 2018, https://islamophobiaisracism.wordpress.com.

7   *U.S. v. Cartozian* referenced Supreme Court cases *Ozawa v. U.S.* (1922), which
     disallowed Japanese from naturalizing, and *U.S. v. Baghat Singh Thind* (1923),
     which ruled against an Indian Sikh man (referred to as a "high-caste Hindu"
     to delineate his Indian identity).

8   George Fredrickson, *Racism: A Short History* (Princeton: Princeton Universi-
     ty Press, 2002), 19.

9   Kellie B. Gormly et al., "Suspect in Pittsburgh Synagogue Shooting Charged
     with 29 Counts in Deaths of 11 People," *Washington Post*, October 27, 2018,
     https://www.washingtonpost.com/nation/2018/10/27/pittsburgh-police
     -responding-active-shooting-squirrel-hill-area/?noredirect=on&utm_term=
     .cbc78fabb492.

10   See Tomoko Masuzawa, *The Invention of World Religions* (University of Chi-
     cago Press, 2005), for a critique of the World Religions model.

11   See Faiza Patel and Meghan Koushik, *Countering Violent Extremism* (New
     York: Brennan Center for Justice at NYU School of Law, 2017) for a critique of
     CVE. The following array of websites illustrates its presence in interreligious
     research and projects: "Can Interfaith Contact Reduce Extremism among
     Youth? Implications for Countering Violent Extremism in Pakistan and Sri
     Lanka," United States Institute of Peace, accessed March 2, 2019, https://www
     .usip.org/events/can-interfaith-contact-reduce-extremism-among-youth;
     Brian J. Adams, "Violent Extremism and the Value of Interfaith Dialogue,"
     Medium.com, February 23, 2015, accessed March 2, 2019, https://medium
     .com/the-machinery-of-government/violent-extremism-and-the-value-of
     -interfaith-dialogue-9926b6766d68; and "Countering Violent Extremism
     and Interfaith Programming in Tanzania," Center for Intercultural Dialogue,
     accessed March 2, 2019, https://centerforinterculturaldialogue.org/2016/03/
     12/countering-violent-extremism-and-interfaith-programming-in-tanzania
     -grant-us-dos/.

12   A small sampling of books addressing religious violence includes Bruce Lin-
     coln, *Holy Terrors: Thinking About Religion after September 11* (Chicago: Uni-
     versity of Chicago Press, 2003); Mark Juergensmeyer, *Terror in the Mind of
     God: The Global Rise of Religious Violence* (Berkeley: University of California
     Press, 2003); Mark Juergensmeyer, Margo Kitts, and Michael Jerryson, eds.,
     Violence and the World's Religious Traditions: An Introduction (Oxford: Ox-
     ford University Press, 2016); Charles Selengut, *Sacred Fury: Understanding
     Religious Violence* (New York: Rowman-Altamira, 2003); Lloyd Steffen, *Holy
     War, Just War: Exploring the Moral Meaning of Religious Violence* (New York:
     Rowman & Littlefield, 2007); and Karen Armstrong, *Fields of Blood: Religion
     and the History of Violence* (New York: Anchor, 2015).

13   Edward Said, *Orientalism* (New York: Random House Vintage, 1994), 332.

14   William Scott Green, "Otherness Within: Towards a Theory of Difference in
     Rabbinic Judaism," in *To See Ourselves as Others See Us: Christians, Jews, Oth-
     ers in Late Antiquity*, ed. Jacob Neusner and Ernest S. Frerichs (Chico, Calif.:
     Scholars, 1985), 50–51. He relies on the work of anthropologists like James A.

Boon, *Other Tribes, Other Scribes: Symbolic Anthropology in the Comparative Study of Cultures, Histories, Religions, and Texts* (Cambridge: Cambridge University Press, 1982).

References

Adams, Brian J. "Violent Extremism and the Value of Interfaith Dialogue." *Medium.com*, February 23, 2015. Accessed March 2, 2019. https://medium .com/the-machinery-of-government/violent-extremism-and-the-value-of -interfaith-dialogue-9926b6766d68.

Armstrong, Karen. *Fields of Blood: Religion and the History of Violence.* New York: Anchor, 2015.

Bayoumi, Moustafa. "Racing Religion." *CR: The New Centennial Review* 6, no. 2 (2006): 267–93.

Boon, James A. *Other Tribes, Other Scribes: Symbolic Anthropology in the Comparative Study of Cultures, Histories, Religions, and Texts.* Cambridge: Cambridge University Press, 1982.

Center for Intercultural Dialogue. "Countering Violent Extremism and Interfaith Programming in Tanzania." Accessed March 2, 2019. https:// centerforinterculturaldialogue.org/2016/03/12/countering-violent-extremism -and-interfaith-programming-in-tanzania-grant-us-dos/.

Commission on British Muslims and Islamophobia. *Islamophobia: A Challenge for Us All.* London: Runnymede Trust, 1997. Available at www .runnymedetrust.org/companies/17/74/%20Islamophobia-A-Challenge-for -Us-All.html.

Duss, Matthew, Yasmine Taeb, Ken Gude and Ken Sofer. "Fear Inc. 2.0: The Islamophobia Network's Efforts to Manufacture Hate in America." Center for American Progress. 2015. Available at https://cdn.americanprogress.org/wp -content/uploads/2015/02/FearInc-report2.11.pdf.

Fredrickson, George. *Racism: A Short History.* Princeton: Princeton University Press, 2002.

Gormly, Kellie B., Avi Selk, Joel Achenbach, Mark Berman, and Alex Horton. "Suspect in Pittsburgh Synagogue Shooting Charged with 29 Counts in Deaths of 11 People." *Washington Post*, October 27, 2018. https://www .washingtonpost.com/nation/2018/10/27/pittsburgh-police-responding-active -shooting-squirrel-hill-area/?noredirect=on&utm_term=.cbc78fabb492.

Green, Todd H. *The Fear of Islam: An Introduction to Islamophobia in the West.* Minneapolis: Fortress, 2015.

Green, William Scott. "Otherness Within: Towards a Theory of Difference in Rabbinic Judaism." In *To See Ourselves as Others See Us: Christians, Jews, Others in Late Antiquity*, edited by Jacob Neusner and Ernest S. Frerichs, 49–69. Chico, Calif.: Scholars, 1985.

Haas Institute for a Fair and Inclusive Society at the University of California–Berkeley. "New Database Exposes Anti-Muslim Legislation across the US: Searchable Tool Names Bills' Backers." Press release. April 25, 2018. Accessed February 27, 2019. https://haasinstitute.berkeley.edu/new-database-exposes -anti-muslim-legislation-across-us.

Juergensmeyer, Mark. *Terror in the Mind of God: The Global Rise of Religious Violence*. Berkeley: University of California Press, 2003.

Juergensmeyer, Mark, Margo Kitts, and Michael Jerryson, eds. *Violence and the World's Religious Traditions: An Introduction*. Oxford: Oxford University Press, 2016.

Khabeer, Su'ad, Arshad Ali, Evelyn Alsultany, Sohail Daulatzai, Lara Deeb, Carol Fadda, Zareena Grewal, Juliane Hammer, Nadine Naber, and Junaid Rana. "Islamophobia Is Racism: Resource for Teaching & Learning About Anti-Muslim Racism in the United States." Public syllabus. Accessed December 11, 2018. https://islamophobiaisracism.wordpress.com.

Lincoln, Bruce. *Holy Terrors: Thinking About Religion after September 11*. Chicago: University of Chicago Press, 2003.

Masuzawa, Tomoko. *The Invention of World Religions*. Chicago: University of Chicago Press, 2005.

Patel, Faiza, and Meghan Koushik. *Countering Violent Extremism*. New York: Brennan Center for Justice at NYU School of Law, 2017.

Said, Edward. *Orientalism*. New York: Random House Vintage, 1994.

Selengut, Charles. *Sacred Fury: Understanding Religious Violence*. New York: Rowman-Altamira, 2003.

Steffen, Lloyd. *Holy War, Just War: Exploring the Moral Meaning of Religious Violence*. New York: Rowman & Littlefield, 2007.

United States Institute of Peace. "Can Interfaith Contact Reduce Extremism among Youth? Implications for Countering Violent Extremism in Pakistan and Sri Lanka." Accessed March 2, 2019. https://www.usip.org/events/can-interfaith-contact-reduce-extremism-among-youth.

26

Confronting Xenoglossophobia

Caryn D. Riswold and Guenevere Black Ford

In February 2018, the Council on American Islamic Relations (CAIR) filed a lawsuit on behalf of a young man who was removed from a Southwest Airlines flight after another passenger complained about him speaking Arabic.[1] In 2016, CAIR requested a federal investigation of the removal of a Muslim couple from a Delta Air Lines flight after a flight attendant "claimed that Faisal Ali tried to hide his cell phone and was sweating and that he said the word 'Allah.'"[2] These are just two of several incidents of racial and religious profiling in recent years. What they share is the role that language played in the alleged racial profiling, specifically the role of a "foreign"[3] language, Arabic. They highlight a dimension of Islamophobia to which scholars of religion and interfaith studies have yet paid little attention: xenoglossophobia. The fear of foreign languages manifests one form of a fear of otherness with distinctive relevance to interfaith and interreligious studies. Insofar as language is power, shared language can serve as social capital, while a lack of shared language can function as a barrier if one lacks curiosity and a commitment to learn and to bridge difference.

Eboo Patel describes how interfaith leadership requires a series of skills and commitments, including the ability to build relationships and mobilize religiously diverse communities, in part by facilitating interfaith conversations with a religiously diverse group.[4] He notes how those interfaith conversations require multiple levels of communication generated by good questions, concrete activities, and respectful listening. At the most basic level, however, is either a shared language or a willingness to not let a difference of language stand in the way. Qualities like "grit," the ability to navigate tension and conflict, as well as "craft," a long-term commitment to doing something well, are precursors to this type of communication.[5] When it is not immediately easy to understand another person, because of either the content or the linguistic delivery of their beliefs, foundational commitments to pluralism can make a significant difference.

That some of the current events involving suspicion of Arabic speakers result in "racial" profiling complaints highlights the intersectional nature of this issue. "Even if religion may be highly salient, it is always intersecting with other identities like race, class, gender, geography, politics, ethnicity, nationality, and sexuality."[6] Religion is itself embedded in webs of power and privilege, including racial bias and, though missing from the list of identity markers here, views of language. In a study and critique of the "English Only" movement in the United States, Donaldo Macedo points out that "the ideological principles that sustain those debates are consonant with the structures and mechanisms of a colonial ideology."[7] He points out that this is an ideology that negates another culture's symbolic systems, "including the native language."[8] Lindsay Perez Huber uses the phrase "racist nativist microaggressions"[9] to capture the intersection of race, language, and power in her study of the effects of English dominance in public education. She notes that "racist nativist discourses and English hegemony articulate the systemic process of subordination and domination."[10] Research shows that this phenomenon, which we capture here with the term "xenoglossophobia," has been studied primarily in relationship to teaching and learning in public educational contexts. It is time for scholars and researchers to apply these insights to their field.

Unpacking the ways that xenoglossophobia functions as a layer of bias and stereotype at work in interfaith encounters can help us remove yet another barrier to interfaith cooperation. This is because, as Jenna Shim suggests, "people's attitudes about different languages/accents/dialects are political and thus show prevalent power relations."[11] In the United States, systemic power has long been afforded to white native speakers of English. This is not a new phenomenon, nor is it limited to the fear of Arabic that often makes the twenty-first-century news. In the early and mid-twentieth century, anti-Catholic bias was informed by many things, including racist ethnocentrism and xenoglossophobia. Congressman Ira G. Hersey of Maine, who served in the U.S. House of Representatives from 1917 to 1929, included in his anti-immigration views a warning about people from Asia and Southern Europe "with their strange and pagan rites, their babble of tongues."[12] Inextricable from religious ritual, language was a key factor in perceptions of "otherness" that pervaded nineteenth- and twentieth-century views of Catholicism. They "babbled." "On Christmas Eve 1806, in one of the many demonstrations outside of St. Peter's [in Manhattan], the building was surrounded by people enraged by the service of 'popish superstition' occurring inside, otherwise known as Christmas Mass."[13] At that time in the young English-speaking United States, the Mass would have been spoken in Latin.

The emerging field of interfaith and interreligious studies depends on a multi- and interdisciplinary understanding of human interactions and the role of religions in culture. Much of the research on linguistic bias has come out of the field of language education, and lessons may be drawn from understanding classroom dynamics as one significant location of interpersonal exchange. In her study of teachers who work with English-language learners, Shim concludes that self-reflection about one's beliefs about other languages is essential to build bridges necessary for student learning. She also notes that this "entails uncomfortable and uncertain processes," which takes people into "the space of vulnerability" when they confront their own bias and assumption about "others" that they are in fact dedicated to serving.[14] At the same time, Patel's framework for pluralism includes "respect for identity" wherein "people have a right to form their own identities [and] to express their identity."[15] Language plays a unique role in that it both is part of one's identity and becomes a key mechanism for expression of that identity.

Understanding xenoglossophobia as one of the factors in some religious bias is a first step toward deepening the field of interfaith studies. It also allows those seeking interfaith cooperation to pay attention to the way that linguistic bias may be at work in particular relationships and situations. "People who build barriers are interested in proudly proclaiming the righteousness of their identity and loudly denouncing other identities."[16] The "English Only" movement noted above is a particularly relevant expression of this barrier building. In contrast, Rebecca Dahm argues that "one way to foster active social inclusion is to enable students to develop a positive attitude to 'foreignness.'"[17] Her analysis of one instructional strategy showed that people can "become used to discovering new languages and shed their initial pre-conceived ideas" and that "once they playfully discover the language of their peers, they want to know more about the other's culture."[18] Applying this to interfaith cooperation, we can see that rather than continuing to serve as a barrier, language difference can become one among many opportunities for learning about another person or community. Removing xenoglossophobia can increase the civic goods that Patel associates with pluralism and interfaith cooperation, including strengthening social cohesion, bridging social capital, and reducing isolation.[19] If the scholarship produced by interfaith and interreligious studies is to be a resource for interfaith practitioners and leaders who work to promote understanding across lines of religious difference, then xenoglossophobia is an area ripe for much-needed research.

This research and work on attitudes about "othered" languages can also contribute to understanding what Patel calls a "binding narrative for diverse societies."[20] That this narrative in the United States is often captured with the Latin phrase "e pluribus unum" points toward the socially constructed and flexible nature of attitudes toward language itself. This Latin phrase is understood to capture a foundational American ideal, yet it is written in the same language as the one that incited the Manhattan riot in 1806. Foreignness is determined and dictated by those in power, in concert with other identity markers, whether it be experienced individually or collectively.

Confronting xenoglossophobia in research and practice further develops the field of interfaith studies insofar as it has not yet been attended to as a frequent determinative factor in building barriers between people in a religiously diverse society. Its intersection with race, ethnicity, social class, and geography as well as the way it has manifest in relationship to different languages and religions is apparent as anti-Catholicism gives way to Islamophobia and a resurgent antisemitism in the United States. While the connections these religious prejudices have to national and international politics have been well-documented, the intimate role that language plays in individual and communal religious identities should now be explored comprehensively.

Notes

1   "CAIR and Walkup, Melodia File Suit Challenging Southwest Airlines' Removal of Arabic-Speaking Passenger," Council on American Islamic Relations, press release, February 13, 2018, https://www.cair.com/cair_and_walkup _melodia_law_firm_file_suit_challenging_southwest_airlines_removal_of _arabic_speaking_passenger.

2   Kelly Yamanouchi, "Group Files Complaint against Delta, Alleging Racial Profiling," *Atlanta Journal-Constitution*, August 4, 2016, https://www.myajc .com/business/group-files-complaint-against-delta-alleging-racial-profiling/ tkIXSBVshHyZDm2cZtiXBK/.

3   "Foreign" is here a contextual term, subject to definition by culturally dominant norms.

4   Eboo Patel, *Interfaith Leadership: A Primer* (Boston: Beacon, 2016), 135.

5   Patel, *Interfaith Leadership*, 156–63.

6   Patel, *Interfaith Leadership*, 79.

7   Donaldo Macedo, "The Colonialism of the English Only Movement," *Educational Researcher* 29 no. 3 (2000): 16.

8   Macedo, "Colonialism," 16.

9   Lindsay Perez Huber, "Discourses of Racist Nativism in California Public Education: English Dominance as Racist Nativist Microaggressions," *Educational Studies* 47 (2011): 388.

10 Huber, "Discourses of Racist Nativism," 388.

11 Jenna Shim, "Self-Identified Linguistic Microaggressions among Monolingual Pre-service Teachers: Why They Matter for English Language Learners," *Multicultural Learning and Teaching*, July 7, 2017, 11.

12 Michael C. LeMay, *U.S. Immigration Policy, Ethnicity, and Religion in American History* (Westport: Praeger, 2018), 142.

13 Eboo Patel, *Sacred Ground: Pluralism, Prejudice, and the Promise of America* (Boston: Beacon, 2012), 38.

14 Shim, "Self-Identified Linguistic Microaggressions," 13.

15 Patel, *Interfaith Leadership*, 93.

16 Patel, *Interfaith Leadership*, 63.

17 Rebecca Dahm, "Can Pluralistic Approaches Based upon Unknown Languages Enhance Learner Engagement and Lead to Active Social Inclusion?" *International Review of Education* 63 (2017): 521.

18 Dahm, "Pluralistic Approaches," 540.

19 Patel, *Interfaith Leadership*, 98–99.

20 Patel, *Interfaith Leadership*, 99.

References

Council on American Islamic Relations. "CAIR and Walkup, Melodia File Suit Challenging Southwest Airlines' Removal of Arabic-Speaking Passenger." Press release. February 13, 2018. https://www.cair.com/cair_and_walkup_melodia_law_firm_file_suit_challenging_southwest_airlines_removal_of_arabic_speaking_passenger.

Dahm, Rebecca. "Can Pluralistic Approaches Based upon Unknown Languages Enhance Learner Engagement and Lead to Active Social Inclusion?" *International Review of Education* 63 (2017): 521–43.

Huber, Lindsay Perez. "Discourses of Racist Nativism in California Public Education: English Dominance as Racist Nativist Microaggressions." *Educational Studies* 47 (2011): 379–401.

LeMay, Michael C. *U.S. Immigration Policy, Ethnicity, and Religion in American History*. Westport: Praeger, 2018.

Macedo, Donaldo. "The Colonialism of the English Only Movement." *Education-al Researcher* 29, no. 3 (2000): 15–24.

Patel, Eboo. *Interfaith Leadership: A Primer.* Boston: Beacon, 2016.

———. *Sacred Ground: Pluralism, Prejudice, and the Promise of America.* Boston: Beacon, 2012.

Shim, Jenna. "Self-Identified Linguistic Microaggressions among Monolingual Pre-service Teachers: Why They Matter for English Language Learners." *Multicultural Learning and Teaching*, July 7, 2017.

Yamanouchi, Kelly. "Group Files Complaint against Delta, Alleging Racial Profiling." *Atlanta Journal-Constitution*, August 4, 2016. https://www.myajc.com/business/group-files-complaint-against-delta-alleging-racial-profiling/tkIXSBVshHyZDm2cZtiXBK/.

27

Kairos Palestine and Autoimmune Rejection

Peter A. Pettit

When it was published ten years ago, in late 2009, the *Kairos Palestine* document[1] sent a ripple through the field of interreligious engagement, which, at the time, might have been mistaken for a tsunami. I have suggested elsewhere that activity among several mainline North American Protestant denominations on behalf of Palestinian Christians increased in the several years following the promulgation of *Kairos Palestine*.[2] A "Christian Palestinian Initiative" continues to maintain a website in support of its movement, "which advocates for ending the Israeli occupation and achieving a just solution to the conflict."[3] Responses to the 2009 document came quickly from various quarters and followed familiar patterns. In the end, the impact of *Kairos Palestine* probably was not as great as feared by some or as great as hoped for by others. For the field of interreligious studies, the responses to *Kairos Palestine* offer an informative perspective on the intersection of interreligious study and intra-religious diversity. They provide a case study in the importance of contextual reading and hermeneutics that underscores the value of historical-critical analysis of texts. In addition, they indicate ways in which efforts to ameliorate conflicts with other religious communities can generate or exacerbate strains and conflicts within one's own.

The Jewish community broadly challenged *Kairos Palestine* at its core and in manifold dimensions, as notably exemplified in the statement by the (Reform) Central Conference of American Rabbis Board of Trustees on April 15, 2010. Beyond its detailed critique of the statement as a "morally inconsistent and theologically suspect document" that "echoes supersessionist language of the Christian past," the board noted that "certain . . . individuals and church groups" had accepted and endorsed it. The board said it was "forced to wonder whether these Church organizations do not recognize [the character] of the *Kairos* document or whether they no longer care to share interfaith dialogue with us."[4]

Prominent among the churches that had responded positively to *Kairos Palestine* was the Presbyterian Church (USA), where the Israel-Palestine Mission Network published a three-week congregational study plan, which was printed and distributed by an Episcopal Church affiliate, Friends of Sabeel–North America. The guide likened *Kairos Palestine* to the anti-Nazi Barmen Declaration of 1934, the American civil rights "Letter from Birmingham Jail" of 1963 penned by Martin Luther King Jr., and the South African *Kairos Document* of 1985. It set out to facilitate engagement with the Palestinian statement, commended for study by the General Assembly of the Presbyterian Church (USA) in 2010, by providing "a common understanding of some of the political and religious issues that are a consequence of Israel's annexation of East Jerusalem and military occupation of the West Bank and Gaza."[5]

On the international interfaith stage, the International Council of Christians and Jews (ICCJ) drew on the language of a prominent Jewish interfaith professional, Rabbi Leon Klenicki, in assessing *Kairos Palestine* under the exhortation "Let Us Have Mercy upon Words."[6] Building on a workshop at the ICCJ 2010 annual conference in Istanbul, the board enumerated "admirable aspects" in the statement and deplored the "heated climate" in which the statement was being received. It noted that "certain charged phrases," in a wider context of "increasing polarization in the discourse between Jews and Christians and also within each community," "can trigger reflexive condemnations [with] a degree of vehemence . . . reaching an unprecedented crescendo in many places."

An accompanying letter sent to the authors of *Kairos Palestine* from the ICCJ board pressed some of the key questions it had raised in the statement about ambiguities and contradictions within the *Kairos Palestine* document. The Kairos Palestine organization in the fall of 2010 sent a reply that addressed six specific points raised in the ICCJ letter. The reply affirmed that *Kairos Palestine* is against polarization and invited a meeting that would "reflect on the role of the Palestinian people that is conspicuously absent in most Christian-Jewish dialogue."[7] The principal concern of the reply was the "displacement theology" that the authors saw undermining Palestinian life as a result of

Western Christian efforts to reject "replacement theology" in regard to the Jewish people.

The several responses noted here characterize basic positions on a more densely populated spectrum and illustrate a truism of theological analysis. That is, the theological concerns and positions that are expressed reflect the context within which each community engages the issue at hand. American Jews largely engage from a concern for the well-being of the State of Israel, notwithstanding their robust debate about its policies and its place in relationship to diasporic Jewish life. The mainline American Protestant denominations engage from a century and a half of missionary activity with Arabs in the region, as well as a more recent theological emphasis on liberation theology and God's "preferential option for the poor." Advocates within the international interfaith dialogue community engage from a background in countering Christianity's long-standing "teaching of contempt" for Jews and Judaism. The Palestinian liberation theologians who penned *Kairos Palestine*, self-evidently, engage from their position among a people living under military occupation and feeling itself in exile from at least a portion of their ancestral homeland.

Of particular note in this regard is the fact that three of the groups just characterized include Christians and two include Jews. Add to that the fact that the *Kairos Palestine* authors ensured the participation of leaders in Jewish-Christian dialogue in the release of their statement, just as mainline Protestants have regularly enlisted Jewish groups within their circles whenever they raise criticisms of Israeli policy, and the complexity of intra-communal engagement with these issues becomes even clearer.

This has two implications for interreligious studies. First, when one is speaking about a religious community and its self-understanding, it is crucial to understand the context within which its self-expression is set. Much as we might hope that this is obvious today, we must also recognize it as applicable to engagement with texts and self-representations of religious communities in the past. That is, the quaintly "modern" practice of historical-critical analysis is not as irrelevant or bankrupt as one might imagine from the past several decades of emphasis on post-structuralist, reader-response, narrative, ideological, and other similar schools of interpretation.

Our understanding of texts as recent as the last decade on a topic as current as the Israeli-Palestinian conflict demands that we know the sociopolitical and cultural contexts from which they emerge. How, then, can we imagine that we understand the texts of another era or particular culture without as clear a profile as we can gain of the contexts from which those emerge? The texts can be used in any way we choose, to be sure, in a reading that is guided solely

208

or primarily by our own perspectives and concerns. In order to construct an understanding of them in relation to other religious communities with which they were interacting, or with which we may want to compare and contrast them, it would seem essential that we undertake the most rigorous analysis possible to situate them in a concrete setting. The simple facts that no such analysis can claim to be unaffected by the analyst's own context and background, and that no such analysis can claim to generate a perfectly accurate profile of the text's context, do not eliminate the evident value in striving for the best we can attain.

Second, the participation of both Jews and Christians in nearly all the efforts related to *Kairos Palestine* makes it impossible to characterize a singular "Jewish" or "Christian" view of the issues involved. That should give us pause in mounting efforts in interreligious studies that rely on broad portraits of religious communities by the common-language labels applied to them. We are unable to characterize a singular "Christian" or "Jewish" view of something as proximate to us as contemporary communities engaging the Israeli-Palestinian conflict. How, then, do we suppose that we can characterize what is (generally) "Jewish" or "Christian" at any more remote period or cultural context when we study those "religions" in relation to other religious communities?

Here a cardinal insight of Michael Barnes provides a helpful guide. In his introduction to religious pluralism in *The Routledge Companion to the Study of Religion*, Barnes engages what he calls "the three-fold paradigm," familiar from the work of John Hick and others. He traces that paradigm to its logical and pragmatic failure to account for both "the living out of the heritage which grounds and gives coherence to the faith of communities" and "the rich complexity of inter-religious relations."[8] Rather than focusing on the objects of theological study that we might call "religions," Barnes proposes turning our attention to "the nature of the theological *subject*, the community of faith which exists by seeking to articulate its relationship with God."[9]

Those communities, as we see in the case of *Kairos Palestine* and responses to it, are complicated and variegated as much as they are concretely situated. Thus, Barnes' counsel "to shift attention . . . to the skills, dispositions and virtues which sustain persons in their pursuit of meaning"[10] will lead us into a productively nuanced, non-categorical exploration of interreligious realities.

A final corollary of this last point is worth mentioning for practitioners of interreligious engagement, whether or not they are also part of the field of interreligious studies. One of the most salutary outcomes of the *Kairos Palestine* episode was the increased awareness it gave to those involved of the wide disparities in perspectives among coreligionists. When engaging in interreligious dialogue and study, there is a tendency so to focus on understanding the fine points and differences presented by the religious other that the diversity within one's own community can be overlooked. Some community members' efforts to engage interreligiously in healing and compensatory ways for harm done to another can trigger a volatile response from coreligionists.

Even within our communities, across different cultures and times, we have developed widely different "skills, dispositions, and virtues" by which we sustain our pursuits of meaning and our self-understandings as religious people. We do justice more fully to others who share our broad label and we are more honest with those in other religious communities when we acknowledge the particularity with which we—and all people—embody and express what it is that we call "our religion."

Notes

1   The document, issued by the Kairos Palestine organization in Bethlehem in December 2009, is "the word of Christian Palestinians to the world about what is happening in Palestine" (https://www.kairospalestine.ps/sites/default/files/English.pdf).

2   Peter A. Pettit, "Mainline Protestant Churches and Israel" (presentation at the Institute for Jewish-Catholic Relations, Saint Joseph's University, Philadelphia, March 19, 2018, part 2 in *The Land and State of Israel in Christian Theologies*), video available online at IJCR website: https://sites.sju.edu/ijcr/ (listed by date under "Institute Archives," time-stamp 25:00).

3   Kairos Palestine website: http://www.kairospalestine.ps/.

4   Central Conference of American Rabbis, "CCAR Resolution on the 2009 *Kairos* Document," April 15, 2010. https://www.ccarnet.org/ccar-resolutions/ccar-resolution-2009-kairos-document/.

5   Israel-Palestine Mission Network of the Presbyterian Church (U.S.A.), *Three-Week Congregational Study Plan: "Kairos Palestine"; A Moment of Truth* (Portland, Ore.: Friends of Sabeel–North America, 2010), 1.

6   International Council of Christians and Jews, "Let Us Have Mercy upon Words: A Plea from the International Council of Christians and Jews to All Who Seek Interreligious Understanding," Heppenheim, Germany, 2010. http://www.iccj.org/redaktion/upload_pdf/201402221306270.ICCJ%20-%20Mercy%20Upon%20Words.pdf.

7   "Letter from Kairos Palestine Authors to ICCJ," Council of Centers on Jewish-Christian Relations, October 23, 2010, accessed April 15, 2019, https://ccjr.us/dialogika-resources/themes-in-today-s-dialogue/isrpal/kairos-iccj2010oct23.

8   Michael Barnes, "Religious Pluralism," in *The Routledge Companion to the Study of Religion*, 2nd ed., ed. John Hinnells (London: Routledge, 2010), 434.

9   Barnes, "Religious Pluralism," in Hinnells, *Routledge Companion*, 434 (emphasis in original).

10 Barnes, "Religious Pluralism," in Hinnells, *Routledge Companion*, 434.

References

Barnes, Michael. "Religious Pluralism." In *The Routledge Companion to the Study of Religion*, 2nd ed., edited by John Hinnells, 426–41. London: Routledge, 2010.

Central Conference of American Rabbis. "CCAR Resolution on the 2009 *Kairos* Document." April 15, 2010. https://www.ccarnet.org/ccar-resolutions/ccar-resolution-2009-kairos-document/.

Council of Centers on Jewish-Christian Relations. "Letter from Kairos Palestine Authors to ICCJ." October 23, 2010. Accessed April 15, 2019. https://ccjr.us/dialogika-resources/themes-in-today-s-dialogue/isrpal/kairos-iccj2010oct23.

International Council of Christians and Jews. "Let Us Have Mercy upon Words: A Plea from the International Council of Christians and Jews to All Who Seek Interreligious Understanding." Heppenheim, Germany, 2010. http://www.iccj.org/redaktion/upload_pdf/201402221306270.ICCJ%20-%20Mercy%20Upon%20Words.pdf.

Israel-Palestine Mission Network of the Presbyterian Church (U.S.A.). *Three-Week Congregational Study Plan: "Kairos Palestine"; A Moment of Truth*. Portland, Ore.: Friends of Sabeel—North America, 2010.

Kairos Palestine. Bethlehem, Palestine, 2009. https://www.kairospalestine.ps/sites/default/files/English.pdf.

Pettit, Peter A. "Mainline Protestant Churches and Israel." Presentation at the Institute for Jewish-Catholic Relations, Saint Joseph's University, Philadelphia, March 19, 2018. Part 2 in *The Land and State of Israel in Christian Theologies*. Video available online at IJCR website: https://sites.sju.edu/ijcr/. Listed by date under "Institute Archives," time-stamp 25:00.

V
PRAXIS AND POSSIBILITY

28

Cross-Cultural Leadership as Interfaith Leadership

Barbara A. McGraw

It goes without saying that travelers ought to study cultural practices before they visit, do business, or conduct other endeavors in countries around the world. There are numerous online sites that address what people from this or that culture do—their habits and practices. However, organizational and international leadership today require much greater understanding than what one can glean from studying how one bows or how and what food is consumed in various countries. Rather, effective leadership in today's global context requires investigating the deep roots of culture in a region's traditional religion for an in-depth understanding of underlying values that shape people's vision of the good society and the good life within it. Leadership that employs such understanding, therefore, is at its core interfaith leadership.

In other words, interreligious studies can deepen cultural studies, leadership studies, and especially the practice of cross-cultural leadership significantly not only by providing knowledge of the deep value roots of each region's culture founded in its traditional dominant religion but also by generating important insights that can lead to greater understanding about how to engage in intercultural encounters more respectfully and effectively. Furthermore, such leadership not only is critical for endeavors that occur within countries other than one's own but is applicable within organizations whose culturally diverse constituents have come from all across the world. Consequently, meaningful and practical knowledge for effective cross-cultural leadership ought to have interreligious understanding and interfaith competence at heart.

Understanding the Deep Religious Roots of Culture

Both religion and culture are notoriously difficult to define. Edward B. Tylor, the founder of cultural anthropology, was the first to define culture as a learned social construct—"that complex whole which includes knowledge, belief, art, morals, law, custom and any other capabilities and habits acquired by man as a member of society."[1] Thus, culture consists of the "symbolic construction, articulation, and dissemination of meaning" in various forms—for example, music, images, social norms, and ideas.[2] Definitions of religion generally reflect particular biases about what it entails—for example, definitions that pose a supernatural power as the creator[3] or focus on belief (Tylor)[4] or something set apart (Durkheim)[5]—thus limiting the term to what is recognized as "religion" in the West. Livingston offers a "working definition," which serves our purposes here, as it does not reflect such deficiencies: "Religion is that system of activities and beliefs directed toward that which is perceived to be of sacred value and transforming power."[6]

Livingston's definition encompasses cultural expressions that scholars and practitioners of the West may not recognize as "religion." Significantly, especially in the United States due in large part to the legal doctrine of separation of church and state, religion is often defined as something that can be distinguished from other aspects of society.[7] Here, however, the argument is that the traditional religion of a region is the foundation of cultural norms and practices. That is, culture encompasses "knowledge, beliefs, art, morals, law, custom" and "symbolic construction, articulation, and dissemination of meaning in various forms" and so forth that reflect the ideals expressed in the "activities and beliefs" that are "perceived to be of sacred value and transforming power."[8] Therefore, attempts to marginalize religion or ignore it altogether obscure the critical role religion plays in shaping culture, including in the United States.

Significantly, research shows considerable correlations between today's peoples and their national cultures,[9] although of course there are variations (e.g., exceptions, subgroups, counter cultures). Still, as Hofstede, Hofstede, and Minkov have argued, national institutions reflect their general cultural milieu. Unless such institutions are imposed by an outside authority, they reinforce the "mental programming [i.e., culturally acquired mental maps] on which they were founded," even when there is internal diversity.[10] Consequently, it is useful for leaders whose purview involves international relations (public or private) to consider culture at the national level and to consider such national cultural influences on diverse individuals from around the world within an organization.[11]

Researchers generally agree that culture and values intersect, and some conclude that "values, more than practices, are the stable element in culture." However, often they conclude that values are inferred "from people's activity."[12] I suggest, however, that rather than focusing on what people do and then inferring values, it would be better to develop multireligious knowledge as a resource for understanding values, and therefore the inherent meaning of customs, social assumptions, and motivations. Such an approach would lead to a richer, thicker, and more stable understanding of a region's underlying values than what we generally find in cultural studies.

Cultural studies tend to underappreciate or even ignore the religious roots of values and the practices and motivations that derive from them, treating them as a minor aspect of culture. An example is when religious foundations are noted but considered overbroadly,[13] or mentioned as important but not explored,[14] or relegated to the realm of the "supernatural" and therefore treated as being unworthy of more than a brief mention.[15] Or religion is viewed as an anomaly or as a problem to be avoided, or as a threat because it is viewed as mainly a generator of conflict.[16] As a result, the nuanced deep religious value differences that are critical to understanding the particularities of national cultures are obscured.

Because a region's traditional religion is marginalized in the literature, the underlying deep motivations for people's cultural practices are not considered. The tendency, then, is for attention to turn to the derivative *effects* of what lies deeper—which I refer to as the *artifacts* of a culture's religious value roots. Examples referenced in the literature include power distance and uncertainty avoidance and the issue of "face-saving" in Asian cultures.[17] My argument here is that without an understanding of the deep value roots of culture in their traditional religion, those artifacts are disembodied from what actually animates them.

Implications for Cross-Cultural Leadership

The West's leadership literature often glosses over differences with a focus on "global" or "universal" needs, definitions, and dimensions that apply cross-culturally rather than on particularities. An example involves theory and research on global leadership,[18] especially where the focus is global mindset.[19] There, the overall identified theories and competencies reflect a search for global paradigms, despite recognition that there are cultural differences. Similarly, when religious dimensions are considered in this context, the erroneous assumption that aspects of the dominant religion of one's home nation are universally applicable in other nations sometimes prevails. For example, Christianity-centered influences—such concepts as "a calling" and such values as "altruistic love"—have been proposed as universally applicable.[20] Even when world religions are taken into account, they are collapsed into generalities that are assumed to apply to all, which disregards critical differences,[21] or are only considered in general ways as relevant to leadership styles and followers' cultural expectations of leaders.[22]

Further, scholars who ignore religion often do not recognize the religious roots of their own religio-cultural perspectives, which can obscure the potential for bias. (The attempted universalizing of Christian particularities referenced above illustrates this point.) It follows that leaders who do not recognize their own particular religio-cultural influences, which inform leaders' habits and practices, can undermine their efforts at effective leadership.

Focus on the artifacts of culture, rather than on deep religious roots and values, can result in leaders conflating or missing cultural cues in their own behavior and in others' behavior in ways that can lead to misunderstandings or even missed opportunities to advance common goals or to gain new perspectives on problems to be solved or for innovative ideas to emerge. As a result, leaders can end up causing significant organizational dysfunction when managing constituents with diverse religio-cultural orientations or may undermine the potential for cooperation on important initiatives with potential partners around the world.

Consider the American businessman who recently recounted to me that he had experienced difficulty obtaining a contract with a potential partner in China. He said, "All they wanted to do was talk and share tea and alcoholic beverages—over two years!" He noted, however, that after those two years, they did finally do business together, and, when they did, they "didn't need a contract." Puzzled, he said, "I don't know why." I suggest that if he had understood the Confucian influence on Chinese culture, he would have had an appreciation for the important value of honor in relationships and how it is through such relationships that the aspirational ideal of social harmony is thought to be achieved to further the common good.[23]

Consider also the often-referenced frustration that Americans say they experience when conducting business abroad. American businesspersons' values of efficiency and productivity in the service of profit run headlong into cultural expectations abroad where other values take precedence over the Americans' profit-maximizing imperative. Generally, Americans are unaware that they bring with them their famous Protestant work ethic, focused on worldly success, especially the accumulation of wealth, as evidence of being one of the "chosen"—now no longer by God, but by the capitalist market system itself. That ethic focuses Americans, whose efficiency in the service of productivity is legendary, on the value of work over almost everything else, often at the cost of relationships and consideration of the common good.

These admittedly essentialized accounts, which obviously would require much more explanation and analysis in a longer work, nevertheless illustrate the dilemma. It is not difficult to imagine the differences in expectations for behavior, leadership, and followership from these two very different religio-cultural orientations when they run headlong into each other in an organizational setting or in an international endeavor. Yet too often no one has considered what leadership ought to entail in the midst of diverse interactions such as these or in organizations with many constituents coming from different nations. That is, they have not recognized that such interactions actually are interfaith interactions.

New-Genre Leadership and the Deep Value Roots of Culture

There are many theories of leadership, including traditional approaches such as the Great Man Theory and the Charismatic Leader Theory, both of which focus on the characteristics of the leader.[24] With his influential work on leadership, however, James MacGregor Burns signaled a departure from such traditional leadership approaches,[25] which primarily involve a series of transactions between leaders and followers. Known as "transforming leadership," Burns' approach is a creative process of leader–follower interaction. Rather than addressing a leader's characteristics/traits and competencies, as do many other leadership theories,[26] transforming leaders galvanize followers by appealing to their intrinsic needs and higher values and aim at a common aspirational moral purpose.[27] Burns' transforming leadership has been an influence on other "new-genre leadership" approaches, which involve leader–follower motivational relationships and activity based on values and purpose—for example, shared, servant, collaborative, relational, authentic, and spiritual leadership.[28] Such leadership has been shown to be effective for inspiring teams and for follower satisfaction,[29] and it is particularly relevant for innovative business leaders who employ creative collaboration and/or adopt corporate social responsibility strategies, especially for moral reasons.[30]

Such dynamic, collaborative, and values-based approaches to leadership, which focus on followers as much as leaders and their interaction, require a much more nuanced understanding of the particularities of constituents' cultural perspectives. As shown above, deep religious roots shape their perspectives, values, and customs, and the social assumptions and orientations that inform them. This can be so even when individuals within a nation or region—or who bring those orientations from many nations into an organization—do not identify as being religious or have a commitment to a religion that is not the traditional religion of their home nation or region. Those individuals are nevertheless shaped by the overall cultural milieu of their origins. Consequently, it is especially important for leaders who adopt such new genre leadership approaches to recognize that it is critical not only to take account of cross-cultural considerations but also to become knowledgeable about the religious roots of those cultures—in effect becoming interfaith leaders.

Further Study

The argument in this brief chapter is intended to establish a foundation for cross-cultural leadership as interfaith leadership that will generate further discussion. And the implications for future research and improved practice are many. Future scholarship could include engagement of leadership scholars with religion scholars who have a specific, in-depth expertise on the religions that have influenced the deep values of specific nations and regions around the world—and the customs and social assumptions and orientations derived from them—for relevant organizations and international projects. Also, there is potential for scholar–practitioner engagement for more effective organizational and global leadership—to raise awareness of the importance of multireligious knowledge and understanding of interfaith practice for effective leadership. Furthermore, scholars of cultural diversity, leadership, and organizations, on the one hand, and religion scholars, on the other hand, would benefit from engaging each other's work to enrich explorations in their own fields and to expand the scholarly discourse in the largely unexplored avenues of research suggested here that could be produced by their interactions.

Conclusion

If appeals to values and advancement of aspirational purposes are to be employed in leadership that aims to galvanize others to achieve worthy common goals in cross-cultural contexts, attention to the particularities of the values and motivations of culturally diverse constituents is needed. That requires understanding of the deep values, motivations, and social aspirations found in the traditional religious orientation of regions of the world and operationalizing that understanding in cross-cultural leadership as interfaith leadership.

Notes

1   Edward Burnett Tylor, *Primitive Culture: Research into the Development of Mythology, Philosophy, Religion, Art, and Custom* (London: John Murray, 1871), 1:1.

2   Manfred B. Steger, *Globalization: A Very Short Introduction*, 3rd ed. (Oxford: Oxford University Press), chap. 5.

3   American Heritage Dictionary, s.v. "Religion" (def. 1), accessed January 21, 2019, https://ahdictionary.com/word/search.html?q=religion&submit.x=30 &submit.y=21.

4   Tylor, *Primitive Culture*.

5   Émile Durkheim, *The Elementary Forms of Religious Life*, trans. Karen E. Fields (New York: Free Press, 1995 [original publication 1912]).

6   James C. Livingston, *Anatomy of the Sacred: An Introduction to Religion* (New York: Macmillan, 1993), 11.

7   J. O. Usman, "Defining Religion: The Struggle to Define Religion under the First Amendment and the Contributions and Insights of Other Disciplines of Study Including Theology, Psychology, Sociology, the Arts, and Anthropology," *North Dakota Law Review* 83, no. 1 (2007): 123–223.

8   See notes 1, 2 and 6, above.

9   Research also shows considerable correlations of individuals' personality traits and their national cultures, although there are variations (Geert Hofstede, Gert Jan Hofstede, and Michael Minkov, *Cultures and Organizations: Software of the Mind* [New York: McGraw-Hill, 2010], 21–22, 39).

10 Hofstede, Hofstede, and Minkov, *Cultures and Organizations*, 24.

11 Of course, it is always important to avoid stereotypes: one ought to consider the particularities of the persons, groups, and subnational regions encountered (Hofstede, Hofstede, and Minkov, *Cultures and Organizations*, 40). That said, taking into account national cultures around the world is an important starting point for a discussion of cross-cultural leadership and the importance of considering the deep values derived from national cultures' traditional religious roots.

12 See, e.g., Hofstede, Hofstede, and Minkov, *Cultures and Organizations*, 28.

13 See, e.g., Hofstede, Hofstede, and Minkov, *Cultures and Organizations*, 246–48.

14 See, e.g., Susan R. Komives, Nance L. Lucas, and Timothy R. McMahon, *Exploring Leadership: For College Students Who Want to Make a Difference*, 3rd ed. (San Francisco: Jossey-Bass, 2013), 176.

15 See, e.g., Gary P. Ferraro and Elizabeth K. Briody, *The Cultural Dimension of Global Business*, 8th ed. (London: Routledge, 2017), 17.

16 See, e.g., Hofstede, Hofstede, and Minkov, *Cultures and Organizations*, 14, 45.

17 See, e.g., Ferraro and Briody, *Cultural Dimension of Global Business*.

18 See, e.g., Mark E. Mendenhall, Torsten Kühlmann, and Gunter K. Stahl, *Developing Global Business Leaders: Policies, Processes, and Innovations* (Westport, Conn.: Quorum, 2001).

19 Mansour Javidan, Richard M. Steers, and Michael A. Hitt, eds., *The Global Mindset (Advances in International Management, Volume 19)* (Bingley, U.K.: Emerald Group, 2007); Nakiye Boyacigiller et al., "The Crucial yet Elusive Global Mindset," in *The Blackwell Handbook of Global Management: A Guide to Managing Complexity*, ed. Henry W. Lane et al. (Malden, Mass.: Blackwell, 2006), 81–93.

20 Louis W. Fry, "Introduction to the Leadership Quarterly Special Issue: Toward a Paradigm of Spiritual Leadership," *Leadership Quarterly* 16 (2005): 621.

21 Mark Kriger and Yvonne Seng, "Leadership with Inner Meaning: A Contingency Theory of Leadership Based on the Worldviews of Five Religions," *Leadership Quarterly* 16 (2005): 771–806. Stephen Prothero argues that religious differences are more important than religious commonalities when religious literacy is the goal (*God Is Not One: The Eight Religions That Run the World—and Why Their Differences Matter* [New York: HarperCollins, 2010]).

22 Rasa Pauliené, "Transforming Leadership Styles and Knowledge Sharing in a Multicultural Context," *Business, Management and Education* 10, no. 1 (2012): 91–109, doi:10.3846/bme.2012.08.

23 Robert S. Ellwood and Barbara A. McGraw, *Many Peoples, Many Faiths: Women and Men in the World Religions*, 10th ed. (Upper Saddle River, N.J.: Pearson, 2014), chap. 4; John G. Oetzel et al., "Historical, Political, and Spiritual Factors of Conflict: Understanding Conflict Perspectives and Communication in the Muslim World, China, Colombia, and South Africa," in *The Sage Handbook of Conflict Communication: Integrating Theory, Research, and Practice*, ed. John G. Oetzel and Stella Ting-Toomey (Thousand Oaks, Calif.: Sage, 2006), 549–74.

24 Komives, Lucas, and McMahon, *Exploring Leadership*, chap. 2.

25 James MacGregor Burns, *Leadership* (New York: HarperCollins, 1978).

26 Dmitry Khanin, "Contrasting Burns and Bass," *Journal of Leadership Studies* 1, no. 3 (2007): 7–25.

27 James MacGregor Burns, *Transforming Leadership* (New York: Grove), 2003.

28 Bruce Avolio, Fred Walumbwa, and Todd J. Weber, "Leadership: Current Theories, Research, and Future Directions," *Annual Review of Psychology* 60 (2009): 421–49, doi:10.1146/annurev.psych.60.110707.163621.

29 Pauliené, "Transforming Leadership Styles," 93; and David A. Waldman, Donald S. Siegel, and Mansour Javidan, "Components of CEO Transforma-

tional Leadership," *Journal of Management Studies* 43, no. 8 (2006): 1705, doi: 10.1111/j.1467-6486.2006.00642.x.

30 Khanin, "Contrasting Burns and Bass"; Waldman, Siegel, and Javidan, "Components of CEO Transformational Leadership," 1704 (citing Richard L. Daft, *The Leadership Experience*, 2nd ed. [Cincinnati: South-Western, 2002]).

References

Avolio, Bruce, Fred Walumbwa, and Todd J. Weber. "Leadership: Current Theories, Research, and Future Directions." *Annual Review of Psychology* 60 (2009): 421–49. doi:10.1146/annurev.psych.60.110707.163621.

Boyacigiller, Nakiye, Schon Beechler, Sully Taylor, and Orly Levy. "The Crucial yet Elusive Global Mindset." In *The Blackwell Handbook of Global Management: A Guide to Managing Complexity*, edited by Henry W. Lane, Martha L. Maznevski, Mark E. Mendenhall, and Jeanne McNett, 81–93. Malden, Mass.: Blackwell, 2006.

Burns, James MacGregor. *Leadership*. New York: HarperCollins, 1978.

———. *Transforming Leadership*. New York: Grove, 2003.

Daft, Richard L. *The Leadership Experience*. 2nd ed. Cincinnati: South-Western, 2002.

Durkheim, Émile. *The Elementary Forms of Religious Life*. Translated by Karen E. Fields. New York: Free Press, 1995 (original publication 1912).

Ellwood, Robert S., and Barbara A. McGraw. *Many Peoples, Many Faiths: Women and Men in the World Religions*. 10th ed. Upper Saddle River, N.J.: Pearson, 2014.

Ferraro, Gary P., and Elizabeth K. Briody. *The Cultural Dimension of Global Business*. 8th ed. London: Routledge, 2017.

Fry, Louis W. "Introduction to the Leadership Quarterly Special Issue: Toward a Paradigm of Spiritual Leadership." *Leadership Quarterly* 16 (2005): 619–22.

Hofstede, Geert, Gert J. Hofstede, and Michael Minkov. *Cultures and Organizations: Software of the Mind*. New York: McGraw-Hill, 2010.

Javidan, Mansour, Richard M. Steers, and Michael A. Hitt, eds. *The Global Mindset (Advances in International Management, Volume 19)*. Bingley, U.K.: Emerald Group, 2007.

Khanin, D. "Contrasting Burns and Bass." *Journal of Leadership Studies* 1, no. 3 (2007): 7–25.

Komives, Susan R., Nance L. Lucas, and Timothy R. McMahon. *Exploring Leadership: For College Students Who Want to Make a Difference*. 3rd ed. San Francisco: Jossey-Bass, 2013.

Kriger, Mark, and Yvonne Seng. "Leadership with Inner Meaning: A Contingency Theory of Leadership Based on the Worldviews of Five Religions." *Leadership Quarterly* 16 (2005): 771–806.

Livingston, James C. *Anatomy of the Sacred: An Introduction to Religion*. New York: Macmillan, 1993.

Mendenhall, Mark E., Torsten Kühlmann, and Gunter K. Stahl. *Developing Global Business Leaders: Policies, Processes, and Innovations*. Westport, Conn.: Quorum 2001.

Oetzel, John G., Babiana Arcos, Phola Mabizela, A. Michael Weinman, and Qin Zhang. "Historical, Political, and Spiritual Factors of Conflict: Understanding Conflict Perspectives and Communication in the Muslim World, China, Colombia, and South Africa." In *The Sage Handbook of Conflict Communication: Integrating Theory, Research, and Practice*, edited by John G. Oetzel and Stella Ting-Toomey, 549–74. Thousand Oaks, Calif.: Sage, 2006.

Paulienė, Rasa. "Transforming Leadership Styles and Knowledge Sharing in a Multicultural Context." *Business, Management and Education* 10, no. 1 (2012): 91–109. doi:10.3846/bme.2012.08.

Prothero, Stephen. *God Is Not One: The Eight Religions That Run the World—and Why Their Differences Matter*. New York: HarperCollins, 2010.

Steger, Manfred B. *Globalization: A Very Short Introduction*. 3rd ed. Oxford: Oxford University Press.

Tylor, Edward Burnett. *Primitive Culture: Research into the Development of Mythology, Philosophy, Religion, Art, and Custom*. Vol. 1. London: John Murray, 1871.

Usman, J. O. "Defining Religion: The Struggle to Define Religion under the First Amendment and the Contributions and Insights of Other Disciplines of Study Including Theology, Psychology, Sociology, the Arts, and Anthropology." *North Dakota Law Review* 83, no. 1 (2007): 123–223.

Waldman, David A., Donald S. Siegel, and Mansour Javidan. "Components of CEO Transformational Leadership." *Journal of Management Studies* 43, no.8 (2006): 1703–25. doi:10.1111/j.1467–6486.2006.00642.x.

29

Interreligious Empathy

Catherine Cornille

If the field of interfaith studies consists of the knowledge and skills necessary to live together harmoniously in a pluralistic society, then reflection on the possibility and limits of interreligious empathy would seem to constitute an important critical and constructive ingredient of the field. Since experience forms an essential component of religious life, empathy contributes in important ways to a comprehensive understanding of the religious other. The ability to resonate with the beliefs and practices of the other helps to break down barriers, while the inability to do so tends to cast the religious other as strange and threatening. Empathy may be located somewhere on the border between knowledge and skill. It involves experiential knowledge of the other that may be more innate as a personal skill in some, while requiring more effort in others. This chapter examines empathy in the context of interreligious encounter and makes the case for not only why interfaith studies might play an important role in cultivating interreligious empathy but also why the field of interfaith and interreligious studies ought to critically reflect on variables that enhance or impede empathy.

Though empathy forms an essential dimension of interreligious understanding, it is rarely discussed explicitly in interfaith studies, as also more broadly in the study of religion. Early phenomenologists of religion such as Gerardus van der Leeuw and Max Scheler gave it due attention.[1] In time, however, it came to be regarded as too subjective, unpredictable, and uncontrollable a skill to be part of a systematic or scholarly study of religion. Of late, there has been a resurgence of philosophical interest in empathy, especially in its relation to morality. Empathy is generally regarded as an aggression-curber and a helping-accelerator. It is used in schools to avoid conflict and in companies to promote collaboration and productivity. Martin Hoffman points out that little has made as much difference in changing white Americans' attitudes toward slavery as Harriet Beecher Stowe's novel *Uncle Tom's Cabin*.[2] On the other hand, empathy can also be used effectively to punish the other or to manipulate their emotions for one's own ends. To "urinate on the Bible or the Koran," Frans de Waal points out, "rests on our ability to assume their viewpoint and realize what will hurt or harm them the most."[3]

The term "empathy" is of surprisingly recent origin. While the experience may be essentially human and of all times, the term was coined by Robert Vischer in 1873 to describe the process of aesthetic enjoyment and later popularized by Theodore Lipps to apply to the understanding of mental states and experiences of others. Though it is often used interchangeably with "sympathy," Scheler drew a clear distinction between "sympathy" as "fellow-feeling" and "empathy" as "all such attitudes as merely contribute to our comprehending, understanding, and in general reproducing (emotionally) the experiences of others, including their states of feeling."[4] Sympathy may thus be regarded as empathy with the added desire to contribute to the welfare of others.[5] Scholars have come to distinguish between different types of empathy: cognitive versus affective empathy (Antti Kauppinene), basic versus re-enactive empathy (Karsten Stueber), passive versus active empathy (Richard Garrett and George Graham), and self-focused versus other-focused empathy (Martin Hoffman).[6] Of particular interest for interfaith studies is the general acknowledgment that empathy flows more easily toward friends than toward strangers, toward in-group more than toward out-group, toward people one considers fair and honorable than toward those one considers unfair and dishonorable, toward those one likes than toward those one envies and dislikes.[7] On the other hand, there is vast evidence of the possibility of empathy across religious traditions, of resonance with teachings and practices both similar to and different from one's own, of profound identification with certain experiences leading to conversion as well as of aversion for certain forms of religious experience leading to condemnation. Interreligious empathy does not always lead to sympathy or agreement. As Halpbern points out, "The work of empathy is precisely trying to imagine a view of the world that one does not share, and in fact may find it quite difficult to share. Notably, while empathy involves perceiving the other's complex point of view, it does not require accepting the other's views."[8]

While empathy does not presuppose endorsement, it does at least require some degree of openness to the plausibility or the meaningfulness of the beliefs and practices of the other. This represents a challenge for interreligious empathy. Insofar as the beliefs of one tradition often directly contradict those of another, such openness requires considerable doctrinal humility and a reconsideration of traditional exclusive religious claims.[9] Experiences of empathy may themselves in turn engender greater doctrinal or religious openness. Changes in the attitudes toward other religions of the second Vatican council were brought about by empathy with the suffering of Jews under prior doctrinal views and by greater empathy with the religious teachings and practices of other religions in general.

In addition to doctrinal openness, interreligious empathy also requires or at least relies on experience, participation, and imagination.[10] Interreligious empathy presumes some familiarity with certain types of religious experience and religious desire. Each religion contains a vast diversity of types of religious experiences such that, as has been pointed out, it is at times easier to resonate with experiences of individuals of other religious traditions than with individuals belonging to one's own tradition.[11] Interreligious empathy is thus made possible, but also constrained by, one's own religious repertoire. Since religious experiences are often generated by ritual action, participation in the religious and ritual life of the other contributes to empathy. This, however, also points to the limits of interreligious empathy, since it draws attention to the occasional ritual exclusion of individuals not belonging to a particular religion. It also sheds light on the fact that religious experiences are shaped by a particular faith commitment and that the lack of such commitment inevitably impedes identification with the experience of the other.

In the absence of actual faith or the possibility of ritual participation, interreligious empathy may still feed on the powers of the imagination. This forms one of the most essential and elusive ingredients of interreligious empathy. It involves the ability of conceiving of things existing otherwise. Since the imagination plays a crucial role in all religious life, it may also serve to conceive of alternatives to one's own religious beliefs and images, male conceptions of the divine referring to the possibility of female gods, or belief in the resurrection of the body suggesting the possibility of reincarnation, and vice versa. Insofar as religions offer answers to the same fundamental questions, it is possible to imagine alternative answers. This does not mean that the imagination offers a certain bridge to the religious world of the other. It may also run wild or falter when encountering entirely new religious images and worlds. While participation in the religious life of the other may feed and properly steer the imagination, it remains a highly personal faculty, difficult to predict or control.

It must be clear that interreligious empathy does not involve duplicating the experience of the other. Any resonance with the religious life of the other will be colored by one's own religious background, experiences, and dispositions. Rather than using the term "empathy" in interreligious relations, Gavin Flood therefore uses Bakhtin's term "live-entering."[12] This ensures recognition of the alterity of the other, and it cautions against simply projecting one's own feelings upon the other.

Even though the experiential life of other religions may not be perfectly or fully penetrable, any degree of resonance with the beliefs and practices of religious others goes a long way to overcoming fear and animosity and to developing respect and solidarity. The very attempt to understand the religious other from within may also open up a new register of religious experience that may enrich one's own religious life.

The field of interfaith studies may play an important role in cultivating interreligious empathy. It seeks to offer the necessary tools and opportunities for individuals from different religions to know one another and to participate in the religious life of the other. While empathy may not in itself become a distinctive academic subject, the field of interfaith studies should include critical reflection on the variables that enhance or impede such empathy, particularly when engaging in case studies.

Notes

1   Gerardus van der Leeuw, *Religion in Essence and Manifestation* (Princeton: Princeton University Press 1964), 671–78. Max Scheler, *The Nature of Sympathy* (London: Routledge & Kegan Paul, 1954).

2   Martin Hoffman, "Empathy, Justice and Social Change," in *Empathy and Morality*, ed. Heidi Maibom (Oxford: Oxford University Press, 2014), 87.

3   Frans de Waal, *The Age of Empathy: Nature's Lessons for a Kinder Society* (New York: Random House, 2009), 211.

4   Scheler, *Nature of Sympathy*, 8.

5   Heidi Maibom, "Introduction," in Maibom, *Empathy and Morality*, 3.

6   All these distinctions are developed in Maibom, *Empathy and Morality*.

7   Shlomo Hareli and Bernard Weiner, "Dislike and Envy as Antecedents of Pleasure at Another's Misfortune," *Motivation and Emotion* 26 (2002): 257–77.

8   Jodi Halpbern, "Rehumanizing the Other: Empathy and Reconciliation," *Human Rights Quarterly* 26, no. 3 (2004): 581.

9   This is worked out in an area of theological reflection called "Theology of Religions."

10   Catherine Cornille, *The Im-possibility of Interreligious Dialogue* (New York: Crossroads, 2008), 137–76.

11   Perry Schmidt-Leukel, *Religious Pluralism and Interreligious Theology* (Maryknoll, N.Y.: Orbis, 2017), 222–47.

12   Gavin Flood, *Beyond Phenomenology: Rethinking the Study of Religion* (London: Cassell, 1999), 159–68.

References

Cornille, Catherine. *The Im-possibility of Interreligious Dialogue.* New York: Crossroads, 2008.

de Waal, Frans. *The Age of Empathy: Nature's Lesson for a Kinder Society.* New York: Random House, 2009.

Flood, Gavin. *Beyond Phenomenology: Rethinking the Study of Religion.* London: Cassell, 1999.

Halpbern, Jodi. "Rehumanizing the Other: Empathy and Reconciliation." *Human Rights Quarterly* 26, no. 3 (2004): 561–83.

Hareli, Shlomo, and Bernard Weiner. "Dislike and Envy as Antecedents of Pleasure at Another's Misfortune." *Motivation and Emotion* 26 (2002): 257–77.

Hoffman, Martin. "Empathy, Justice and Social Change." In Maibom, *Empathy and Morality*, 71–96.

Maibom, Heidi, ed. *Empathy and Morality.* Oxford: Oxford University Press, 2014.

———. "Introduction." In Maibom, *Empathy and Morality*, 1–40.

Palmisano, Joseph. *Beyond the Walls: Abraham Joshua Heschel and Edith Stein on the Significance of Empathy for Jewish-Christian Dialogue.* Oxford: Oxford University Press, 2012.

Rifkin, Jeremy. *The Empathic Civilization: The Race to Global Consciousness in a World in Crisis.* New York: Penguin, 2009.

Scheler, Max. *The Nature of Sympathy.* London: Routledge & Kegan Paul, 1954 (1913).

Schmidt-Leukel, Perry. *Religious Pluralism and Interreligious Theology.* Maryknoll, N.Y.: Orbis, 2017.

Smart, Ninian. *Concept and Empathy: Essays in the Study of Religion.* London: MacMillan, 1986.

Stein, Edith. *On the Problem of Empathy.* The Hague: Martinus Nijhoff, 1964.

Stueber, Karsten. *Rediscovering Empathy: Agency, Folk Psychology and the Human Sciences.* Cambridge, Mass.: MIT Press, 2006.

van der Leeuw, Gerardus. *Religion in Essence and Manifestation.* Princeton: Princeton University Press, 1964 (1933).

30

Howard Thurman's Mentorship of Zalman Schachter-Shalomi

Or N. Rose

A highly creative and controversial Jewish leader, Rabbi Zalman Schachter-Shalomi, founder of the Jewish Renewal Movement, was a pioneering inter-religious practitioner in post–World War II North American life. By the time of his death in 2014 he was widely regarded as a leading interpreter of Juda-ism (particularly the mystical tradition) and a wise religious bridge-builder.[1] Schachter-Shalomi participated in public and private gatherings with such re-nowned figures as His Holiness the 14th Dalai Lama, Archbishop Desmond Tutu, and Father Thomas Keating, and from 1995 to 2002 he held the World Wisdom Chair at the Buddhist Naropa University in Boulder, Colorado. How-ever, long before he grew into the role of international Jewish sage and spiritual elder, Schachter-Shalomi began an idiosyncratic journey that took him from the world of HaBaD-Lubavitch Hasidism[2] into dialogue with an array of prac-titioners, practices, and texts from the world's religions.

In this brief essay, I explore Schachter-Shalomi's first encounters with the renowned African American clergyman and public intellectual Howard Thurman[3] at Boston University (BU) in the fall of 1955. At the time Thurman served as dean of Marsh Chapel and professor of spiritual disciplines and re-sources at BU's School of Theology, and Schachter-Shalomi[4] was a new student in the M.A. program in psychology and religion, while also working as a pulpit rabbi in a small Orthodox congregation in New Bedford, Massachusetts. The rabbi regarded this relationship as pivotal in his development as a religious leader and educator.

As a scholar in the burgeoning field of interreligious studies, I think it is crucial that we learn from the experiences of our forebears—researchers and practitioners alike—and those, like Schachter-Shalomi, who moved between these distinct but related spheres of activity. Further, it is essential to examine both the public and the private efforts of such figures to better understand the efficacy of different forms of engagement and the connections among them. A robust and nuanced history of interreligious activity in North America (and elsewhere)—including success and failures—is a desideratum in the study of religion that would benefit researchers and grassroots participants alike.[5] I view this chapter as a kind of historical "case study" in interreligious leadership formation, with the practice of hospitality emerging as a central virtue and practice in this episode.

A Chance Encounter?

As a commuter student Schachter-Shalomi had to leave his home in New Bedford at 5:00 a.m. daily to arrive in time for morning classes. This meant that he departed before sunrise and could not, therefore, recite the *Schacharit* (Morning) service before heading off to Boston. And so, after arriving at BU, he had to find an appropriate place to pray. The only building he could find that was open at that early hour was the university chapel. However, as Schachter-Shalomi writes, navigating this Christian holy space was challenging for him:

> The main chapel upstairs was full of statues of Jesus and the Evangelists. As an Orthodox Jew, I simply wasn't comfortable praying there. Downstairs was a smaller, more intimate chapel for meditation, but there I was likewise inhibited by a big brass cross on the altar. Having no other option, I chose a public room called the Daniel Marsh Memorabilia Room in the same building. There I found myself a corner facing east, toward Jerusalem, and began to pray.[6]

While the young rabbi was apprehensive, a few previous constructive interfaith experiences helped him cross this threshold.[7]

Schachter-Shalomi continued to pray by himself in the Marsh Memorabilia Room for the next several days, before he attracted the attention of one of the chapel employees:

> Just after completing my prayers, a middle-aged black man came into the room and said in a casual way: "I've seen you here several times.

Wouldn't you like to say your prayers in the small chapel?" I shrugged my shoulders, not knowing what to say. The man was so unpretentious that I thought he might have been the janitor. And his offer was so forthcoming that I did not want to hurt his feelings. But how could I explain that I couldn't pray in the chapel because of the cross on the altar? After a moment of looking at me earnestly, he said: "Why don't you stop by the chapel tomorrow morning and take a look? Maybe you'd be comfortable saying your prayers there."[8]

Curious to see what his enigmatic host had in mind, Schachter-Shalomi the next morning went to look at the small chapel. To his surprise, it had been significantly reconfigured:

There I found two candles burning in brass candleholders, and no sign of the big brass cross! The large, ornate Bible was open to the Book of Psalms, Psalm 139, "Whither shall I flee from Thy presence." From then on, I understood that I was at liberty to move the cross and say my morning prayers in the chapel. Afterward, I would always put the cross back and turn the page to Psalm 100, the "Thank you" psalm.

As Schachter-Shalomi would soon learn (much to his embarrassment), the man he mistook for the janitor was, in fact, the dean of Marsh Chapel, the reverend Howard Thurman. He made this revelation when he initiated a meeting with the dean to discuss his course work.

Sometime after this, I read an announcement about a new course in Spiritual Disciplines and Resources, which would include "labs" for spiritual exercises to be taught by the Dean of the Chapel. The course intrigued me, but I was apprehensive about taking it. The Dean of the Chapel was also a minister, and I worried that he might feel obliged to try and convert me.[9]

To Schachter-Shalomi's surprise, Thurman used a dramatic pedagogic tool to invite the apprehensive new student into his course:

He [Dean Thurman] put his coffee mug down on his desk and began to examine his hands. He looked at them slowly as if considering the light and dark sides of an argument. . . . He did this with such a calm certainty that he seemed to possess great power. . . . Finally, he spoke—"Don't you trust the *Ru'ah Ha'Kodesh*?"[10]

And how did Schachter-Shalomi respond to this gesture? "I was stunned. He had used the Hebrew for the Holy Spirit, something I had not expected from a Gentile. And in so doing, he brought that question home to me in a powerful way."[11] While it took Schachter-Shalomi some time to respond to Thurman's provocative question, the eventual answer was yes; he trusted that his relationship with God and commitment to Jewish life and practice—his "anchor chains"—were strong enough to take the risk of studying with this Christian teacher. Clearly, he also trusted this kind, perceptive, and challenging man, who had humbly welcomed him into the chapel, rearranging the prayer space for him with great attention to religious and aesthetic detail.[12] Additionally, Thurman chose not to say anything about the chapel experience, letting his actions speak for themselves.

Thurman's gestures could have easily fallen flat had his younger interlocutor not been receptive to his brand of hospitality. Another person may have not returned to the chapel after their initial encounter or, if that person did return, might not have been able to play the sophisticated, nonverbal game of moving the cross and flipping from psalm to psalm. Further, other students may have found the dean's challenge about the Holy Spirit too forceful, presumptuous, or even manipulative.

Since Thurman was an older, erudite, and charismatic religious leader, Schachter-Shalomi was perhaps more open to learning from him, based on the young rabbi's training and relationships with his Hasidic teachers and mentors. While he was expanding his religious horizons, Schachter-Shalomi still valued the guidance of a seasoned (male) teacher, even if that man was a black, Baptist minister. The private office meeting may have even felt familiar to the rabbi from his experiences in *yehidut*, one-on-one counseling sessions with his *rebbes* (Hasidic masters).[13]

While neither man says so in their writings, I wonder if the fact that both were from minority communities and had personally experienced the pain of marginalization and oppression helped them forge their relationship. It is interesting to note that because of his experience with the burning of crosses by the Ku Klux Klan, Thurman carried with him great ambivalence about this ubiquitous Christian symbol. As he wrote, "Even to this day [1959], I find that whenever I see the cross my mind and my spirit must do a double take because the thing that flashes instinctively in my mind is that of the burning cross of the Klan."[14] I would imagine that this made it easier for Thurman to move the large brass cross in the chapel, knowing that this weighty symbolic object could alienate Schachter-Shalomi as a Jew, whose people had lived in the shadow of the cross for centuries.

Learning from Our Forebears

One foundational teaching that emerges from this story is the power of *inter-religious hospitality*. In using the term, I mean a display of thoughtful welcome by a person from one religious tradition to someone from a different tradition, keeping in mind the specific religious needs of one's guest. As evidenced above, gestures of interreligious hospitality can be particularly important when forging relationships across communities, whether individual or group, as they can help establish trust and respect. Of course, in order to serve as an effective host interreligiously, one must be both knowledgeable enough about the needs of one's guest and willing to accommodate a person (or persons) whose beliefs and practices may differ from, even challenge, one's own. As the French monk Pierre-François de Béthune writes, "Offering such hospitality does involve a risk . . . [as evidenced by the fact that the words] 'hospitality' and 'hostility' share the same Indo-European root. . . . The guest, the stranger . . . always arouses a certain anxiety."[15] Further, the host also risks alienating the guest through the host's chosen gestures of hospitality, even when acting with the best of intentions. Of course, one must also carefully consider how much one can accommodate another without compromising one's integrity.

De Béthune also notes the importance of being able to *offer* and *receive* hospitality; learning to serve in both roles is crucial to this bridge building work. As he writes, "The first side, the offering of hospitality, has been more often studied. But if this is the only kind of hospitality we are engaged in, we are running the risk of want of balance."[16] In thinking about such issues, one must also carefully consider matters of power and privilege as it relates to religion, race, gender, and the like. The case of Thurman and Schachter-Shalomi is an interesting one given their respective identities and the roles each played in the context of their relationship at BU and in the wider world. It is noteworthy that Schachter-Shalomi went on to study closely with Thurman while at BU and invited his teacher—whom he came to lovingly call his "Black *Rebbe*"[17]— to lecture at the University of Manitoba in the spring of 1963, where the rabbi served as a professor and Hillel director (Jewish student life) after completing his studies at BU. Both men wrote effusively about the spiritual significance of their encounter in Winnipeg.[18]

Conclusion

While Zalman Schachter-Shalomi and Howard Thurman are both well-known figures in their respective religious communities and in related scholarly, spiritual, and activist circles, few people are aware of their relationship. Thurman's thoughtful welcome of Schachter-Shalomi to BU—and his subsequent mentorship of the young rabbi—was decisive in the formation of this iconoclastic Jewish leader. While it is harder to evaluate the impact of this relationship on Thurman, as he was an older, well-established intellectual and leader when the two men met, it is clear from his reflection on his visit to Winnipeg in 1963 that their interactions touched him deeply and inspired him to continue his own idiosyncratic and impactful interreligious journey.

It is my hope that by uncovering such stories of interreligious engagement, particularly the work of pioneering figures like Thurman and Schachter-Shalomi, we can better understand the history of the North American interfaith movement. As scholars and practitioners, it is crucial that we study both the public and the private efforts of our forebears so that we can learn from their struggles and successes. Otherwise, we will not only be "doomed to repeat" their mistakes but also lose the opportunity to gain from their acts of courage and compassion.

Notes

1   See the obituaries in the *New York Times,* https://www.nytimes.com/2014/07/09/us/zalman-schachter-shalomi-jewish-pioneer-dies-at-89.html?_r= 1, and *The Huffington Post,* https://www.huffpost.com/entry/rabbi-zalman -schachtersha_b_5555879.

2   See Naftali Lowenthal, "Lubavitch Hasidism," Yivo Encyclopedia of Jews in Eastern Europe, accessed February 9, 2019, http://www.yivoencyclopedia .org/article.aspx/Lubavitch_Hasidism.

3   For an introduction to Thurman's life and work, see, Luther E. Smith, ed., *Howard Thurman: Essential Writings* (Maryknoll, N.Y.: Orbis, 2006).

4   At the time, his name was Zalman Schachter; he added the name Shalomi (from the Hebrew word *Shalom,* "Peace") later as a way of balancing his inherited family name, which means "ritual slaughter" in Yiddish (the family occupation for several generations). See his comments on this matter in Zalman Schachter-Shalomi (with Edward Hoffman), *My Life in Jewish Renewal: A Memoir* (Lanham, Md.: Rowan & Littlefield, 2012), 182.

5   One important example of this type of research is Kevin M. Schultz, *Tri-faith America: How Catholics and Jews Held Postwar America to Its Protestant Promise* (New York: Oxford University Press, 2011).

6   Zalman Schachter-Shalomi, "What I Found in the Chapel," in *My Neighbor's Faith: Stories of Interreligious Encounter, Growth, and Transformation*, ed. Jennifer Howe Peace, Or N. Rose, and Gregory Mobley (Maryknoll, N.Y.: Orbis, 2012), 208. He retold this story several times in print with minor differences.

7   Zalman Schachter-Shalomi, *My Life in Jewish Renewal*, chaps. 10–14. Many Orthodox Jews will not enter a church because of theological and historical reasons woven into Jewish legal positions.

8   Schachter-Shalomi, "What I Found in the Chapel," in *My Neighbor's Faith*, 209.

9   Schachter-Shalomi, *My Life in Jewish Renewal*, 209.

10 Schachter-Shalomi, *My Life in Jewish Renewal*, 210.

11 Schachter-Shalomi, *My Life in Jewish Renewal*, 210.

12 Thurman had an abiding interest in religious aesthetics, including the use of the arts in worship services (Smith, *Howard Thurman*, 21–24). This was a passion he and Schachter-Shalomi shared in common.

13 Thanks to Netanel Miles-Yepez, a close disciple of Schachter-Shalomi, for our discussion of this matter.

14 See Howard Thurman, *Footprints of a Dream: The Story of the Church for the Fellowship of All Peoples* (New York: Harper & Row, 1959), 17.

15 See Pierre-François de Béthune, "Monastic Inter-religious Dialogue," in *The Wiley-Blackwell Companion to Inter-religious Dialogue*, ed. Catherine Cornille (Chichester: Wiley-Blackwell, 2013), 45.

16 De Béthune, "Monastic Inter-religious Dialogue," in Cornille, *Wiley-Blackwell Companion to Inter-religious Dialogue*, 48.

17 See my 2004 interview with Schachter-Shalomi: Or N. Rose, "On the Growing Edge of Judaism: Reb Zalman at Eighty," in *Tikkun Reader: Twentieth Anniversary*, ed. Michael Lerner (Lanham, Md.: Rowan & Littlefield, 2007), 145–49.

18 Schachter-Shalomi, *My Life in Jewish Renewal*, 91–92; Howard Thurman, "The Wider Ministry and the Concept of Community," unpublished sermon, July 28, 1963. My thanks to Dr. Walker Fluker and Dr. Peter Eisenstaedt of the Howard Thurman Papers Project at Boston University for sharing this document with me.

References

de Béthune, Pierre-François. "Monastic Inter-religious Dialogue." In *The Wiley-Blackwell Companion to Inter-religious Dialogue*, edited by Catherine Cornille, 34–50. Chichester: Wiley-Blackwell, 2013.

Lowenthal, Naftali. "Lubavitch Hasidism." Yivo Encyclopedia of Jews in Eastern Europe. Accessed February 9, 2019. http://www.yivoencyclopedia.org/article.aspx/Lubavitch_Hasidism.

Rose, Or N. "On the Growing Edge of Judaism: Reb Zalman at Eighty." In *Tikkun Reader: Twentieth Anniversary*, edited by Michael Lerner, 145–49. Lanham, Md.: Rowan & Littlefield, 2007.

Schachter-Shalomi, Zalman. *My Life in Jewish Renewal: A Memoir.* With Edward Hoffman. Lanham, Md.: Rowan & Littlefield, 2012.

———. "What I Found in the Chapel." In *My Neighbor's Faith: Stories of Interreligious Encounter, Growth, and Transformation*, edited by Jennifer Howe Peace, Or N. Rose, and Gregory Mobley, 207–10. Maryknoll, N.Y.: Orbis, 2012.

Schultz, Kevin M. *Tri-faith America: How Catholics and Jews Held Postwar America to Its Protestant Promise.* New York: Oxford University Press, 2011.

Smith, Luther E., ed. *Howard Thurman: Essential Writings.* Maryknoll, N.Y.: Orbis, 2006.

Thurman, Howard. *Footprints of a Dream: The Story of the Church for the Fellowship of All Peoples.* New York: Harper & Row, 1959.

———. "The Wider Ministry and the Concept of Community." Unpublished sermon. July 28, 1963.

31

Peacebuilding

Navras J. Aafreedi

Of all the species on earth, it is only the *Homo sapiens* that perpetrate genocides and feel so threatened by their own kind that they maintain standing armies to defend themselves against any possible attack. Even when they are unable to fulfill their basic needs of food, clothing, and shelter, they spend on armament. Although many other species too draw boundaries to assert control of certain territories, none of them obsessively divides land, water, and sky the way humans do. On top of it all, they have the superciliousness to look down upon all the other species. It may not be easy to undo the divisions on earth. However, it should not disappoint us to the extent of throwing us into complacence, for in spite of all this we still have reasons to be optimistic. After all, we have at least agreed not to repeat the mistake beyond our own planet by agreeing, through the Outer Space Treaty, not to divide other celestial bodies among nations. This brief chapter sketches a few ways interreligious and interfaith studies can play a role in the prevention of intolerance and promote peacebuilding, primarily through providing educational opportunities.

Human beliefs are not necessarily based on logic and reason. This is something we do not generally realize. Hence, instead of being content with just clinging to our own belief(s), we even resist other points of view and try ceaselessly to convert others to our views or to impose them. Needless to say, this creates friction and tension in society.

Whether we talk of antisemitism, communalism, homophobia, Islamophobia, misogyny, nationalism, racism, regionalism, tribalism, xenophobia, or discrimination on linguistic, gender, or ethnic lines, the solution to each of these problems lies in an educational revolution. Ignorance leads to stereotypes. Stereotypes in turn fuel prejudice. Prejudice progresses into hatred. Hatred more often than not finds expression in violence. It would be utopian to think that we would ever be able to eliminate prejudices that lead to violence. However, this realization should certainly not make us complacent, for complacency often makes the situation worse than it already is. Only sincere and genuine efforts keep the situation from worsening. What we need to do is to take stock of our efforts up to this point.

It would be unfair and incorrect to blame religion for all the strife in the world. According to the *Encyclopedia of Wars*, in a survey of 1,800 conflicts it was found that less than 10 percent involved religion at all.[1] The BBC-commissioned survey "God and War" found that religion did play some part in 40 percent of conflicts but usually a minor one.[2] Yet we cannot deny that how we interpret and practice religion is surely responsible for a whole lot of worldly strife.

According to a report produced by the Woolf Institute in Cambridge (U.K.), interfaith activism still has a long way to go.[3] More often than not, interfaith activists talk in echo chambers and hesitate to confront the real issues, lest they derail dialogue. Another criticism is that interfaith initiatives generally "preach to the converted." They generally attract participants who are already sympathetic, while they fail to reach out to skeptics or outsiders.

Hatred thrives on falsehood. Only education aimed at raising awareness can combat it effectively. To take one example, Jews and Muslims, who are sadly seen as natural adversaries today, have produced beautiful examples of religious harmony in South Asia, wherever they happen to be neighbors in places like Kochi (Cochin), Kolkata (formerly Calcutta), Mumbai (formerly Bombay), Ahmedabad, Thane, and so forth. However, it is the Muslims who have not had the chance to directly interact with Jews over a long period that develop prejudices and biases against Jews based on the many anti-Semitic stereotypes propagated by certain *ulama*[4] and promoted by a section of their press, guilty of yellow journalism.

It is neither easy nor required to make people abandon their faith. The problem is not with faith but with its interpretation of texts. It may not be permissible to make any changes to any text considered sacred and revealed. However, people need to be increasingly educated to understand their texts metaphorically in the polemics instead of interpreting them literally. In situations where it may not be possible, the polemic, wherever encountered, should be juxtaposed with a similar reference to the same people the polemic is directed against from the same text, as Ed Kessler recommends. According to him:

> We can juxtapose contrasting texts from the same Scripture. For example, when dealing with New Testament accounts of abrasive arguments between Jesus and the Pharisees one might turn to passages which demonstrate their close relationship (e.g., Luke 13:1). One might compare verses such as "No-one comes to the Father except through Me" (John 14:6) with passages such as "Other sheep I have which are not of this fold" (John 10:16). The more violent passages in the Hebrew Bible can be contrasted with passages such as Isaiah 19:23-4, "Blessed is Egypt My people, and Assyria the work of My hands, and Israel My inheritance." Likewise when confronted with Qur'an 9:30, "The Jews said, Ezra is the son of God; and the Christians said, the Messiah is the son of God; they said this with their own mouths, repeating what earlier disbelievers had said; may God confound them!"; one might respond with 2:136, "Say [you believers], We believe in God and what was sent down to us and what was sent down to Abraham, Ishmael, Isaac, Jacob, and the tribes; and what was given to Moses and Jesus and all the Prophets by their Lord. We make no distinction between any of them."[5]

Both the rabbis and the church fathers agree that texts have multiple meanings. Origen was of the view that Scripture has three meanings: literal, moral, and spiritual. It has been a tradition with the rabbis to follow a fourfold method: simple or straightforward, allusion, homiletical or drawn-out, and mystical; one *midrash* claims that it is possible to interpret the Torah in forty-nine ways. This approach is described as exegetical pluralism. Its existence implies that traditional interpretations of Scripture provide space for a breadth and plurality of viewpoint. According to Kessler, "Exegetical pluralism and a hermeneutic of ambiguity demonstrate that" religious communities "can learn from and help one another."[6] There is a long tradition of *ijtihād*, or independent reasoning and debate in Islam.

Victimhood and injustice more often than not cause hatred. What emerges as a major obstacle in achieving reconciliation is selective amnesia. We tend to remember only the suffering caused to the group we claim to be a member of, not the suffering caused by our group to the other. And, even if our group did cause the suffering, we still tend to perceive the other as having started it.

The primary steps to constructive peacebuilding begin with agreeing to a historical narrative, abstaining from negative portrayals of the other, recognizing the sufferings of the other, and admitting the wrongs done by us to the other. Although this is difficult to achieve, there are some glimmers of hope such as *Nostra aetate*, *Dabru emet*, "A Common Word between Us and You," and "Towards a Global Ethic" (Hans Küng and the Parliament of the World's Religions). Another significant example is that of Mohammed S. Dajani Daoudi, the Palestinian scholar and academic who for several years has been devotedly making efforts to raise awareness of the Holocaust (Shoah) among the Arabs by taking Palestinian students to Auschwitz and by regularly speaking against the denial, minimization, and trivialization of the Holocaust. He has had to pay a heavy price for it. He lost his professorial position, his car was burnt, and there is a constant threat to his life.[7]

There is always a great reluctance to admitting the wrongdoings of one's own tradition, for it is feared that the fallout can lead to a demand for apology, which may, in the future, entail being compelled to pay reparations or compensation. There is a long list of genocides and pogroms still waiting to be recognized, which would be the very first step toward justice and reconciliation. It should go without saying that there cannot be any lasting peace without justice and reconciliation.

Often our differences are more imaginary than actual. And, even if there are differences, we must learn to agree to disagree. And, more often than not, we talk of religious, cultural, and civilizational distinctions without paying attention to the fuzzy boundaries and overlaps.

As one conscious of the frequent communal clashes in India, often involving mass violence, I made a modest attempt to promote a better understanding of interfaith relations by creating an undergraduate course—Reading Interfaith Relations in World History—at Presidency University, Kolkata. In this course, we examine seven different aspects of interfaith relations: (1) amity, (2) bigotry, (3) conflicts, (4) clashes, (5) interfaith activism, dialogue, and reconciliation, (6) the role of religion in journalism and how matters related to religion are reported in the media, and (7) the state and religion. World history is more or less a record of amity and enmity between peoples of different religious persuasions. The history of their relations continues to shape our present and would in turn affect our future. The course aims to provide a comprehensive understanding of interfaith relations in world history.

Social awareness of minority religion contributions is also very important, lest the minorities come to be seen as burdens living a parasitical existence and as groups that only exploit national resources without contributing to nation building. For democracy to thrive it needs to be nurtured; and one of the prerequisites for its flourishing is to raise awareness among the citizenry of the cultural, religious, and ethnic diversity within the country. Without such awareness, democracy can too easily turn into majoritarianism. An effective way to avoid this is to promote the study of minority religious and cultural groups. The treatment of minorities remains the benchmark of how civilized a society is. Mostly minority communities, though desirous of integration, resist assimilation. It is for every society to determine and ascertain what efforts to take to integrate its minority groups into the mainstream so that they do not feel marginalized or left out of the nation-building process, without depriving them of their separate identity (a common consequence of assimilation). An example of this is the launch of a master's course (history) at Presidency University, Kolkata, titled "A History of Small Communities of Foreign Origin in Colonial India," which examines six of India's religious micro-minorities, each of whom made significant contributions to Indian economy and culture in spite of their numerical insignificance. Intolerance emerges and increases in any society where contributions made by minorities go unrecognized. History testifies to the fact that even if religious intolerance initially targets only minorities, later it will victimize the whole of society, including the majority. Intolerance toward one is a threat to all. Interfaith studies can surely play an important role in the prevention of intolerance and the promotion of peace and understanding through some of the directives outlined in this short chapter.

Notes

1   C. Phillips and A. Axelrod, *Encyclopedia of Wars* (New York: Facts on File, 2004).

2   G. Austin, T. Kranock, and T. Oommen, *God and War: An Audit and an Exploration* (London: BBC, 2003).

3   John Fahy and Jan-Jonathan Bock, *Beyond Dialogue: Interfaith Engagement in Delhi, Doha & London* (Cambridge: Woolf Institute, 2018).

4   Muslim scholars recognized as having authoritative or specialized knowledge of Islamic law and theology. A few examples of *ulama* who have resorted to anti-Semitic rhetoric are Sayyid Abul Ala Mawdudi, Abul Hasan Ali Nadwi, Israr Ahmed, Ayatollah Rouhallah Mausavi Khomeini, and Kalb-e-Jawad, among many others.

5   Edward Kessler, "Religious Texts, Tolerance and Intolerance," blog of the Woolf Institute, Cambridge, U.K., February 25, 2016, https://www.woolf.cam .ac.uk/blog/religious-texts-tolerance-and-intolerance.

6   Edward Kessler, *An Introduction to Jewish-Christian Relations* (New York: Cambridge University Press, 2010), 211.

7   Aleisa Fishman's interview with Mohammad S. Dajani as part of the United States Holocaust Memorial Museum's podcast series *Voices on Antisemitism*, accessed April 10, 2019, https://www.ushmm.org/confront-antisemitism/ antisemitism-podcast/mohammed-dajani.

References

Austin, G., T. Kranock, and T. Oommen. *God and War: An Audit and an Exploration*. London: BBC, 2003.

Fahy, John, and Jan-Jonathan Bock. *Beyond Dialogue: Interfaith Engagement in
Delhi, Doha & London*. Cambridge: Woolf Institute, 2018.

Fishman, Aleisa. Podcast interview with Mohammad S. Dajani Daoudi. June 4,
2015. United States Holocaust Memorial Museum's *Voices on Antisemitism*.
Accessed April 10, 2019. https://www.ushmm.org/confront-antisemitism/
antisemitism-podcast/mohammed-dajani.

Kessler, Edward. *An Introduction to Jewish-Christian Relations*. New York: Cambridge University Press, 2010.

———. "Religious Texts, Tolerance and Intolerance." Blog of the Woolf Institute,
Cambridge, U.K., February 25, 2016. https://www.woolf.cam.ac.uk/blog/
religious-texts-tolerance-and-intolerance.

Phillips, C., and A. Axelrod. *Encyclopedia of Wars*. New York: Facts on File, 2004.

32

Nation Building

Asfa Widiyanto

This chapter argues that interfaith engagement is not only significant for nurturing peace but also for deepening the process of nation building. There are three concerns of this chapter. *First*, it highlights the modalities of interfaith activism for peacemaking. *Second*, it assesses the potential contribution of interfaith activism toward the nurturance of nation building most specifically within the framework of post-secular nation-state. *Third*, it explores an appropriate model of religious education in the context of post-secular nation-state. In addressing these concerns, this chapter makes the case for scholars of inter-religious studies to take on the responsibility of scholar-activist. Their contribution to the field can (1) play a role in building peace and mutual harmony among different faith communities by accentuating the spirit of peace inherent within most traditions, (2) deepen cohesion in divided nation-states by helping to build trust, and (3) make a substantial contribution to a curriculum of religious education that values and accommodates minority faiths.

Interfaith Activism and Peacemaking

Hans Ucko reveals the apprehension of one bishop who said, "How can I sing my song of praise of Jesus without offending the other?"[1] This praise appears to declare that other faiths and praises are not legitimate. The bishop's question touches upon the inherent truth claims within the religions. These truth claims will pose a threat to peace, if the believers in question embrace them exclusively in a theological sense.

Hans Küng's saying "no peace among the nations without peace among the religions"[2] clearly demonstrates the vital role that the religions may play in the creation of world peace. This is due to the fact that religion constitutes one of the most important identity markers for people. Interfaith activists, aware of these ideals, accordingly take necessary arrangements in the dialogues among faith communities to eliminate any tensions among them and to promote cooperation. Similarly, Irvin-Erickson portrays interfaith activists as striving to "unite what cannot be united, trying to resolve conflicts among groups of people who have incompatible belief sets that fate them toward violence."[3] These activists serve as bridge builders who work toward strengthening the civic fabric[4] within religiously diverse nation-states.

Nietzsche is reported to have said that "convictions are more dangerous enemies of truth than lies."[5] Convictions are possible signals of exclusivist theological commitments. In the context of our digital age, these convictions and beliefs may be exploited (by politicians, for example) to support false narratives and fabricate information with hidden agendas. Many politicians are aware of the emergence of post-truth, in which information is considered true not because it accords with hard reality but rather because it resonates with people's convictions and beliefs. Here the interfaith activist can play a role in the peace-building process and work toward the creation of mutual harmony among different faith communities by underlining the universal messages of religions and by accentuating the spirit of peace that is inherent within the esoteric dimension of religions. The role of the interreligious scholar and researcher, who is often also the interfaith activist to varying degrees, is to focus his or her investigative lens on contexts in which truth has been fabricated to stir distrust and division among religious communities for political, personal, or financial gain at the expense of truth, social cohesion, and harmony.

Interfaith Activism and Nation Building in a Post-secular Nation-State

Nation building here is understood as the course of constructing a shared identity that might function as the basis for people to live together peacefully, to recognize shared laws, and to distribute resources in a just manner.[6] We observe at least two components in building the nation, namely the cultural-symbolic and the civic-instrumental. The cultural-symbolic facet deals with the production of cultural-symbolic capital inside the society and the reorganization of shared identity and its symbolic essences. The civic-instrumental feature has to do with the material and the utilitarian, and the problems of administration and resource management.[7]

Interfaith activism, which can play a role in the cultural-symbolic dimension of the nation building, is not a taboo in the post-secular nation-state. Rather, it is highly needed for the well-being of the nation-state. A healthy public sphere does not refer to the absence of religion in the public space, but it can also designate the active presence of religion and religious communities in the public sphere,[8] with their commitment to common good and nation building. It is interfaith activists, religious scholars, and academic scholars who nurture positive interreligious relations that tend to be most supportive of efforts to promote the common good and nation building. The common good becomes the shared concern of these activists and scholars, and it is what often allows them to cooperate and come to the same table.

Interfaith activists, with their various theological commitments, represent civil society actors willing to cooperate within, between, and among the many faith communities. These activists perceive that the general well-being of humanity and that of their particular nation is addressed by the ideals of religion. In short, their position is, in general, that religion ought to serve humanity for the common good.

Religion contains both unifying and dividing elements, to be sure. Although most religions have features that can promote division and conflict, interfaith activism can counter these divisive elements by nurturing pluralism (both theological pluralism and civic-political pluralism), which also helps to deepen the process of nation building. Interfaith activists serve as actors of social cohesion, especially within their locally lived communities and countries. They seek to draw attention to and to live out the common platform many religions share as a starting point for interreligious cooperation.

Interfaith activism is also of significance in deepening cohesion in divided nation-states, as Daniel Weinstock argues. In such states, Weinstock reports, "trust-building" is more appropriate than "nation building." [9] Trust-building in this sense refers to the search for a basis for solidarity that allows all citizens to work together and thus develop mutual trust and respect among the communities.

"Transformed Religious Education": Nation Building and Interfaith Activism

In some countries, religious education (RE) rarely makes any significant contribution toward the establishment of mutual harmony among its citizens. In some cases, RE contributes to disharmony. In other cases, RE contends with the state's vision. In still other cases, RE has been exploited by the majority and used to discriminate against and oppress minority religious groups. Some of

this can be attributed to the fact that RE in some countries is focused on cultivating the personal piety of the students and pays little attention to interfaith
literacy and civic values.

In response to this problem, there are at least two trajectories that can be
pursued in order to reform RE: "secularized religious education" and "transformed religious education." The *first trajectory*, secularized RE, refers to the
enterprise of secularizing religious education curriculum by stressing interfaith literacy[10] and peace studies.[11] Another proposal for cultivating secularized RE is to foster "global citizenship," which refers to the kind of citizenship
that enforces intergroup empathy and values religious diversity.[12]

Secularization of RE entails yielding the management of RE to the secular state. Its main goal is to achieve public order, social cohesion, and mutual
harmony. This kind of venture, however, does not aim at forming the religious
piety of the students. Consequently, the students would seek other educational
and religious institutions—namely, the private ones—that could offer resources and support for shaping their personal piety. Fuad Jabali argues that leaving
RE to private institutions is not without risk since the state would be absent
in such an arrangement and therefore would have little influence on the curricula.[13] Nor could the state have a hand in helping to prevent RE from being
reduced to exclusivism and fundamentalism.

The *second option* is transformed RE, which pays appropriate attention to
personal piety, interfaith literacy, and civic values. In transformed RE, religion
or religious piety is not perceived as a threat to peace and coexistence but rather appreciated for its potential capital to build social cohesion. Religious piety
is observed in a way that does not run counter to multiculturalism and citizenship. It is a piety that has undergone the process of "re-hermeneuticisation"[14]
in order to be in line with the spirit of the time and, most specifically, with
recent sociopolitical developments.

This proposal for a transformed RE has the potential to empower civil society, which, in the long run, will contribute to the well-being of the nation-
state. Transformed RE still needs to be developed and adapted to each nation
within which it is employed. There is no one model of transformed RE fit to
be applied to all countries, especially since the specific contexts of the various
countries differ in constitution, majority religious group, and other significant
nation-building factors.

Interfaith activists, progressive religious scholars, and academic scholars
constitute the main actors who should lead this reformation of RE. As potential agents for change, those in positions of power are best able to perceive RE

in a critical manner and thusly offer constructive ways forward in shaping the content of RE in their respective countries.

In order to exercise this enterprise properly, these activists and scholars need a certain degree of academic freedom that allows them to articulate and communicate their vision to the public without fear of censorship, intimidation, or persecution. However, the reality is sometimes far from ideal. Governments sometimes restrain activists and scholars, especially when particular ideas for and visions for reformation are perceived as threatening to, or encroaching on, their governmental power and authority. Nonetheless, some activists and scholars continue to seek reformation by their own volition.

In many countries, nation building is based on the majority or dominant "societal culture."[15] Certainly, this kind of model influences the nature of RE in respective countries. The dominant religious group has significant power, persuasion, and possibility to exert their influence on the course of both nation building and RE. Clearly, the politics of RE in one particular country will be related to, embedded in, and deeply influenced by the politics of nation building that exist in that country.

Transformed RE, within the context of a multinational state that has a clear dominant religious majority or societal culture, has to account for the minority faiths if it wants to succeed on the highest level. Although minority faiths do not play a significant role in the course of nation building, their existence cannot be neglected. They remain citizens with the same rights of their fellow citizens. Amplifying the voices of these religious minorities, and helping to turn the ears of the majority, remains a significant part of the overall task for interfaith activists and academic scholars—that is, if they desire to make any substantial or long-term contribution to the creation of an RE curriculum that values and accommodates all faiths. These scholars and activists are often the ones with the freedom, agency, and resources to effect change to public policy and to stimulate negotiation with key stakeholders on matters related to reforming and transforming RE.

Notes

1   Hans Ucko, "Truth or Truths: How Does This Fit in a World of Religious Plurality," *Journal of Ecumenical Studies* 52, no. 1 (2017): 15–27.

2   Hans Küng, *Christianity: Essence, History, and Future* (New York: Continuum, 1995).

3   Douglas Irvin-Erickson, "Introduction: Interfaith Contributions to Nurturing Cultures of Peace," in *Violence, Religion and Peacemaking: Contribution of*

Interreligious Dialog, ed. Douglas Irvin-Erickson and Peter C. Phan (London: Palgrave Macmillan, 2016), 1–20.

4   Eboo Patel, "Toward a Field of Interfaith Studies," *Liberal Education* 99, no. 4 (2013): 38–43.

5   Ucko, "Truth or Truths."

6   Rene Grotenhuis, *Nation-Building as Necessary Effort in Fragile States* (Amsterdam: Amsterdam University Press, 2016).

7   Michael Hill and Lian Kwen Fee, *The Politics of Nation-Building and Citizenship in Singapore* (London: Routledge, 1995).

8   José Casanova, *Public Religions in the Modern World* (Chicago: University of Chicago Press).

9   Daniel Weinstock, "Building Trust in Divided Societies," *Journal of Political Philosophy* 7, no. 3 (1999): 287–307.

10 Ali Munhanif, in discussion with the author, January 15, 2019.

11 David Smock, foreword to *Violence, Religion and Peacemaking: Contribution of Interreligious Dialog*, ed. Douglas Irvin-Erickson and Peter C. Phan (London: Palgrave Macmillan, 2016), v–vii

12 Rito Baring, in discussion with the author, January 15, 2019.

13 Fuad Jabali, in discussion with the author, January 15, 2019.

14 See Benjamin Tallis, "Living in Post-truth: Power/Knowledge/Responsibility," *New Perspectives* 24, no. 1 (2016): 7–18.

15 Will Kymlicka, *Politics in the Vernacular: Nationalism, Multiculturalism, and Citizenship* (Oxford: Oxford University Press, 2001).

References

Casanova, José. *Public Religions in the Modern World*. Chicago: University of Chicago Press.

Grotenhuis, Rene. *Nation-Building as Necessary Effort in Fragile States*. Amsterdam: Amsterdam University Press, 2016.

Hill, Michael, and Lian Kwen Fee. *The Politics of Nation-Building and Citizenship in Singapore*. London: Routledge, 1995.

Irvin-Erickson, Douglas. "Introduction: Interfaith Contributions to Nurturing Cultures of Peace." In *Violence, Religion and Peacemaking: Contribution of Interreligious Dialog*, edited by Douglas Irvin-Erickson and Peter C. Phan, 1–20. London: Palgrave Macmillan, 2016.

Küng, Hans. *Christianity: Essence, History, and Future*. New York: Continuum, 1995.

Kymlicka, Will. *Politics in the Vernacular: Nationalism, Multiculturalism, and Citizenship*. Oxford: Oxford University Press, 2001.

Patel, Eboo. "Toward a Field of Interfaith Studies." *Liberal Education* 99, no. 4 (2013): 38–43.

Smock, David. Foreword to *Violence, Religion and Peacemaking: Contribution of Interreligious Dialog*, edited by Douglas Irvin-Erickson and Peter C. Phan, v–vii. London: Palgrave Macmillan, 2016.

Tallis, Benjamin. "Living in Post-truth: Power/Knowledge/Responsibility." *New Perspectives* 24, no. 1 (2016): 7–18.

Ucko, Hans. "Truth or Truths: How Does This Fit in a World of Religious Plurality." *Journal of Ecumenical Studies* 52, no. 1 (2017): 15–27.

Weinstock, Daniel. "Building Trust in Divided Societies." *Journal of Political Philosophy* 7, no. 3 (1999): 287–307.

33

Scholarship as Activism

Jeannine Hill Fletcher

When historians look back at the moment in which interreligious studies emerges as a discipline in the context of the United States, they may tell a story of the flourishing of civil and human rights in a multireligious, multiracial America. We are, after all, heirs of a tremendous civil rights movement and the historic change in immigration legislation of the 1960s that fundamentally shifted the body politic to create a new religious America. As forerunner of our field, Diana Eck alerted us at the turn of the twenty-first century that the United States had become "the world's most religiously diverse nation."[1] But the rhetorical framing of more recent titles should remind the reader that changes to our body politic have not been celebrated by everyone. For some, studies like *The End of White Christian America* raises a sound of alarm.[2] While the emergence of interreligious studies may have once been buoyed on the wave of change in the post-1965 era, the rise in public displays of white nationalism and legislative refusal of diversity (in various immigration policies) reminds us that this work is emerging from within a dangerously contested space and must respond to the social and political realities of our moment.

In considering the role of scholars in this emergent field, I am guided by the theoretical framing of Max Horkheimer in his 1937 essay, "Traditional and Critical Theory."[3] In Horkheimer's view, traditional theorists take themselves to be merely describing the realities under consideration in their studies; but critical theorists recognize the role their studies play within the dynamics of the social present. For too long, Horkheimer muses, the disciplines have produced knowledge sustaining a status quo that benefits those who hold the reins of power and production, validating a description of an unjust reality without challenging it. He insists, however, that the critical theorist has a different purpose: "If, however, the theoretician and his specific object are seen as forming a dynamic unity with the oppressed class, so that his presentation of societal contradictions is not merely an expression of the concrete historical situation but also a force within it to stimulate change, then his real function emerges."[4] Through this lens, the question for the emergent field of interreligious studies is whether and how scholars "form a dynamic unity with the oppressed class" and commit themselves to be a force to "stimulate change" within our concrete historical situation.

I propose that interreligious studies is indeed a socially engaged field and that we might need to prepare future scholars in the field with the tools of scholarly activism. That is to say, we will not be crafting scholars who will be content with placing their bodies in the desk chairs of the libraries, but we will be seeking disciplinary tools for active social and political engagement. By allowing our socially engaged projects to define the trajectories of our research, we invite an orientation to our work that does not begin first with previous studies that originate in the academy. While indeed research is the heart of our work, it is not the origin. The scholar-activist begins instead with a view from the struggles of those without power in our society and asks what research is needed to address the reality at hand. For such a method of research, we will need to equip scholars of interreligious studies with interdisciplinary approaches that include political science, sociology, anthropology, and ethnography; we will want to be conversant with our colleagues in law as well as in theology. But the mobilizing of these interdisciplinary tools will first ask, *Who is it in our interreligious landscape that needs our work in this moment?* We will also, therefore, need resources that help scholars bridge academy and community to partner for social change, and relationships through which to form mutually beneficial partnerships oriented to the needs of those who need our work. In addition to the best tools of current scholarship in a range of disciplines, Paolo Freire's *Pedagogy of the Oppressed* (1970) should be standard reading in our field.

Religion, sociology, education, and law will help us importantly engage our social present. But, I am increasingly convinced that scholars of interreligious studies in the United States must know the history of America as a white Christian nation. The transformation of the 1965 legislation and the backlash of 2016 are realities of our social present that emerge from out of a carefully crafted Christian America built from the lives and losses of people of color and

people of the world's faiths. Interreligious studies *must* include careful attention to the history of how "religion" was used legally to dispossess, displace,
dehumanize, and deface the countless people of color in the American systems of colonization, enslavement, nation building, education, housing, and
law, which prioritized white Christian well-being. Our moment not only is
charged with competing interests but also carries the weight of our history
that has sustained the well-being of some (white and Christian) at the expense
of others (people of color and the world's faith traditions). If we can see the
way ideas emerging from white Christian traditions have shaped a landscape
in which whiteness and Christianness continue to afford privileges within our
social present, the critical theorist and activist-scholar might see interreligious
studies as an applied tool for creating a more humane world through a truly
multiracial and multireligious America.

If we need help summoning the courage to articulate our ideological commitments to the future of humanity up front in our research and teaching, we
might learn from recent work about the role of the theologian and scholar of
religion in producing our unjust status quo. Perhaps we need to be awakened
from our naiveté that our work has been for the good of humanity by scholars
of our discipline who help us to see the crimes against humanity that theologians and scholars have committed. To this end, I recommend the work of
Susannah Heschel's important book *The Aryan Jesus*, which chronicles how
twentieth-century German scholarship produced "knowledge" about Jesus
and "the Jews" that had a direct impact on nationalist ideology and legislation.[5] I also recommend historian Craig Wilder's *Ebony and Ivy*, in which the
author shows the myriad ways religious thinkers in our universities benefited
from and produced ideas to sustain the enslavement of people identified as
"non-white" and "non-Christian."[6] When we recognize the ways in which the
production of knowledge participates in the generation of symbolic capital
that structures rights and access in our society, we might understand why Heschel employs the term "desk murderers" for those scholars who produce the
ideas that will make death-dealing practices of exclusion and oppression seem
reasonable.[7]

The orientation of the scholar-activist is compelled to resist the possibility
that we might instead simply engage in neutral scholarship. In Horkheimer's
view, if the theorist looks out and sees a social reality of injustice and does
nothing, this too is a force at work in constructing the social present. Contemporary theorist Barbara Applebaum responds to the charge of a "liberal bias"
in today's education system by reminding us that "academic neutrality . . . can
support oppression by default."[8] The critical theorist, thus, recognizes that her

work is not neutral in its commitment to employ the systems of meaning-making and knowledge production toward liberatory ends, because the alternative is to do nothing and allow an unjust reality to continue as the status quo.

When historians look back at the emergence of interreligious studies in *our* moment, I hope they will see courageous scholar-activists who embraced the tasks of expanding religious literacy and deepening the human engagement with systems of religion as work done in solidarity with one another, in solidarity with those under threat and in commitment to a more just and humane world. If they do, they will also see that sharpening our tools of critical-theoretical understanding and shaping the next generation of scholar-activists with interdisciplinary, socially engaged methods have been crucial to our work.

Notes

1   In her 2001 book *A New Religious America*, Diana L. Eck opens with the recognition of the historic Johnson-Reed legislation of 1965 that allowed a much wider range of religious and cultural diversity to characterize new immigrants to the United States. *A New Religious America: How a "Christian Country" Has Become the World's Most Religiously Diverse Nation* (San Francisco: HarperCollins, 2001).

2   Robert P. Jones, *The End of White Christian America* (New York: Simon & Schuster, 2016).

3   Max Horkheimer, "Traditional and Critical Theory" (1937), in *Critical Theory: Selected Essays*, ed. M. O'Connell (New York: Continuum, 1999), 188–243.

4   Horkheimer, "Traditional and Critical Theory," in O'Connell, *Critical Theory*, 215.

5   Susannah Heschel, *The Aryan Jesus: Christian Theologians and the Bible in Nazi Germany* (Princeton: Princeton University Press, 2008).

6   Craig Wilder, *Ebony and Ivy: Race, Nation and the Troubled History of America's Universities* (New York: Bloomsbury, 2013).

7   Heschel, *Aryan Jesus*, 16.

8   Barbara Applebaum, "Is Teaching for Social Justice a 'Liberal Bias'?" *Teachers College Record* 111, no. 2 (2009): 384.

References

Applebaum, Barbara. "Is Teaching for Social Justice a 'Liberal Bias'?" *Teachers College Record* 111, no. 2 (2009): 376–408.

Eck, Diana L. *A New Religious America: How a "Christian Country" Has Become the World's Most Religiously Diverse Nation.* San Francisco: HarperCollins, 2001.

Heschel, Susannah. *The Aryan Jesus: Christian Theologians and the Bible in Nazi Germany*. Princeton: Princeton University Press, 2008.

Horkheimer, Max. "Traditional and Critical Theory" (1937). In *Critical Theory: Selected Essays*, edited by M. O'Connell, 188–243. New York: Continuum, 1999.

Jones, Robert P. *The End of White Christian America*. New York: Simon & Schuster, 2016.

Wilder, Craig. *Ebony and Ivy: Race, Nation and the Troubled History of America's Universities*. New York: Bloomsbury, 2013.

34

Dialogue and Christian–Muslim Relations

Douglas Pratt

Interreligious studies is neither theology nor religious studies (*Religionswissenschaft*). But it draws methodologically from both. It is something of an amalgam, yet more than that. This relatively new field is in process of developing its own methods and strategies, which address the spaces and connections between ("inter") religious identities and differences. It engages in the study of what is going on within the context of dialogical and other encounters between and among religions. This encompasses what religious peoples do—their actions and behaviors;[1] what religious people think—their beliefs, concepts, perceptions and ideas; and what might be happening in regard to formal or informal religious self-reflection—ideologies, statements, and formulations. Drawing upon my own research in the field, my focus here is on interreligious studies' engagement with interreligious dialogue and Christian–Muslim relations, with reference to some specific examples and including some reflective comment arising from that.[2]

Interreligious Dialogue

The wider context of interreligious relations and dialogue today, and the focus of much allied studies, is the indisputable fact of religious diversity.[3] This sets the context for interfaith engagement and raises the question of the relativities of religious identities and presumptions of absolute truth.[4] In a mono-religious context, interreligious relations and allied engagements do not figure: they are not issues as such. Matters of interreligious understanding simply do not arise;

there is no "inter." However, in a religiously plural context, it is the fact of religious diversity, the plurality of religions rubbing shoulders and seeking a mode of peaceful coexistence or engaged in combative encounter, that sets the scene.[5] And although religious extremism and religiously motivated terrorism have become the combative feature of our time,[6] people of different religions, in pursuit of dialogical relationship with one another, have yet the possibility of transcending histories of combative clash in favor of a future marked by co-operative engagement. The "inter" can be negative, but it can also be positive.[7] The rise of bilateral and multilateral interreligious dialogue activities and other engagements, together with the advent of multi-faith or interfaith groups and councils in many parts of the world, bear witness to the fact that, indeed, we live in a dialogical and cross-cultural and multireligious relational age. All of this calls for close study.[8]

As for the positive dimension of interreligious engagement, members of other religions join with Christians at dialogue conferences, or as partners in interfaith organizations, or in many common quests and cooperative ventures of one sort or another. Leaders from different religions receive hospitable welcome at the Vatican,[9] and the religious "other" is received and welcomed as an honored guest at Assemblies of the World Council of Churches.[10] Where, previously, friendly and accommodating relational detente on the basis of mutual respect would have been the exception, it is now an effective rule.

Christian–Muslim Relations: A New Dialogical Era

In the first decade of the twenty-first century, two significant initiatives in the field of Christian–Muslim relations arose.[11] With the aim of establishing a new environment for theological bridge building between Muslims and Christians, the *Building Bridges Seminar* series was begun in 2002 by the archbishop of Canterbury, George Carey. In the same year the *Theologisches Forum Christentum–Islam* (Christian–Muslim Theological Forum) was initiated by an ecumenical group of young scholars in Germany. Both quickly settled into a pattern of annual conference-style meetings. They each produce quality published outcomes.

At the initial meeting of *Building Bridges*, Archbishop Carey regarded the series' potential as being to achieve greater understanding, to build relational bridges, and to attain fuller recognition of "responsibilities as religious leaders and scholars to help our communities live together in ways which do not suppress our own identities but open us up to the riches which the other offers."[12] He noted that "there are many around us who believe that the world would be better off without faith and all its apparent capacity to generate division, hatred and violence," and he regarded that as a challenge: therefore, he urged that the two faiths need to play "our part in trying to ensure that the wider world may reap the best—not fear the worst—of what our faiths have to offer."[13] *Building Bridges* falls into the category of dialogical projects marked by both religious conviction and academic rigor. Its style, according to Rowan Williams, "has been patient, affirming, and celebrating."[14] Attention to scriptural and other authoritative texts has been of primary importance.

In a similar fashion, interest in fostering a dialogue with Muslim scholars led to the founding of the *Theologisches Forum Christentum–Islam* within Germany. The driving motivation was to foster theological dialogue that was balanced and equal in terms of the level of the engagement and the expertise of the interlocutors. Two preliminary conferences were held with Christian participants who had particular interest or specialty in Christian–Muslim relations.[15] This was to enable preparatory reflection and discussion about the task of engaging in the dialogue and led to the establishment of a joint Christian–Muslim steering group. The forum has since been something of a seedbed for new and emerging scholarship in the area of Christian–Muslim dialogue more widely, as well as the development of Islamic theological scholarship and teaching within the German context.

A major theme to emerge out of the preliminary conferences was recognition that mutual *internal plurality* leads to *diverse interreligious relations*. Each religion manifests multiple internal diversities, or identities, so there is a multiplicity of possible relationships between them. The lived reality is that there is no one Islam and no singular Christianity that dialogically engage— there is great diversity within each. The dialogue takes place in the context of a matrix of various Christian–Muslim relationships and settings. The context of the "inter" is itself highly diverse, and greater recognition of this often grows out of appreciation for the internal diversity that exists within each tradition.

In reflecting on dialogical developments, I have suggested that a theology (or religious ideology) of dialogue may be understood in terms of three dynamic "moments," or dimensions—namely, theology *for, in* (or *within*), and *after* dialogue.[16] A theology of dialogue must address the reasons *for* dialogue as such; it must identify the agenda, principles, and substance of what takes place *within* dialogue; and it ideally engages in self-reflection *after* dialogue on the theological meaning or implications of the dialogical encounter. After the case for dialogue is made, the tasks of identifying the agenda of any dialogue and then asking what the dialogue suggests by way of the need for consequential reflection are, in my view, natural corollaries.[17] This threefold theological analysis of dialogue can enable further rethinking of the rationale for subsequent and continued engagement, as well as recasting the dialogue agenda so as to address relevant new issues.[18] It facilitates an enriching dialogical circle.

"Christian–Muslim Relations, a thematic history" (CMRTH) is a subproject of the international *Christian–Muslim Relations—A Bibliographical History* (CMR) research project, which traces the history of relations between the followers of the world's two most-populous religions from the first days of interaction down to the end of the "long" nineteenth century (1914). This project is based at the University of Birmingham, England.[19] Its first phase covered the period 600–1500 and resulted in five large volumes of bibliographical data of works written by a Muslim or a Christian about, for, or against the other. In other words, it is a bibliographical compendium of works of apologetics, polemics, or inquiry and instruction, broadly speaking. It is focused on the "inter" dimension, the interactions, between Muslims and Christians, as recorded in known texts. A second phase, which commenced in 2012, covers the sixteenth to the eighteenth centuries in a further nine volumes, and by the end of 2019 it has reached the point of dealing with the nineteenth century. This is expected to produce another eight volumes.[20]

At a relatively early stage the idea emerged that the bibliographical history needed to be complemented and capped by a thematic history, in two volumes of essays, that would draw upon the bibliographical resource. This would have the twofold aim of demonstrating the value and usefulness of the bibliographical history itself and of beginning to highlight the complex interactions and diverse issues that the bibliographical data show. The first volume, of some twenty essays, was published in 2020.[21] A second volume, to continue and expand the themes up to 1914, will follow once the full bibliographical history is compiled.

The focus of the thematic history subproject is on themes and topics that reflect and reveal something of the relational dynamics that have engaged the two faiths down through the centuries. The themes selected aim to strike a balance of Christian and Muslim perception and experience, the diversity of relational interaction (positive, negative, neutral), some of the key recurring theological topics, differences in reaction (Christian response to Islam and Muslim response to Christianity), broad common motifs, and local, specific elements. Four dynamic categories of relationship—*antipathy, affinity, appeal, accommodation*—have been identified in respect of Christian–Muslim interaction. Together they constitute a heuristic device that provides something of an overarching structure to an analysis of the history of interaction.

Antipathy signals the rather dominant feature of mutual rejection by asserting superiority one over the other, deriding the other as false, devilish, or evil, and much else besides. *Affinity* refers to the motif of sensing commonality, of an open inquiry in respect of the other premised on a sense of "sameness," more or less. Within this category, instances of mutual inquiry, theological debate, and other aspects of relatively positive relational engagement may be examined. *Appeal* is made by one to the other whether in respect to the dynamic of apologetics ("We are different, but you should listen to our worthy argument and explanation"), or in consequence of affinity ("We are nearly the same, so come on over"), or as an alternate to the outright rejection of antipathy ("You are clearly in the wrong—but we don't attack you; rather, here is why you should come on over"). Finally, *accommodation* is a long-standing dynamic, whether seen in the Muslim institution of *dhimmi* communities that locates and proscribes Christian (and other) existence within *dar al-Islam* as a "Peoples of the Book," or in Christian attitudes toward Muslim presence framed in terms of law or sociocultural realpolitik.

Arguably the first millennium of Christian–Muslim engagement sets the scene for the modern era, and, together, they provide the backdrop for what is often referred to as the postmodernity of the twentieth and twenty-first centuries. Further, by the end of the first millennium a transitional phase (fifteenth to sixteenth centuries, broadly speaking), incorporating developments that feature heavily later on (e.g., the impact of the Ottoman Empire; the incursion of Christianity and Islam into West Africa), was clearly underway. A thematic history is not a narrative work as such; the aim is not to tell the story of the first thousand years in the first volume, then commence the second at the point where the first ends. Rather, there will be a measure of overlap chronologically as the second volume continues to explore themes that reflect the four categories—with some themes within those categories clearly flowing through in terms of both chronological and geographic expansion down to the terminus of 1914.

The study of interreligious engagement and dialogue, and of Christian–Muslim relations, can be undertaken from a wide variety of scholarly perspectives—theological, historical, philosophical, and so on.[22] Interreligious studies may utilize these approaches, but the focal interest is in the dynamics that obtain in respect of the "inter" dimensions. So, for example, whereas each religion may have a narrative concerning the origin, purpose, and end point of material existence, the interreligious studies' interest is on a deep scrutiny of the narrative structures as it is the narrative dynamics, rather than the accompanying beliefs born of the narratives, that yield insight into the religions themselves and what might obtain between them. Dynamic parallels are often of deeper significance than beliefs themselves. Thus, the field and focus of interreligious studies is poised to offer a valuable perspective from which to engage the study of contemporary interreligious phenomena such as dialogue and Christian–Muslim relations.

Notes

1   Cf. Douglas Pratt, "Religion Is as Religion Does: Interfaith Prayer as a Form of Ritual Participation," in *Ritual Participation and Interreligious Dialogue: Boundaries, Transgressions and Innovations*, ed. Marianne Moyaert and Joris Geldhof (London: Bloomsbury, 2015), 53–66.

2   Cf. Douglas Pratt, *The Challenge of Islam: Encounters in Interfaith Dialogue* (Abingdon: Routledge, 2017); Risto Jukko, Douglas Pratt, and Michael Ipgrave, "The Churches and Christian–Muslim Relations," in *The Routledge Handbook of Christian–Muslim Relations*, ed. David Thomas (Abingdon: Routledge, 2017), 247–56.

3   Cf. Douglas Pratt, "Religion Fixed and Fickle: The Contemporary Challenge of Religious Diversity," in *Sacred Selves—Sacred Settings: Reflecting Hans Mol*, ed. Douglas Davies and Adam J. Powell (Farnham, U.K.: Ashgate, 2015), 101–22.

4   E.g., see Michael Barnes, S.J., *Religions in Conversation: Christian Identity and Religious Pluralism* (London: SPCK, 1989); Israel Selvanayagam, *Relating to People of Other Faiths* (Tiruvalla, India: CSS-BTTBPSA Joint Publication, 2004); Douglas Pratt, "Pluralism, Postmodernism and Interreligious Dialogue," *Sophia* 46, no. 3 (2007): 243–59.

5   Cf. Douglas Pratt, "Religious Pluralism and Dialogue," in *Theological Issues in Christian–Muslim Dialogue*, ed. Charles Tieszen (Eugene, Ore.: Wipf and Stock, 2018), 112–24.

6   Cf. Douglas Pratt, *Religion and Extremism: Rejecting Diversity* (London: Bloomsbury, 2018); Pratt, "Reactive Co-radicalization: Religious Extremism as Mutual Discontent," *Journal for the Academic Study of Religion* 28, no. 1 (2015): 3–23; Pratt, "Religion and Terrorism: Christian Fundamentalism and Extremism," *Terrorism and Political Violence* 22, no. 3 (2010): 438–56.

7   Cf. Douglas Pratt, "The Persistence and Problem of Religion: Modernity, Continuity and Diversity," *Australian Religion Studies Review* 25, no. 3 (2012): 273–92.

8   See, for example, David Cheetham, Douglas Pratt, and David Thomas, eds., *Understanding Interreligious Relations* (Oxford: Oxford University Press, 2013); Douglas Pratt, *The Church and Other Faiths: The World Council of Churches, the Vatican, and Interreligious Dialogue* (Bern: Peter Lang, 2010); Pratt, "Interreligious Dialogue: Ecumenical Engagement in Interfaith Action," in *International Handbook of Inter-religious Education*, ed. Kath Engebretson et al. (Dordrecht: Springer, 2010), 1:103–22; Pratt, "Religious Identity and the

Denial of Alterity: Plurality and the Problem of Exclusivism," in *The Relation of Philosophy to Religion Today*, ed. Paolo Diego Bubbio and Philip Andrew Quadrio (Newcastle-upon-Tyne: Cambridge Scholars, 2011), 210–14.

9   Douglas Pratt, "The Vatican in Dialogue with Islam: Inclusion and Engagement," *Islam and Christian–Muslim Relations* 21, no. 3 (2010): 245–62.

10   Douglas Pratt, "The World Council of Churches in Dialogue with Muslims: Retrospect and Prospect," *Islam and Christian–Muslim Relations* 20, no. 1 (2009): 21–42.

11   See Douglas Pratt, *Christian Engagement with Islam: Ecumenical Journeys since 1910* (Leiden: Brill, 2017).

12   Michael Ipgrave, *The Road Ahead: A Christian–Muslim Dialogue* (London: Church House, 2002), x.

13   Ipgrave, *Road Ahead*, x.

14   Rowan Williams, preface to *Prayer: Christian and Muslim Perspectives*, ed. David Marshall and Lucinda Mosher (Washington, D.C.: Georgetown University Press, 2013), xvi–xvii.

15   The record of these conference meetings (*Tagungen*) can be found in Andreas Renz, Hansjörg Schmid, and Jutta Sperber, eds., *Herausforderung Islam: Anfragen an das christliche Selbstverständnis Theologisches Forum Christentum–Islam* (Stuttgart: Akademie der Diözese Rottenburg-Stuttgart, 2003); and idem, eds., *Heil in Christentum und Islam: Erlösung oder Rechtleitung? Theologisches Forum Christentum–Islam* (Stuttgart: Akademie der Diözese Rottenburg-Stuttgart, 2004).

16   See Pratt, *Church and Other Faiths*; also Douglas Pratt, *Being Open, Being Faithful: The Journey of Interreligious Dialogue* (Geneva: WCC Publications, 2014); Pratt, "Theology after Dialogue: Christian–Muslim Engagement Today and Tomorrow," *Islam and Christian–Muslim Relations* 26, no. 1 (2015): 89–101.

17   See, for example, WCC Interreligious Relations and Dialogue Report, "Who Do We Say that We Are? Christian Identity in a Multi-religious World," *Ecumenical Review* 66, no. 4 (2014): 458–501.

18   For example, see Douglas Pratt, "The Praxis of Dialogue: Can We Go Yet Further?" *Current Dialogue* 56 (2014): 50–56.

19   See "The Christian–Muslim Relations Project," University of Birmingham, accessed February 24, 2019, www.birmingham.ac.uk/cmr1900.

20   All CMR volumes are published as a subseries of the *History of Christian–Muslim Relations* (HCMR) series (Leiden: Brill). The data is now also published by Brill online.

21   Douglas Pratt and Charles Tieszen, eds., *Christian–Muslim Relations: A Bibliographical History*, vol. 15, *Thematic Essays (600–1600)* (Leiden: Brill, 2020).

22   Cf. Douglas Pratt, "Christianity and Other Faiths: Exploring Interfaith Engagement," *Studies in Interreligious Dialogue* 26, no. 1 (2016): 5–19; Pratt, "Ini-

tiative and Response: The Future of Christian–Muslim Dialogue," in *Contemporary Muslim–Christian Encounters: Developments, Diversity and Dialogues*, ed. Paul Hedges (London: Bloomsbury, 2015), 117–33.

References

Barnes, Michael, S.J. *Religions in Conversation: Christian Identity and Religious Pluralism*. London: SPCK, 1989.

Bubbio, Paolo Diego, and Philip Andrew Quadrio, eds. *The Relation of Philosophy to Religion Today*. Newcastle-upon-Tyne: Cambridge Scholars, 2011.

Cheetham, David, Douglas Pratt, and David Thomas, eds. *Understanding Interreligious Relations*. Oxford: Oxford University Press, 2013.

Davies, Douglas, and Adam J. Powell, eds. *Sacred Selves—Sacred Settings: Reflecting Hans Mol*. Farnham, U.K.: Ashgate, 2015.

Engebretson, Kath, Marian de Souza, Gloria Durka, and Liam Gearon, eds. *International Handbook of Inter-religious Education*. Vol. 1. Dordrecht: Springer, 2010.

Hedges, Paul, ed. *Contemporary Muslim–Christian Encounters: Developments, Diversity and Dialogues*. London: Bloomsbury, 2015.

Ipgrave, Michael. *The Road Ahead: A Christian–Muslim Dialogue*. London: Church House, 2002.

Jukko, Risto, Douglas Pratt, and Michael Ipgrave. "The Churches and Christian–Muslim Relations." In Thomas, *Routledge Handbook*, 247–56.

Marshall, David, and Lucinda Mosher, eds. *Prayer: Christian and Muslim Perspectives*. Washington, D.C.: Georgetown University Press, 2013.

Moyaert, Marianne, and Joris Geldhof, eds. *Ritual Participation and Interreligious Dialogue: Boundaries, Transgressions and Innovations*. London: Bloomsbury, 2015.

Pratt, Douglas. *Being Open, Being Faithful: The Journey of Interreligious Dialogue*. Geneva: WCC Publications, 2014.

———. *The Challenge of Islam: Encounters in Interfaith Dialogue*. Abingdon: Routledge, 2017.

———. *Christian Engagement with Islam: Ecumenical Journeys since 1910*. Leiden: Brill, 2017.

———. "Christianity and Other Faiths: Exploring Interfaith Engagement." *Studies in Interreligious Dialogue* 26, no. 1 (2016): 5–19.

———. *The Church and Other Faiths: The World Council of Churches, the Vatican, and Interreligious Dialogue*. Bern: Peter Lang, 2010.

———. "Initiative and Response: The Future of Christian–Muslim Dialogue." In Hedges, *Contemporary Muslim–Christian Encounters*, 117–33.

———. "Interreligious Dialogue: Ecumenical Engagement in Interfaith Action." In Engebretson et al., *International Handbook*, 1:103–22.

———. "The Persistence and Problem of Religion: Modernity, Continuity and Diversity." *Australian Religion Studies Review* 25, no. 3 (2012): 273–92.

———. "Pluralism, Postmodernism and Interreligious Dialogue." *Sophia* 46, no. 3 (2007): 243–59.

———. "The Praxis of Dialogue: Can We Go Yet Further?" *Current Dialogue* 56 (2014): 50–56.

———. "Reactive Co-radicalization: Religious Extremism as Mutual Discontent." *Journal for the Academic Study of Religion* 28, no. 1 (2015): 3–23.

———. *Religion and Extremism: Rejecting Diversity*. London: Bloomsbury, 2018.

———. "Religion and Terrorism: Christian Fundamentalism and Extremism." *Terrorism and Political Violence* 22, no. 3 (2010): 438–56.

———. "Religion Fixed and Fickle: The Contemporary Challenge of Religious Diversity." In Davies and Powell, *Sacred Selves*, 101–22.

———. "Religion Is as Religion Does: Interfaith Prayer as a Form of Ritual Participation." In Moyaert and Geldhof, *Ritual Participation*, 53–66.

———. "Religious Identity and the Denial of Alterity: Plurality and the Problem of Exclusivism." In Bubbio and Quadrio, *Relation of Philosophy*, 210–15.

———. "Religious Pluralism and Dialogue." In Tieszen, *Theological Issues*, 112–24.

———. "Theology after Dialogue: Christian–Muslim Engagement Today and Tomorrow." *Islam and Christian–Muslim Relations* 26, no. 1 (2015): 89–101.

———. "The Vatican in Dialogue with Islam: Inclusion and Engagement." *Islam and Christian–Muslim Relations* 21, no. 3 (2010): 245–62.

———. "The World Council of Churches in Dialogue with Muslims: Retrospect and Prospect." *Islam and Christian–Muslim Relations* 20, no. 1 (2009): 21–42.

Pratt, Douglas, and Charles Tieszen, eds. *Christian–Muslim Relations: A Bibliographical History*. Vol. 15, *Thematic Essays (600–1600)*. Leiden: Brill, 2020.

Renz, Andreas, Hansjörg Schmid, and Jutta Sperber, eds. *Heil in Christentum und Islam: Erlösung oder Rechtleitung? Theologisches Forum Christentum–Islam*. Stuttgart: Akademie der Diözese Rottenburg-Stuttgart, 2004.

———, eds. *Herausforderung Islam: Anfragen an das christliche Selbstverständnis Theologisches Forum Christentum–Islam*. Stuttgart: Akademie der Diözese Rottenburg-Stuttgart, 2003.

Selvanayagam, Israel. *Relating to People of Other Faiths*. Tiruvalla, India: CSS-BTTBPSA Joint Publication, 2004.

Thomas, David, ed. *The Routledge Handbook on Christian–Muslim Relations*. Abingdon: Routledge, 2017.

Tieszen, Charles, ed. *Theological Issues in Christian–Muslim Dialogue*. Eugene, Ore.: Wipf & Stock, 2018.

University of Birmingham. "The Christian–Muslim Relations Project." Accessed February 24, 2019. www.birmingham.ac.uk/cmr1900.

Williams, Rowan. Preface to Marshall and Mosher, *Prayer*.

World Council of Churches Interreligious Relations and Dialogue Report. "Who Do We Say that We Are? Christian Identity in a Multi-religious World." *Ecumenical Review* 66, no. 4 (2014): 458–501.

35

Gender and Christian–Muslim Relations

Deanna Ferree Womack

If interreligious studies is to gain traction as a field of research, then its scope will need to be defined broadly—but not so broadly that contributing scholars must set aside their particular areas of expertise.[1] Recent publications on interreligious curriculum and pedagogy take a general approach, emphasizing methods for teaching and skills for dialogue and critical engagement that are adaptable to multiple religious and interreligious contexts. This approach is essential for equipping students to live and work in a religiously plural society. Yet to develop interreligious studies (IRS) as a *scholarly* field and not only an area of teaching, we need to include more narrowly focused research too.

With scholars of religious and theological studies in mind, in this chapter I argue that IRS could become an inviting home for historians, anthropologists, sociologists, theologians, and others whose work examines at least two religions comparatively, and especially for those whose expertise centers on *only* two traditions. Few have the training to publish substantively on all five of the so-called world religions, and we should make it clear that this is not what IRS requires. Further, I see a unique opportunity for IRS to bring together areas of research that remain marginal in conversations on religion and theology. As one example of how this might be done, I focus here on gender and Christian–Muslim relations, noting that gender is not yet a significant subject for IRS and that it is rarely treated substantively in Christian–Muslim studies.

In the following three sections, I begin with the potential for integrating Christian–Muslim studies and gender studies into IRS. Second, I explore existing research on Christian–Muslim relations and identify the need for deeper investigation of gender norms in Christian–Muslim encounters. Finally, I envision the nascent field of IRS including scholarship that promotes relations between two contemporary communities, such as Christians and Muslims in the United States. That is to say, like IRS as an area of teaching, the scholarly field of IRS can be distinct in its concrete impact on society.

IRS, Christian–Muslim Relations, and Gender Studies

The *inter*-relational emphasis of IRS calls to mind comparisons between multiple traditions or, more practically speaking, dialogue and relationship building between people of diverse faiths. Emphasizing the inclusive scope of the field, foundational texts like Leirvik's *Interreligious Studies: A Relational Approach to Religious Activism and the Study of Religion* and the edited volume *Interreligious/Interfaith Studies: Defining a New Field* suggest that IRS is a big tent.[2] Such texts advocate approaches that are adaptable to many forms of teaching, activism, and scholarship. Yet must researchers become generalists to fully engage in the field? Few scholars today have expertise in "comparative religions" in the traditional sense of studying Judaism, Christianity, Islam, Hinduism, and Buddhism together. This is one reason why pedagogies for IRS have shifted away from an "Intro to World Religions" method where the instructor endeavors to cover all five traditions.[3]

At the same time, a comparative emphasis remains in religious studies, and a growing number of scholars are interested in relations between two different faith communities. Consider, for example, the publications *Journal of Hindu–Christian Studies, Studies in Christian–Jewish Relations*, and *Islam and Christian–Muslim Relations*. Can these comparative explorations find a place in IRS? Indeed, IRS might provide a forum for reflection on the value of such scholarly sub-guilds and for exploring what Hindu–Christian, Muslim–Christian, Buddhist–Christian, and Jewish–Christian studies have in common (like the strong and at times dominating Christian presence in many interreligious conversations). As a historian interested in Christian–Muslim encounters, I would welcome such a forum. For Islamic–Christian history is marginal within the church history guild, and Islamic studies and Christian theology understandably center upon specific Muslim or Christian subjects. In contrast, as indicated by IRS theorists and practitioners—like Leirvik, Patel, Howe Peace, and Silverman—conversations about IRS are occurring among scholars with significant academic or personal experience navigating diverging faith traditions. Source materials and regions of study may differ, but questions about community, conflict, and collaboration across religious difference similarly drive Christian–Muslim studies and the existing IRS corpus.

The connection between IRS and the study of gender may not be quite as apparent. As Elizabeth Kubek has shown, however, feminist scholars are already contributing to IRS. Kubek sees the historical development of women's and gender studies as a potential model for building this new field.[4] I would take her argument further to emphasize that the question of gender itself is a relevant and necessary one for IRS to take up—not intermittently or in select panels marked for specialists, but consistently and comprehensively. Understandings of gender and sexuality shape most faith traditions and are embedded in religious expectations for behavior and norms for relating to insiders and outsiders. For this reason, such issues—which can generate tension in interreligious conversations—ought to receive more attention from scholars of religion. Rather than ignoring potential fault lines, IRS should distinguish itself as a field by bringing such neglected subject matter, like gender in Christian–Muslim relations, to the forefront.

Filling the Gaps in Christian–Muslim Studies

When it comes to the study of gender and religion, over the past two decades or so feminist scholars have produced rich research on women in Islam, Christianity, and Judaism (sometimes in comparative volumes).[5] Publications on gender, sexuality, and religion more generally have also increased, but very little research has been done on the influence of gender norms upon Christian–Muslim relationships. Feminist scholarship on this topic is sparse, consisting of a few regional case studies on Christian and Muslim women,[6] while works in Christian–Muslim studies on history, doctrine, and scriptural comparison tend not to address gender at all.

Why should gender be a significant category of analysis within Christian–Muslim studies? One reason is that current rhetoric about Christian–Muslim conflict is framed in gendered language, as we see in the U.S. public sphere and in American Christian discourses. Along with the collective marking of Muslim men as violent and threatening, I find that gendered reasoning leads conservative and progressive American church members alike to view Muslim women as passive and oppressed. For such western Christians, Gayatri Spivak's famous critique of white men (and women) in colonial contexts intent on "saving brown women from brown men" usually holds true, whether they speak with concern or disparagement about women and Islam. Imperial logic and a "rescue mission" mentality merge together, collapsing the distinctions between

Muslim women of vastly different cultural and theological backgrounds and silencing their voices.[7] As Lila Abu-Lughod argued in the wake of 9/11, rather than denying them the same agency that we readily afford to American Christian women fighting against patriarchy, if we listened to Muslim women, we might find that they do not really need saving.[8]

Many Christians, however, persist with narrow views of women and Islam, and many Muslims similarly lack clarity on gender norms in various Christian traditions. Feminist theology and studies like Abu-Lughod's are excellent resources for those who wish to learn more about either Christian or Muslim women's experiences. Yet few of these studies specifically promote Christian–Muslim dialogue, in part because Christian and Muslim scholars who work on gender are often more intent on changing their own traditions. I believe IRS could bridge this gap by elucidating why gender is such a critical issue for Christian–Muslim relations. Scholars in IRS could also provide guidance for using discussions of gender to improve Christian–Muslim understanding at a more practical level. With the field's distinct emphasis on *inter*relations, then, gender in Christian–Muslim encounters (and in Hindu–Christian or Jewish–Muslim encounters, for that matter) is a ripe subject for investigation.

The Practical Impact of IRS Inclusivity

Finally, with its inclusive scope, IRS might link together scholars in multiple fields whose interests overlap but whose disciplines are rarely in conversation (like Christian feminist theology and anthropology of Islam and gender). Few of us will be interested in joining a new scholarly enclave, but the unique emphases of IRS—on the contact between two or more traditions and on advancing better interfaith relationships today—can be maintained while integrating particular niche areas (like work on Christians, Muslims, and gender) into a broad and open academic network. Because IRS invites reflection on the practical impact of research, the field could have much to offer for scholars who wish to influence social change.

As researchers in IRS navigate the challenges of this new field, a number of questions will loom large, questions such as: *What counts as good scholarship? For whom do we write? Will interreligious studies ever become a field for doctoral study?* On the one hand, IRS may gain slower recognition in the academy if it is viewed as a practitioner field. On the other hand, to limit IRS research to theoretical questions would drain the field of its energy and distinctiveness. And to impose a facade of scholarly objectivity and disengagement seems contradictory to the aim of many IRS pioneers to encourage community-building interaction between people of all religious and secular backgrounds.[9]

For one model of rigorous scholarship that also supports a desired practical outcome, we can look to Christian–Muslim studies. Whether Christian, Muslim, or unaffiliated, scholars in this area usually hope to cultivate better contemporary relations between Muslims and Christians, and they often practice a form of sophisticated interfaith dialogue among themselves. Even with such apparent concrete goals and named religious affiliations, the subfield known as Christian–Muslim studies is growing in the academy. New publications, academic organizations, and conferences centering on Christian–Muslim relations indicate as much.[10]

IRS might therefore build upon this model, while also facilitating a broad research network of scholars from Christian–Muslim studies, scholars of Hindu–Christian and Jewish–Muslim relations, and scholars working on marginalized subjects like gender.

Notes

1   I am grateful for the research grant from the Gerda Henkel Foundation in Düsseldorf, Germany, which made the writing of this chapter possible.

2   Oddbjørn Leirvik, *Interreligious Studies: A Relational Approach to Religious Activism and the Study of Religion* (London: Bloomsbury Academic, 2015); Eboo Patel, Jennifer Howe Peace, and Noah J. Silverman, eds., *Interreligious/ Interfaith Studies: Defining a New Field* (Boston: Beacon, 2018).

3   Kevin Minister, "Transforming Introductory Courses in Religion: From World Religions to Interreligious Studies," in Patel, Peace, and Silverman, *Interfaith/Interreligious Studies*, 60–71.

4   Elizabeth Kubek, "Common Ground: Thinking Critically About Interfaith Studies and the Interfaith Movement," in Patel, Peace, and Silverman, *Interfaith/Interreligious Studies*, 26–35.

5   For one collaborative example, see Yvonne Haddad and John L. Esposito, eds., *Daughters of Abraham: Feminist Thought in Judaism, Christianity, and Islam* (Gainesville: University of Florida Press, 2001).

6   See Anne Hege Grung, *Gender Justice in Muslim-Christian Readings: Christian and Muslim Women in Norway Making Meaning of Texts from the Bible, the Koran, and the Hadith* (Leiden: Brill, 2015); Kathleen McGarvey, *Muslim and Christian Women in Dialogue: The Case of Northern Nigeria* (New York: Peter Lang, 2009).

7   Gayatri Chakravorty Spivak, "Can the Subaltern Speak?" in *Marxism and the Interpretation of Culture*, ed. Cary Nelson and Lawrence Grossberg (Urbana: University of Illinois Press, 1988), 293. On the imperial rescue paradigm and Spivak's work in relation to Islamic feminism, see Miriam Cook, "Islamic

Feminism before and after September 11th," *Duke Journal of Gender Law &
Policy* 9, no. 2 (2002): 227–35.

8   Lila Abu-Lughod, *Do Muslim Women Need Saving?* (Cambridge, Mass.: Harvard University Press, 2013).

9   Interreligious interaction is a major theme for interreligious studies cours-
es. Kristi Del Vecchio and Noah J. Silverman, "Learning from the Field: Six
Themes from Interfaith/Interreligious Studies Curricula," in Patel, Peace, and
Silverman, *Interreligious/Interfaith Studies*, 50–52.

10 The University of Edinburgh's Christian–Muslim Studies Network, for example, has organized international conferences and promoted books like Fadi
Daou and Nayla Tabbara's *Divine Hospitality: A Christian–Muslim Conversation* (Geneva: World Council of Churches, 2017).

References

Abu-Lughod, Lila. *Do Muslim Women Need Saving?* Cambridge, Mass.: Harvard
University Press, 2013.

Cook, Miriam. "Islamic Feminism before and after September 11th." *Duke Journal of Gender Law & Policy* 9, no. 2 (2002): 227–35.

Daou, Fadi, and Nayla Tabbara. *Divine Hospitality: A Christian–Muslim Conversation.* Geneva: World Council of Churches, 2017.

Del Vecchio, Kristi, and Noah J. Silverman. "Learning from the Field: Six Themes
from Interfaith/Interreligious Studies Curricula." In Patel, Peace, and Silverman, *Interfaith/Interreligious Studies*, 50–52.

Grung, Anne Hege. *Gender Justice in Muslim–Christian Readings: Christian and
Muslim Women in Norway Making Meaning of Texts from the Bible, the Koran,
and the Hadith.* Leiden: Brill, 2015.

Haddad, Yvonne, and John L. Esposito, eds. *Daughters of Abraham: Feminist
Thought in Judaism, Christianity, and Islam.* Gainesville: University of Florida
Press, 2001.

Kubek, Elizabeth. "Common Ground: Thinking Critically About Interfaith Studies and the Interfaith Movement." In Patel, Peace, and Silverman, *Interfaith/
Interreligious Studies*, 26–35.

McGarvey, Kathleen. *Muslim and Christian Women in Dialogue: The Case of
Northern Nigeria.* New York: Peter Lang, 2009.

Minister, Kevin. "Transforming Introductory Courses in Religion: From World
Religions to Interreligious Studies." In Patel, Peace, and Silverman, *Interfaith/
Interreligious Studies*, 60–71.

Leirvik, Oddbjørn. *Interreligious Studies: A Relational Approach to Religious Activism and the Study of Religion.* London: Bloomsbury Academic, 2015.

Patel, Eboo, Jennifer Howe Peace, and Noah J. Silverman, eds. *Interreligious/In-
terfaith Studies: Defining a New Field.* Boston: Beacon, 2018.

Spivak, Gayatri Chakravorty. "Can the Subaltern Speak?" In *Marxism and the
Interpretation of Culture*, edited by Cary Nelson and Lawrence Grossberg,
271–313. Urbana: University of Illinois Press, 1988.

36

Conclusion

Hans Gustafson

Several scholars in this volume refer to interreligious studies (IRS) as a burgeoning and nascent field, pointing to its relatively recent emergence in Western academia. The use of "interreligious studies" in the context of academia, to my knowledge, first appeared in 1999 in the Faculty of Theology at the University of Oslo (Norway).[1] Two decades later, as this field continues to forge a foothold in the wings of academia by emphasizing teaching and research, several questions emerge. In particular, as a multidisciplinary field of study, what will be its enduring and dominant research methods and pedagogical practices? Within an academic institution, university, or college, where ought such a program or department be housed? Should it stand on its own as an inter- or multidisciplinary program or department, or should it be located within an existing department or program, such as religious studies or sociology? As such, is it truly "a field of its own,"[2] or is it more appropriately a subfield of a broader or more established field? Perhaps it is more akin to an interdisciplinary "area studies" such as American studies, Irish studies, women's studies, environmental studies, African American studies, justice and peace studies, international studies, Jewish studies, Islamic studies, or Catholic studies. Certainly, these are not all structured the same, nor do they all share the same normative commitments (if they espouse them at all). How might IRS locate itself in relation to these programs and within the halls of academia? What lessons might IRS learn from their histories of journeying into the university and legitimizing themselves alongside other established fields and disciplines?

What is IRS's relation to interfaith practitioners and activists who actively work in the trenches to bring about interreligious understanding, cooperation, and social cohesion? How does IRS serve, critique, balance, and learn from them? What responsibilities do IRS scholars share in exposing and combatting hateful and oppressive movements and trends in history and today, including those implicitly perpetuated by those in the interfaith movement itself? If IRS is to remain a truly academic pursuit of truth and knowledge generation, will it have to remain ever aware and suspicious of developing too close of relations with interfaith practitioners, political bodies, and policymakers? Should IRS be concerned with becoming tied too closely to political and social agendas and embedded within activism, or should IRS embrace its normative, activist, and socially transformative dimensions? Ought the scholar be an activist or strive to separate these complex identities within herself? Does IRS run the risk of being dubbed, unfairly, a so-called "grievance study" devoid of any serious scholarly rigor, truth seeking, or knowledge generation? Or is it precisely IRS's commitment to social transformation that creates the conditions necessary for authentic truth seeking and knowledge generation?

If IRS is truly a field of its own, does it have subfields of its own, and/or does it envelop several existing fields, including various theological subfields (e.g., interreligious theology, intercultural theology, comparative theology, etc.) and nontheological fields (e.g., interreligious and intercultural dialogue studies)? What voices are missing? Currently IRS is dominated by Western European and North American voices, and the bulk of these scholars tend to cluster in the fields of religious studies and theology. The two most notable gatherings of these scholars occur at the Interreligious and Interfaith Studies group at the annual American Academy of Religion in North America and the biennial gathering of the European Society of Intercultural Theology and Interreligious Studies in Europe. Will the field expand (and is there a need) by establishing an explicit presence within other significant academic societies and associations? Will IRS heed Paul Hedges' call to "decolonize" by looking beyond the West for scholarly wisdom to advance the field and avoid various pitfalls the study of religion has fallen into?

This volume represents but one step toward a greater self-definition of IRS, specifically as it relates to research and scholarship. As the field expands, and as (inter)religious relations becomes increasingly apparent in the ways that influence major and minor facets of life today, other pressing questions, tensions, and challenges will no doubt surface. Scholars committed to IRS will be charged with the task to remain ever aware of these tensions and their implications for forging a field that is not only (a) generative of knowledge and truth seeking but also, and no less important, (b) robust and agile enough to engage the practical questions (those with significant "cash value") worthwhile to the contemporary world (including practitioners, activists, policymakers, leaders, and so on). To be sure, these two prongs need not be understood as separate or mutually exclusive but rather understood as interdependent and complementary. An enduring challenge will be for scholars of IRS to maintain mutually enriching relations with interfaith practitioners without falling apart and resulting in an irreparable schism beyond "the Rubicon." At present, such a schism seems rather unlikely given the activist-practitioner commitment of most scholars committed to the healthy formation and flourishing of this field. A primary goal remains to keep these two in a mutually enriching and creative tension to sharpen their respective aims, work, impact, and effectiveness. Scholars researching interreligious relations play a significant role in their investigations of what really takes place in these complex encounters between, within, and among communities and people with various religious, worldview, and lifeway identities. The data from their studies shed light on what and who is at stake, and produce knowledge that can assist in charting new paths going forward for those outside the academy.

Notes

1   "Horizon Document for a Planned Program in Interreligious Studies," Faculty of Theology, University of Oslo, October 16, 2000, accessed May 3, 2019, http://folk.uio.no/leirvik/tekster/horizon_IRS_1999.pdf (faculty mentioned include Notto R. Thelle, Oddbjørn Leirvik, Jone Salomonsen, and Kari Elisabeth Børresen).

2   Joshua Stanton, "Inter-religious Studies: A Field of Its Own," *Huffington Post*, April 24, 2014, https://www.huffpost.com/entry/interreligious-studies-co_b _4827043.

References

"Horizon Document for a Planned Program in Interreligious Studies." Faculty of Theology, University of Oslo. October 16, 2000. Accessed May 3, 2019. http://folk.uio.no/leirvik/tekster/horizon_IRS_1999.pdf.
Stanton, Joshua. "Inter-religious Studies: A Field of Its Own." *Huffington Post*, April 24, 2014. https://www.huffpost.com/entry/interreligious-studies-co_b _4827043.

CONTRIBUTORS

Navras J. Aafreedi is Assistant Professor in the Department of History at Presidency University in Kolkata, India.

Russell C. D. Arnold is Associate Professor of Religious Studies at Regis University in Colorado, U.S.

Ånund Brottveit is Research Director at the Institute for Church, Religion, and Worldview Research (KIFO), Norway.

Catherine Cornille is Professor of Comparative Theology and is the Newton College Alumnae Chair of Western Culture at Boston College in Massachusetts, U.S.

Jeanine Diller is Associate Professor in the Department of Philosophy and Religious Studies at the University of Toledo in Ohio, U.S.

Nelly van Doorn-Harder is Professor of Islamic Studies in the Department for the Study of Religions at Wake Forest University in North Carolina, U.S.

Jeannine Hill Fletcher is Professor of Theology at Fordham University in New York City, U.S.

Guenevere Black Ford is an undergraduate student at Illinois College, U.S.

Anne Hege Grung is Associate Professor of Interreligious Studies in the Faculty of Theology at the University of Oslo, Norway.

Hans Gustafson is Director of the Jay Phillips Center for Interreligious Studies and is Adjunct Faculty in the College of Arts and Sciences at the University of St. Thomas in Minnesota, U.S.

Anna Halafoff is Associate Professor of Sociology at Deakin University, Australia, and is a Research Associate of the UNESCO Chair in Intercultural and Interreligious Relations–Asia Pacific, at Monash University, Australia.

Mark E. Hanshaw is Associate General Secretary, Division of Higher Education, General Board of Higher Education & Ministry, for the United Methodist Church.

Paul Hedges is Associate Professor of Interreligious Studies in the Studies in Interreligious Relations in Plural Societies Programme at the S. Rajaratnam School of International Studies in Nanyang Technological University, Singapore.

Aaron T. Hollander is Associate Director of the Graymoor Ecumenical & Interreligious Institute in New York, U.S.

Thomas Albert Howard is Professor of Humanities and History, Phyllis and Richard Duesenberg Chair in Christian Ethics, at Valparaiso University in Indiana, U.S., and is Senior Fellow of the Lilly Fellows Program in Humanities and the Arts.

J. R. Hustwit is Professor of Philosophy and Religion, and Dean of Arts and Humanities at Methodist University in North Carolina, U.S.

Oddbjørn Leirvik is Professor of Interreligious Studies in the Faculty of Theology at the University of Oslo, Norway.

Jeffery D. Long is Professor of Religion and Asian Studies at Elizabethtown College in Pennsylvania, U.S.

Kate McCarthy is Dean of Undergraduate Education and is Professor of Religious Studies at California State University, Chico, U.S.

Barbara A. McGraw is Professor of Social Ethics, Law, and Public Life, and is the Director of the Center for Engaged Religious Pluralism, in the School of Economics and Business Administration and the School of Liberal Arts, respectively, at Saint Mary's College of California, U.S.

Rachel S. Mikva is Herman Schaalman Chair in Jewish Studies and is InterReligious Institute Senior Fellow at Chicago Theological Seminary in Illinois, U.S.

Kevin Minister is Associate Professor of Religion at Shenandoah University in Virginia, U.S.

Marianne Moyaert is Chair of Comparative Theology and Hermeneutics of Interreligious Dialogue in the Faculty of Religion and Theology and is coordinator of the master program Building Interreligious Relations at Vrije Universiteit Amsterdam, Netherlands.

Timothy Parker is Director of the Graduate Program in Architecture and is Associate Professor of Architectural History and Theory at Norwich University in Vermont, U.S.

Eboo Patel is Founder and President of the Interfaith Youth Core in Chicago, U.S.

Brian K. Pennington is Director of the Center for the Study of Religion, Culture, and Society and is Professor of Religious Studies at Elon University in North Carolina, U.S.

Peter A. Pettit is Director Emeritus of the Institute for Jewish-Christian Understanding of Muhlenberg College and is Teaching Pastor of St. Paul Lutheran Church in Davenport, Iowa, U.S.

Douglas Pratt is Honorary Professor in the Theological and Religious Studies Programme at the University of Auckland, New Zealand, Honorary Senior Research Fellow in the School of Philosophy, Theology and Religion, at the University of Birmingham, UK, and is Adjunct Professor in the Faculty of Theology at the University of Bern, Switzerland.

Caryn D. Riswold is Professor of Religion and Mike & Marge McCoy Family Distinguished Chair in Lutheran Heritage and Mission at Wartburg College in Iowa, U.S.

Or N. Rose is Director of the Miller Center for Interreligious Learning and Leadership at Hebrew College in Newton, Massachusetts, U.S.

Perry Schmidt-Leukel is Professor of Religious Studies and Intercultural Theology and is Faculty of Protestant Theology at University of Münster, Germany.

Geir Skeie is Professor of Religious Education at the University of Stavanger, Norway, and is Guest Professor at the Norwegian University of Science and Technology (NTNU), Norway.

Wolfram Weisse is Professor at Universität Hamburg and is Senior Research Fellow at the Academy of World Religions of the University of Hamburg, Germany.

Asfa Widiyanto is Professor of Islamic Thought at the State Institute for Islamic Studies (IAIN) in Salatiga, Indonesia.

Frans Wijsen is Chair of Empirical and Practical Religious Studies and is Vice Dean of the Faculty of Philosophy, Theology, and Religious Studies at Radboud University in Nijmegen, Netherlands.

Deanna Ferree Womack is Assistant Professor of History of Religions and Multifaith Relations at the Candler School of Theology at Emory University in Georgia, U.S.

INDEX

feminist, 5, 58, 60, 62, 108, 265, 266

Gandhi, 73, 151–52
God, 47, 54–55, 72, 85, 87–88, 98,
    130–31, 150–52, 185–86, 188,
    190n5, 200–208, 217, 225, 231,
    237, 238
grassroots, 11n7, 12n12, 37, 39, 79,
    95, 99, 100, 103, 137, 180, 192,
    229

Hindu, 31, 55, 73, 98, 101–2, 105n23,
    131, 135–36, 144, 145n10,
    147–52, 193, 196n7, 264, 266, 267

intersectional, ix–x, 7, 39, 60, 62,
    157–61, 186, 188, 194, 200
Islamophobia, 7, 31, 36, 191–92, 199,
    202, 236

Jesus, 32, 46, 54, 130, 229, 238, 242,
    251

leadership, xiv, 92, 216–18; civic, 3,
    5, 30; cross-cultural, 7, 213–15,
    218–19, 219n11; development,
    xiii, 4, 10n4, 217–18; interfaith,
    29–31, 45, 178, 180, 199, 213,
    218–19; interreligious, 229; reli-
    gious, 59; studies, 7, 178, 180, 217
lifestance, 192
lifeway, 4, 92, 108, 271
lived religion, ix, 5, 86, 91, 93–95, 99,
    134, 158–59, 162n6

masjid, 29, 32
mosque, 29, 30, 36, 91, 100, 119, 122,
    123
multireligious, 6, 60, 98, 109, 141,
    145n11, 147, 215, 218, 249, 251,
    255

nationalism, 152, 236, 249
nonreligious, ix, xi, 4, 25, 43, 60, 92,
    104n10, 121, 135, 171, 173–75,
    186

orientalism, 164–65

peacebuilding, ix, xi, 8, 11n7, 12n12,
    236, 238
peacemaking, 8, 242
pluralism, 3, 10n4, 13, 74, 130, 173,
    200–201, 244; civic, 11n7, 12n12,
    12n13, 92, 244; exegetical, 238;
    Pluralism Project, 172; religious,
    x, 172, 179–80, 208; theological,
    79, 130, 244
political, 27, 59, 70, 111, 121, 135,
    172, 180, 191–95, 200, 206, 243,
    249–50, 270; action, 99; divide,
    32; imperatives, x; landscape, 8;
    philosophy, 31, 35, 38; pluralism,
    244; power, 49; rhetoric, 100;
    science, 37–38, 111, 171, 250;
    theorist, 62
politics, xiv, 17, 44, 99, 100, 110, 165,
    167, 191–94, 200, 202, 246
postcolonial, 12n13, 58, 60, 62, 79,
    80, 161, 165–66, 168
postcolonialism, 164–65
practitioner, 2, 18, 27, 45, 48, 74, 92,
    111, 115n14, 202, 208, 214, 218,
    228–29, 233, 264, 266, 270–71
prayer, 54–55, 56n6, 188–89, 190n5,
    231
prejudice, 130, 193, 237
prophet, 29, 31, 54, 86–88, 105n24
Protestant, 21, 61, 108, 166–68, 205,
    207, 217
psychology, 35, 38, 44, 81, 171, 228

Qur'an, 71, 87–88, 131, 150, 238